THE
PRINCE
AND THE
POISONER

For Mac and Ida

THE
PRINCE
AND THE
POISONER

THE MURDER THAT
ROCKED THE BRITISH RAJ

DAN MORRISON

The
History
Press

Cover illustration: *New York Daily News*

First published 2024

The History Press
97 St George's Place, Cheltenham,
Gloucestershire, GL50 3QB
www.thehistorypress.co.uk

British Library Cataloguing in Publication Data.
A catalogue record for this book is available from the British Library.

ISBN 978 0 7509 9958 8

Typesetting and origination by The History Press
Printed and bound in Great Britain by TJ Books Limited, Padstow, Cornwall.

Trees for Life

Contents

Cast of Characters

The Accused
- Benoyendra Chandra Pandey: The charismatic Raja of Pakur, a fiefdom bigger than modern New York City; zamindar ruling over thousands of impoverished farmers and tribals; aspiring film producer. Elder half-brother to Amarendra Pandey.
- Taranath Bhattacharjee: Small-time doctor, part-time vaccine maker, and former student at the Calcutta School of Tropical Medicine. Friendly with Benoyendra's mistress, the actress and dancing girl Balika Bala.
- Sivapada Bhattacharjee: Assistant professor at the Calcutta School of Tropical Medicine; former professor of Taranath (no relation); and consulting physician to members of the Pakur Raj clan and other well-to-do families.
- Durga Ratan Dhar: A member of Calcutta's medical elite and a fellow of the Royal College of Physicians.

The Victim
- Amarendra Chandra Pandey: The 22-year-old heir, with his elder half-brother, to the Pakur Raj estate. On the verge of seeking a formal division after years of suspicion that Benoyendra is looting their shared patrimony.

The Law

- E. Henry Le Brocq: Deputy police commissioner in charge of Calcutta's detective department. A genial, aggressive lawman.
- Saktipada Chakrabarty: Assistant police commissioner who launched the Pakur investigation following a secret meeting with Kalidas Gupta (see below).
- N.N. Banerjee: The popular public prosecutor trying his biggest case yet.
- Barada Pain: Wily politician and defence lawyer; future scandal-scarred member of Bengal's wartime Cabinet.
- Thomas Hobart Ellis: Sessions judge and future governor of East Pakistan.
- John Rolleston Lort-Williams: Justice of the Calcutta High Court, and a former Conservative Member of Parliament from south-east London.
- Syed Nasim Ali: Justice of the Calcutta High Court; future chief justice.

The Family and its Affiliates

- Protapendra Chandra Pandey: The late Raja of Pakur, and a supporter of the militant Bengali underground. Died in 1929 of a bacterial infection.
- Rani Surjabati Devi: Aunt and surrogate mother to Benoyendra, Amarendra, and their two sisters; Amarendra's chief protector; target of Benoy's machinations.
- Srimati Pritilata Devi: Benoy's petite, long-suffering wife.
- Prosunendra Chandra Pandey: Benoy's son, a child at the time of Amarendra's death.
- Balika Bala: Stage actress, dancing girl, and Benoyendra's principal mistress.
- Rabindranath Pandey: Amarendra's uncle and defender, and a trained ayurvedic doctor.
- Kalidas Gupta: Diminutive lawyer turned sleuth for the Pandey family and the Calcutta police.

The Doctors
- B.P.B. Naidu: Head of plague research at the Haffkine Institute in Bombay. Part of a new generation of Indian scientists who rose to challenge European dominance of medical research on the subcontinent.
- P.T. Patel: Superintendent of the Arthur Road Infectious Disease Hospital.
- Nalini Ranjan Sen Gupta: Senior Calcutta physician.
- Santosh Gupta: Nalini Ranjan Sen Gupta's nephew and a researcher at the Calcutta School of Tropical Medicine.
- C.L. Pasricha: Professor of pathology at the Calcutta School of Tropical Medicine.
- A.C. Ukil: Calcutta pulmonologist, and director of a laboratory at the All-India Institute of Science.

1

Every Inch an Aristocrat

November 1933: Howrah Station

For most of the year, Calcutta is a city of steam, a purgatory of sweaty shirt-backs, fogged spectacles, and dampened décolletage. A place for melting. In summer the cart horses pull their wagons bent low under the weight of the sun, nostrils brushing hooves, eyes without hope, like survivors of a high desert massacre. The streets are 'the desolate earth of some volcanic valley',[1] where stevedores nap on pavements in the shade of merchant houses, deaf to the music of clinking ice and whirring fans behind the shuttered windows above.

The hot season gives way to monsoon and, for a while, Calcuttans take relief in the lightning-charged air, the moody day-time sky, and swaying trees that carpet the street with wet leaves, until the monotony of downpour and confinement drives them to misery. The cars of the rich lie stalled in the downpour, their bonnets enveloped in steam, while city trams scrape along the tracks. Then the heat returns, wetter this time, to torment again.

Each winter there comes an unexpected reprieve from the furious summer and the monsoon's biblical flooding. For a few fleeting months, the brow remains dry for much of each day, the mind refreshingly clear. It is a season of enjoyment, of shopping for Kashmiri shawls and attending the races. Their memories of the recently passed Puja holidays still fresh, residents begin decking the avenues in red and gold in anticipation of Christmas. With the season's cool nights and determined merriment, to breathe becomes, at last, a pleasure.

Winter is a gift, providing a forgiving interval in which, surrounded by goodwill and a merciful breeze, even the most determined man might pause to reconsider the murderous urges born of a more oppressive season.

Or so you would think.

On 26 November 1933, the mercury in the former capital of the British Raj peaked at a temperate 28°C, with just a spot of rain and seasonally low humidity. On Chowringhee Road, the colonial quarter's posh main drag, managers at the white-columned Grand Hotel awaited the arrival of the Arab-American bandleader Herbert Flemming and his International Rhythm Aces for an extended engagement of exotic jazz numbers.[2] Such was Flemming's popularity that the Grand had provided his band with suites overlooking Calcutta's majestic, lordly, central Maidan with its generous lawns and arcing pathways, as well as a platoon of servants including cooks, bearers, valets, a housekeeper, and a pair of taciturn Gurkha guardsmen armed with their signature curved *kukri* machetes. Calcuttans, Flemming later recalled, 'were *fond* lovers of jazz music'.[3] A mile south of the Grand, just off Park Street, John Abriani's Six, featuring the dimple-chinned South African Al Bowlly, were midway through a two-year stand entertaining well-heeled and well-connected audiences at the stylish Saturday Club.

The city was full of diversions.

Despite the differences in culture and climate, if an Englishman were to look at the empire's second city through just the right lens, he might sometimes be reminded of London. The glimmering of the Chowringhee streetlights 'calls back to many the similar reflection from the Embankment to be witnessed in the Thames', one chronicler wrote.[4] Calcutta's cinemas and restaurants were no less stuffed with patrons than those in London or New York, even if police had recently shuttered the nightly cabaret acts that were common in popular European eateries,[5] and even if the Great Depression could now be felt lapping at India's shores, leaving a worrisome slick of unemployment in its wake.[6]

With a million and a half people, a thriving port, and as the former seat of government for a nation stretching from the plains of Afghanistan to the Burma frontier, Calcutta was a thrumming engine of politics, culture, commerce – and crime. Detectives had just corralled a gang of looters for making off with a small fortune in gold idols and jewellery – worth £500,000 in today's money – from a Hindu temple dedicated to the goddess Kali. In the unpaved, unlit countryside, families lived in fear of an 'orgy' of abductions in which young, disaffected wives were manipulated into deserting their husbands, carried away in the dead of night by boat or on horseback, and forced into lives of sexual bondage.[7]

Every day, it seemed, another boy or girl from a 'good' middle-class family was arrested with bomb-making materials, counterfeit rupees, or nationalist literature. Each month seemed to bring another assassination attempt targeting high officials of the Raj. The bloodshed, and growing public support for it, was disturbing proof that Britain had lost the Indian middle class – if it had ever had them.

Non-violence was far from a universal creed among Indians yearning to expel the English, but it had mass support thanks to the moral authority of Mohandas Gandhi. Gandhi, the ascetic spiritual leader whose campaigns of civil disobedience had galvanised tens of millions, was then touring central India, and trying to balance the social aspirations of India's untouchables with the virulent opposition of orthodox Hindus – a tightrope that neither he nor his movement would ever manage to cross.

And from his palatial family seat at Allahabad, the decidedly non-ascetic Jawaharlal Nehru, the energetic general secretary of the Indian National Congress, issued a broadside condemning his country's Hindu and Muslim hardliners as saboteurs to the cause of a free and secular India.[8] Nehru had already spent more than 1,200 days behind bars for his pro-independence speeches and organising. Soon the son of one of India's most prominent families would again return to the custody of His Majesty's Government, this time in Calcutta, accused of sedition.

It was in this thriving metropolis, the booming heart of the world's mightiest empire, that, shortly after two o'clock in the afternoon on that last Sunday in November, well below the radar of world events, a young, slim aristocrat threaded his way through a crowd of turbaned porters, frantic passengers, and sweating ticket collectors at Howrah, British India's busiest railway station.

He had less than eight days to live.

Amarendra Chandra Pandey, just 21, couldn't know that he was moments away from an incident that would lead to his own agonising death; or that his storied dynasty, one stretching back to the days of the Great Mughals, would in a matter of months be known to the world, broadcast across the globe in tones of horror and amazement, tragically associated with greed, lust, and the perversion of science. All Amarendra wanted was to get home to the comfort of his bungalow in Pakur, 174 miles away, a sprawling country district of black stone mines, forests, and paddy that his clan had ruled for generations.

It had been a trying year. One of Amarendra's elder sisters, Kananbala, had died only months before of what was believed to be a sudden case of the mumps, leaving a husband and teenage daughter. Whatever one's station, life was precarious in the pre-antibiotic era, and the Pandeys were shaken by the pitiless speed with which Kananbala had been lost.

Amar, who had been an avid tennis player and horseman, was himself still recovering from a vicious, bone-wracking bout of tetanus that had left him with lasting heart damage and a crippling secondary infection. Amarendra had spent weeks paralysed, mute with lockjaw, surviving on teaspoons of rice gruel. Still, most tetanus infections ended in death; his troubled recovery was regarded as something of a miracle.

But the young man's troubles weren't only medical in nature. There was a growing, unspoken concern among the close-knit clan that Amarendra's physical challenges were congruent with financial ones. Amid a deluge of evidence that his bullying elder half-brother was looting their shared estate, Amarendra had recently overcome years of reluctance and was now preparing to divide their jointly held property, known as the Pakur Raj.

Benoyendra Chandra Pandey, the powerful Raja of Pakur, had warned Amarendra that he would 'break bones' over any effort to interfere with their shared patrimony. The threat wasn't taken lightly. Benoy's nickname was Sadhan, Bengali for fulfilment. One of his few admirers would later say that Benoy possessed 'physical charm beyond any comparison – a tall physique, generous forehead, doe-eyes', with shoulders like those of an ox and arms as long and thick as the branches of *sal* trees. Benoy, he recalled, was 'every inch an aristocrat'.[9]

Others described a pampered, heavyset man with the latent aggression of a wild boar, a quick mind, and a natural air of even-tempered command. People did as he wished. 'I never saw him angry,' one of Benoy's chief antagonists would later recall. Where slender and dutiful Amarendra was the perfect image of a young, unmarried member of the rural Bengali aristocracy, Benoy was iconoclastic, an open drinker, and a ladies' man who, it seemed, never missed an opportunity to offend the sensibilities of his relatives. Since his father's death from a bacterial infection four years earlier, the new Raja of Pakur had worked relentlessly to seize the properties of his kinsmen and expand the borders – and income – of his back-country fief.

Fratricide is the oldest crime, with many methods available to a brother with the requisite sociopathy. Benoyendra, 32, had that in spades, but he also possessed vision. A would-be impresario of the growing Indian film industry, Benoy hatched a conspiracy that would guarantee Amarendra's death and his own financial freedom. Rather than having his younger brother hacked to death on some rural backroad by hired goons (a not-uncommon practice among the perpetually feuding gentry), shooting him dead in a hunting 'accident', or slowly poisoning Amar with, say, arsenic, as royals and commoners alike had done since at least the Middle Ages, Benoy, a twentieth-century predator loose among Victorians, set his eyes on a thoroughly modern murder.

Inspired by one of English literature's most popular heroes, using medical science in the service of violence, the raja employed a weapon that, he was sure, would make the cause of Amarendra's demise untraceable. The boy's death would easily be chalked up to any one of the grand buffet of viral and bacterial fevers that regularly claimed the lives of Indians and Europeans of all classes in the humid, littoral metropolis.

Benoyendra hatched a plot to strike his brother with stealth, speed, and audacity. By joining forces with a down-and-out physician, and using a well-paid assassin with the nerve to do with his own hands what the doctor and the nobleman could not, Benoy would finally be rid of his troublesome sibling and free to dream and spend as he pleased.

Accompanying Amarendra on platform three that fateful day was his iron-willed aunt, surrogate mother, and would-be protector: the Rani Surjabati Devi. A wealthy dowager, and the widow of their father's brother, Surjabati had raised Benoyendra, Amarendra, and their two sisters. As the boys grew, she struggled to shield Amar from Benoyendra's neglect, and later from his veiled, mounting threats. Not content with looting Amarendra's share of their patrimony, Benoy was also eying the ample properties that the woman he called 'Mother' had inherited from her late husband. The brothers were in line to inherit equal portions of Surjabati's estate, which produced an annual income even bigger than their own.

Surjabati's influence over the younger brother was a constant irritant. 'It is his wish that I should not have any connection to you,' Amarendra wrote to her in 1932. Privately, the aunt and elder nephew loathed one another. In public they performed with Arctic civility. Surjabati, despite her wealth and seniority, was disadvantaged in her long duel with Benoy. He was the *karti*, the undisputed leader of his wing of the family, while the rani was a childless widow, with no biological son of her own, in an era when widows were still expected to live out their days in joyless seclusion. The small, formidable woman in wire-rimmed eyeglasses, who had married into the family as a young teenager, was holding her own against Benoyendra in a contest as old as the aristocracy itself. No one understood he was playing by new rules.

At the East India Railways' Howrah Station, Amarendra collected tickets for his homeward journey on the Pakur Express. Surjabati had already sent ahead instructions for her household servants to burn incense, to wash down the cots and chairs with pest-killing phenyl, to beat and air the cushions and bedding, and to tie fresh leaves to the entry gates in preparation for their arrival. Surjabati, Amar's sister Banabala, and his teenage niece Anima Devi would accompany him on the northbound train. They were joined at the station by a handful of relatives and friends, including, to everyone's surprise, an ebullient Benoyendra who, most uncharacteristically, had also come to see them off.

Amarendra, tickets in hand, led the party in a line towards their waiting train through a clamour of steam whistles, footfalls, and hawkers, his elder brother at the rear. A moment after crossing from the public booking hall to the station hall, with their platform in sight, Amarendra gave a shout.

'I have been pricked!'

2

These Jealous Impulses

As the family gathered in the shadow of their carriage, Amarendra described a collision with a short, muscular stranger, 'not a gentleman', wearing traditional homespun cotton, who'd barrelled into his right side, ricocheted away, and vanished among the thrust of travellers.

Amarendra's beige shirtsleeve was wet with an oily substance the colour of clarified butter; he rolled it up and the party gathered to stare at a damp spot on his upper right shoulder marked by a solitary pinprick. His niece, Anima Devi, stood on her toes and scanned the crowd in a futile search for the assailant. Rani Surjabati felt a chill and leaned on the piled baggage for support. She had experienced the deaths of her husband, her brother-in-law, sisters-in-law, and an adopted daughter. She stared at her young ward, full of foreboding.

As the women boarded the train, Amarendra's cousin, Kamala Prosad Pandey, insisted he remain in Calcutta and have his blood tested, and for a moment Amarendra appeared to waver. Then his *dada*, his elder brother, pushed through the crowd, seized the affected arm and, peering at the strange wound, rubbed the oily red dot with his bare thumb and laughed. Benoyendra accused them of 'making a mountain out of a molehill'. He bore down on Amarendra 'and, in a way,' Kamala recalled, 'forced him into the compartment.'

'That is nothing,' Benoyendra said, manoeuvring Amar to his seat. 'Go home.' The cousin protested, but Benoy cut him off: Amarendra had but one elder brother, and even as an adult he was duty-bound to obey. Everyone knew this, lived this. Kamala backed off. Even in extraordinary conditions, the old ways prevailed. With characteristic obedience, Amarendra stayed on the train, ceremonially touching his brother's feet before Benoy departed.

It was his final capitulation. There the boy sat, miserable. Surjabati lay stretched out on the bench opposite. His sister Banabala produced a bottle of iodine and daubed at the wound. Amarendra asked for a knife to cut away the affected flesh, but no one was carrying a blade. They rattled on.

As the locomotive bore north to the comforts of home, Amarendra's body was already in the opening engagements of a losing battle with a killer that had once consumed half of Europe and that had been scything its way across India for more than two decades. The virulent germs the strange assailant had driven into his arm began to multiply, releasing endotoxins that would in the coming days cause at first scores, and then hundreds of tiny blood clots to form silently throughout Amarendra's body. Their blood supply being choked off by these clots, Amar's organs faced a slow death. With his body's coagulants depleted, and colonies of pathogens growing exponentially, blood from Amarendra's damaged tissue would soon begin seeping into his lungs.

Back home in Pakur, an uncle chastised Amar for having ever left Calcutta, with its world-class doctors, and begged him to return before he became ill with whatever had been stabbed into him.

With a resignation that can be heard, mournful as a bell, from that century to this, Amarendra replied: 'My brother is determined to take my life. What precaution can I take?'

★★★

The Pandeys were wealthy zamindars: local gentry who had ruled over a poor area of subsidence rice farmers, black stone mines, and timber-rich forests since the days of the sixteenth-century Mughal emperor Akbar the Great. Over the course of more than 400 years, the clan had wrung every anna it could from the largely illiterate population of a realm bigger than modern New York City. In 1929, the Raja of Pakur, Protapendra Chandra Pandey, died and left the estate to his two sons, the half-brothers Benoyendra, 27, and Amarendra, 16. From a promontory on the third-floor verandah of the tallest building for miles, Benoyendra and Amarendra could gaze in any direction, over paddy, woodland and hamlet, satisfied that, by law, custom, and divine right, nearly all they surveyed was theirs.

Behind the walls of their whitewashed ancestral palace – a castle-like bastion built to withstand an indigenous peasant uprising – Rani Surjabati Devi raised them as her own. Despite an outward appearance of solidarity, the brothers' relationship was defined by rivalry and resentment, and by Benoyendra's need to assert himself as their father's one true heir. Benoy would battle first for maternal love, and later for money and power.

As the son of a zamindar, Benoyendra had enjoyed a luxurious childhood, raised in a palace, attended by servants, with nannies and tutors to keep him company and assure his proper upbringing. His education would include lessons in English, Bengali, horsemanship, and shooting. Benoy's mother had died when he was just 3 years old, and Surjabati moved into the Gokulpur Palace to care for him and his younger sister Kananbala, serving as a rock of love and continuity. She stayed on after their father remarried and, when the raja's second wife died after childbirth, she took on Benoyendra's half-sister Banabala and the newborn Amarendra, who would never know his birth mother. As the boys grew to adulthood, Surjabati remained a pivotal figure in the household – they called her 'Mom' and 'Mama'.

It would have been natural for Benoyendra to feel some small resentment of the new baby. In a culture where sons were prized well above daughters, Amarendra's arrival represented a dilution of Benoy's supremacy, despite his unassailable position as the eldest male. But when Amarendra's mother died of complications from childbirth, Benoyendra suffered a more severe blow, as Surjabati swept in to care for the motherless newborn and his toddler sister.

The tiny boy was hers from almost his first moment; in an instant, Surjabati's love for Amarendra eclipsed her motherly bond with Benoy. He never forgot it.

Twice robbed of maternal affection, Benoyendra responded to this emotional dethronement with a lifelong resentment of his aunt and the pretender Amarendra. He would evolve into a grandiose figure, rebelling against the careful and rigorous social mores of his community, using money as a weapon against his closest family, and finally turning to violence to excise this narcissistic injury. Sigmund Freud was referring to relations between sisters when he wrote, 'We rarely form a correct idea of the strength of these jealous impulses, of the tenacity with which they persist and of the magnitude of their influence on later development,'[1] but he could just as well have been observing Benoyendra's festering animus for his younger brother. Despite his father's favour and his primacy as the future raja, Benoyendra saw himself as the odd boy out, and now saddled with a co-heir whose well-being he would one day be responsible for.

Compared with most Indians of that era, the Pandeys were unimaginably wealthy. Even by international standards they were rich, with an estate producing income worth a princely £20,000 a year at a time when English farm workers were taking home a little more than a pound a week,[2] and most Indian incomes amounted to mere pocket lint in London and New York. The family's privilege was tethered to the land, and to the time-bound mores of the rural nobility. Long before the forces of Robert Clive defeated Siraj-ud-Daulah at Plassey, before Job Charnok set up the malarial Ganges River post that would become Calcutta (now Kolkata), the forested hills and fertile valleys surrounding Pakur, 174 miles upstream in a region known as the Santhal Parganas, had already been under the rule of 'outsiders' for centuries.

The Pakur Raj dynasty descended from north Indian imperialists, a clan of Kanyakubja Brahmins born on the plains near Lucknow who arrived in the late 1500s to tame the rough lands and peoples found near the eastern margins of the Mughal Empire. They would rule over the region's tillers and indigenous hill people in the name of Akbar the Great.

Their leader was one Sulakshan Tewary, who had seen his ancestral properties in the north turn lifeless from an 'all-pervading pestilence'.[3] Rich, unclaimed lands, however, were available in the east for a freebooter brave or desperate enough to pull up stakes. Tewary secured a land grant, or *jagir*, from the emperor for a wild, unconquered place neither had ever seen. As a zamindar, with the powers of a small monarch, Tewari would fold this virgin territory into the Mughal embrace and convert its thousands of peasants into Akbar's loyal, rent-paying subjects.

Tewary and his followers made a rutted journey halfway across the subcontinent to fulfil this manifest destiny. The train of newcomers made a slow advance through dense jungle dotted with villages and hamlets, until finally it reached a stretch where India's vast, green flatlands gave way to hill country and the great Ganges delta, a place of swaying *sal* trees, Bengal tigers, and small farms raising rice and pulses. This was now home.

Akbar's writ notwithstanding, the local farmers and strongmen, led by a skilled archer named Satyajit Roy, chose to resist the Persian and Awadhi-speaking invaders. The sons of the soil drew first blood but 'were soon pacified and agreed to pay rents out of which the due amount of imperial tribute was remitted to Delhi'.[4] A new dynasty was born. Tewary restored his finances off the backs of his new subjects, while they adjusted to the novelty of having an emperor to support. The new zamindar's grandson later helped Mughal forces defeat the rebellious ruler of Jessore, and the Tewary clan were rewarded with gifts from the emperor, including the hereditary title of 'raja'.[5]

Four centuries later, Tewary's descendants, by now absorbed through marriage into the rural Bengali aristocracy, continued to rule over Pakur, with many of the same powers and responsibilities as their founding figure. Tenant farmers worked the land, and paid rent to Benoyendra and his clan. After taking their generous cut, the Pandeys funnelled a portion of the proceeds to the imperial government in the form of taxes. They had fulfilled this role first under the Mughals, then for the Nawabs of Murshidabad, and finally under the British. Some version of this arrangement obtained on nearly every square inch of rural land across Hindustan.

If poor farmers and other tenants formed the base of this pyramid, the upper layers were taken up by the extracting class, the retinue of hired assessors and collectors paid to manage the estates and squeeze money from the residents, followed by the book-keepers and pleaders who managed a landlord's accounts and his many legal disputes. An estate like the Pakur Raj had diverse income streams, ranging from the rent roll, the zamindar's own crops from land he personally controlled, to the stranglehold loans he made to tenants and local businessmen. A zamindar had to mind his retainers for signs of corruption – they might be taking bribes to accept smaller payments, or they could be creaming off the rent roll. In October 1932, Benoyendra was irritated to learn that Rani Surjabati had hired an employee he had recently dismissed.

'To Your Lotus Feet,' he addressed the woman who raised him, before getting to the point:

> *Boma* [Mother], are you doing well in keeping the man whom I was compelled to dismiss on account of him taking bribe[s] and spoiling our work again and again [?] … You should have at least asked me a word about it … You can, of course, show me disrespect a thousand times, but I hope I shall be able to show you soon whether I can also do so to you once. Do what you think proper. Finis.

She cut the man loose.

Pakur was a money machine, but there was little room for growth. A zamindar could increase his wealth with a strong harvest, by acquiring new land through purchase or litigation, or through efficient management. While Benoy had a zeal for lawsuits, including against members of his own clan, he was considered a disaster as a manager. A friend whose name is now lost to the public record warned him in a letter that without reform, 'You will find within a year or two that you are involved in debts and your property is put up for sale.'

A zamindar's obligations to the Crown were fixed – he was expected to pay up through boomtime, famine, and drought. Those who failed found their properties auctioned off by the government, their income and honour diminished. Two of Benoy's ancestors met worse fates: one was imprisoned by the torture-happy Nawab of Murshidabad in the mid-1700s and forced to abdicate in favour of his brutal father-in-law after failing to extract sufficient tribute from his war-weary tenants. After a famine in 1770 killed one-third of the peasants in lower Bengal, another of Benoy's predecessors was also imprisoned for his arrears, but he somehow managed to gain freedom, keep the throne, and pass it to his son.

'Be on friendly terms with your tenants,' Benoyendra's friend added, 'otherwise they will revolt.' Instead, the new raja kept retainers who were notorious for their greed and cruelty. His trusted estate manager, or *dewan*, the friend warned, 'commits violent oppressions on the tenants, and if a criminal case is started in consequence then it is your money that will be spent [fighting it]'.

Benoyendra should have been especially sensitive to the risks posed by treading on his feudal subjects. Nearly eighty years earlier, one of his predecessors, the wealthy Rani Kshemasundari, narrowly escaped having her throat cut during the Santhal Rebellion of 1855–56, when the region's indigenous tribal people exploded in violence against their overlords. (A despised moneylender wasn't so lucky: a band of Santhals captured and dismembered him alive, joint by joint, after he tried to take control of Pakur in her absence.)[6]

The trusted manager was 'slowly swallowing you just like a snake swallowing a frog, and he is stealing', the friend wrote. The manager, together with a stalwart lawyer from Benoy's court, he added, 'have misappropriated large sums of money belonging to you'. But such was their hold over Benoyendra, he complained, that the raja couldn't recognise the fraud, 'and you have no power to. It is difficult to know these men in their true colours.'

Mistrust was like mother's milk for the gentry, and a zamindar had to believe in somebody. Often it was the cronies of his youth. Forty years earlier, the Bengali writer Lalit Mohan Roy had bemoaned the moral decline of the zamindar class, describing how, in boyhood, a young scion's servants and friends would 'indulge their minor lord into all sorts of wicked pleasures and pastimes with every mischievous device that can minister to his boyish fancies, often purposely impurified – and thus the first seeds of corruption are sown in him'. In an atmosphere of constant competition, other landowners were usually seen as rivals or potential adversaries. 'Among his fellow zamindars he can expect none as a friend.'[7]

As for Benoyendra's young wife, Srimati Pritilata Devi, their marriage existed in a state of partial estrangement. Married in her early teens, Benoy's wife lived in *purdah*, all but confined to the home, with little influence over the family's affairs.

As was the custom, Benoy lived in separate rooms, and dined alone or with male friends. Only occasionally did his wife leave the palace's *zenana*, or women's quarter, to visit him in his chambers. It was considered indecorous for a respectable husband to take daily pleasure in his wife's company and, anyway, there were ample amusements among the household maidservants, to say nothing of the treats available in Calcutta. This domestic formality applied to a zamindar's children as well – the father would see them at pre-arranged times, with no random capering at his feet during the day.

In a dignified photo portrait of the married couple, a moustached Benoyendra is seated on a carved wooden stool, a small slouch to his thick-boned frame, wearing a silk pyjama kurta and sandals, facing to the right. The petite Pritilata stands behind him, her right hand on his shoulder, dressed in a sari she's wrapped around the back and over her shoulder and head, a jewelled belt at the waist. She faces the camera without expression, a hint of confidence in her gaze.

★★★

In a less noxious setting, Amarendra too would have married a girl from a Brahmin clan selected in consultation with his surrogate mother. Living as part of a joint family at the Gokulpur Palace with Benoyendra's wife and three children, Amar would remain closely involved in the estate's affairs, watching the harvests and the rents, advising Benoyendra where his contributions were welcome. His years would be shaped by the rural seasons and the calendar of rituals and festivals, with winter getaways to the theatre and the cinema in Calcutta. But he never got the chance.

The morning after reaching home, Amarendra felt well enough, the events on the platform receding into a kind of bad dream. The following day proceeded without discomfort. The family told almost no one of the incident at Howrah, not even their trusted local doctor. Still, Amar made arrangements to visit Calcutta on Wednesday, 29 November, for a precautionary check-up. There, he was examined by Nalini Ranjan Sen Gupta, a respected doctor who had published both clinical research on tuberculosis and medical commentary defending India's traditional Ayurvedic medicine against the sneers of Western scientists.

When Amarendra, still in outwardly fine health, asked if he could hop on a train back to Pakur that evening, Sen Gupta advised him to stay in town another night. It was prescient advice. Amar awoke the next day with a fever and an ache in his right arm; Sen Gupta ordered a blood sample for culture at the Calcutta School of Tropical Medicine.

It was now clear that the pinprick had caused some kind of infection, but what? An analysis of his blood would lead Amarendra's growing medical team to a diagnosis, but it would take time to culture and identify the pathogen. An uncle telegraphed Surjabati that Amar was quite ill, and she, his sister, and his niece Anima made a beeline for the city. By 1 December, the site of the pinprick had developed into a slightly raised weal, and a lump was forming under his arm. Amarendra's fever worsened the next day, and by Sunday, the 3rd, he was placed on oxygen.

There, in the front room of Surjabati's home on Jatin Das Road (named for a jailed freedom fighter who died after a sixty-three-day hunger strike), Amar's breathing became laboured. Her young uncle was still speaking, Anima recalled, until sometime around 10 p.m., when Amar went silent, his energies concentrated in a vain effort to breathe. Amarendra died before dawn on Monday, 4 December 1933, at age 21. Benoy, who had been so eager to see his younger brother off from the train station just eight days before, was staying in a rented house just a mile away. Not once had he come to visit.

3

The Nervous *Bhaiya*

Shortly after word of Amarendra's death reached Pakur, Benoy received a jaundiced letter of congratulation from his scolding, judgemental friend. Addressing Benoyendra by his nickname, the correspondent wrote: 'Sadhan ..., you are now in luck. All these days you thought that you had a co-sharer, and with this idea you attached no value to properties and squandered away money according to your sweet will. Now you have no further cause for anxiety.

'Then why are you still indifferent to your family affairs?'

Benoyendra's chum was labouring under a misapprehension. Benoy, he imagined, had been burning money not because it was fun – the only way to live, really – but because half the cash he spent was Amarendra's, and it was a joy to spite him. Now, the friend said, there was nothing to keep Benoy from a prodigal's return to the straight and narrow. With Amar out of the way, Benoyendra could finally, at last, be good. Benoy, a hedonist to the core, was deaf to this logic. 'Even now,' the friend complained, 'you do not hesitate to squander away money.' With Amar dead, he said acidly, 'Just think how much you have got to spend now for the two mistresses that you have kept.'

A lawyer close to the Pandey family would later observe that he was running his estate into the ground. 'The staff employed by Benoyendra are incompetent,' he would say in official testimony. 'Money is being spent but the accounts are not written up ... He

comes frequently to Calcutta … He spends it on prostitutes.'
Benoy's expenses included a car and driver, a suite at the Calcutta
Hotel, a rented house in the city, and lots of whiskey. But these
were dwarfed by the small fortune he spent on women.

The raja's local standby was a courtesan named Chanchala, who
he kept at a bungalow in Pakur town. What he apparently didn't
know or perhaps avoided knowing, his friend claimed, was that
Chanchala played with other men on the side. 'Does she depend
only on you?' he asked with a touch of spite. 'If you think so, then
you are quite mistaken.' Rather, Chanchala had been making a
fool of her benefactor, two-timing him with a steady clientele of
low-rent functionaries.

'Jogen is her *dalal*,' or go-between, he wrote. 'He brings
every day big *Bhakats*[1] of Harindanga,[2] Babus of the station,
Sub-Registrars, Deputy Magistrates, and Police Babus who she
entertains. One or two of these men are brought every day.'
Chanchala spent the proceeds of these liaisons on parties for her
friends, while salting the balance away in a postal savings account.
(The fact that Chanchala controlled her own bank account added
scandalous insult to injury; it was unseemly, his friend intimated,
that a woman should have money of her own.)

'But not realising this you are still in love with her,' he admon-
ished Benoy. 'Do you not feel a sense of loathing in the least?'

The answer was no. Benoy's loathing was reserved for stiffs who
followed the rules and the harpies who enforced them. And while
it is possible he was unaware of Chanchala's parallel life and the
betrayal that would represent, another likely explanation was that
Benoyendra had something to gain from her freelance encounters.
The daily parade of second- and third-tier bureaucrats Chanchala
serviced were the nervous system of the Pakur administration –
the men who ran its records office, courts, police, and telegraph. A
wise king, wrote Kautilya, mentor to the great Iron Age emperor
Chandragupta Maurya, 'keeps his eyes open with spies'.[3] Like
a canny intelligence officer, Benoy had built a network of sexually gratified insiders who were happy to lend a hand in his local

conspiracies. Chanchala was more useful to him as an ex-mistress than as a loyal companion.

Besides, he always had Balika.

In Calcutta, Benoyendra maintained a durable romance with a stage actress from the Natya Mandir theatre known as Balika Bala. Balika had appeared in the hit Bengali satirical play *Khas Dakhal* – 'The Land One Possesses' – at the Star Theatre, remembered by critics for the laugh line, 'What, my temperature is 99?' The satirical play 'puts a sling on the so-called advanced people of South Calcutta', one critic recalled.[4]

Balika had been kept by Bhola Nath Pal, an owner of the historic Star Theatre, before she and Benoyendra got together. The new relationship had staying power – they were inseparable when Benoy was in Calcutta. In 1931, he even moved Balika into a house near the Gokulpur Palace in Pakur to keep him company during his stays upcountry. (This outraged Rani Surjabati, who promptly abandoned the palace after three decades.) Benoy and Balika had snuggled up for weeks on a houseboat among the mists of Dal Lake in Kashmir, a popular honeymoon destination 1,400 miles away. When they stayed at Benoy's suite on the top floor of the Calcutta Hotel, Balika would sign the register as the Rani of Pakur, usurping the status of her lover's long-suffering wife, who was living in *purdah* back home in the sticks.

Benoyendra differed from many of his fellow zamindars not in having extra-marital adventures, but by flaunting his indiscretions. It wasn't unusual for upper-class men to keep mistresses or to visit bordellos, nor for the working class to pay for companionship. One-third of Calcutta's population was from outside Bengal,[5] a vast population of overstressed clerks and workmen living far from their families; they supported a booming flesh trade, with an estimated one sex worker for every forty men. In the possibly fictional 1929 memoir *Autobiography of an Educated Fallen Woman*, the upper-class narrator Manada Devi recalls her madame's warning that the neophyte working girl should be prepared 'to run into your own father in my room someday'.

Brothels were registered by the government; military cantonments had even operated official whorehouses to occupy bored British servicemen. (The army bordellos were houses of horror; English social reformers convincingly demonstrated they were often stocked with girls who had been kidnapped and trafficked into sexual slavery.)[6] 'It was generally recognised that religious attitudes were less rigid in India than in England, though social structures were more rigid: prostitutes were not denounced as sinners, but society permitted them no alternative occupation,' historian Kenneth Ballhatchet wrote. 'Also, prostitutes were needed by British soldiers. Rehabilitation was precluded both by Indian realities and by British necessities.'[7]

Authorities took a mostly hands-off approach to urban brothels (as opposed to prostitution in the cantonments), seeing sex work as an unfortunate, if permanent, feature of Indian life – much as it was in Britain. But there was one ironclad exception to this colonial tolerance. In India, one report noted, 'No British woman is allowed under the law to live a life of infamy, either in the houses of ill-fame or with coloured Asiatics'.[8] Christian maids of Albion found working the brothels or living in sin with Indian gentry were promptly deported.

All this semi-open fornication was accompanied by rampant venereal disease. Europeans first brought syphilis to the subcontinent in 1498; the long, deadly, spiral-shaped bacteria had been burrowing into Indian society ever since. By the turn of the twentieth century, British Army manpower was perpetually diminished by the thousands of soldiers laid up with the disease. (Indian *jawans* also suffered from syphilis, but at a rate notably – and, to some, vexingly – lower than their British counterparts.)[9]

Care was poor, especially for members of the Indian public, who recoiled from open discussion of sexual matters. Calcutta, India's biggest city, didn't have a single clinic specialising in venereal disease; in Bombay (now Mumbai), where researchers found syphilis in 30 per cent of all patients admitted to hospital for any reason, there was but one clinic specialising in sexually transmitted infections.[10] If a gentleman passed syphilis to his unfortunate wife; or if his child were to be born blind or with deformities; or if the paterfamilias himself should happen to go unaccountably deaf or mad, the infection could always be blamed on an innocent nick from the unclean razor of a careless barber, leaving the family's honour intact.[11]

In September 1931, Balika Bala was bedridden with what may have been the headache, swollen glands, and fatigue associated with secondary-stage syphilis – a disease Benoy was also carrying. She sent for a doctor she had known since her days with theatre owner Bola Nath Pal. Taranath Bhattacharjee had served as something of a house physician at the Star. He and Balika struck up a lasting friendship; she called the small, nervous doctor *bhaiya*, or brother, and Benoyendra soon recognised that this slim, fastidious, and perpetually cash-strapped sawbones, no stranger to Calcutta's demimonde, might be the boon companion he'd been looking for.

Taranath worked as a journeyman medic, dividing his time between house calls for sick Calcuttans and work at a small laboratory where he prepared serums and vaccines for the market. He had spent a year in the pathology and bacteriology section at the Calcutta Medical College Hospital, performing well enough to earn a recommendation from the department chair. Despite his skill, Taranath had somehow failed to establish a prosperous practice. From 1929 to 1930, he had studied bacteriology at the Calcutta School of Tropical Medicine, but he never paid his fees and did not receive certification. This did not stop Taranath from adding D.T.M., or diploma of tropical medicine, to his list of bona fides. No one doubted his false credential.

And Taranath had until recently earned a small income pulling mutinous teeth from the jaws of clients at a cramped office a half-mile from the white columns of the Grand Hotel. Work as an oral surgeon gave Taranath legal access to strong narcotics. It also required him to master the use of a compact dental syringe.

Benoy, Taranath, and Balika Bala became inseparable. Calcutta was their oyster – rich, debauched, free. Like much of the country, the city seemed perpetually gripped by political and social disruption. After a lull in which the non-violent rebellion had lost steam and the armed resistance to colonial rule had been extinguished,

Mahatma Gandhi's second mass movement against British rule was now gathering strength – and the province was once again on the boil. It was a time of strikes, demonstrations, beatings, arrests, and assassinations. 'The volcano of Indian nationalism never lost its subterranean fire, but it could erupt only periodically,' the great Indian memoirist Nirad Chaudhury wrote, explaining the on-and-off-again nature of open rebellion through the 1920s and '30s. In December 1931, Jawaharlal Nehru was sentenced to two years of rigorous imprisonment in the United Provinces for violating a virtual house arrest. ('This government will be reduced to ashes,' he told the court.) Nearly 67,000 Indians were imprisoned in 1932 as part of the civil disobedience movement; at least 500 of these non-violent protestors were whipped in custody.[12, 13]

Not everyone was sacrificing himself for the nation. Even as anti-British sentiment grew, many Indians were enjoying new forms of entertainment and material comforts produced by the modern age. Benoy and his comrades surfed this wave of amusement and innovation, even as others sounded the alarm. Prafulla Chandra Ray, an eminent chemist and educator, lamented what he saw as a new, vulgar consumerism infecting zamindar and field hand alike:

> Formerly it was quite the custom for ordinary village folks, including the gentry, to walk on foot for four to six miles at a stretch, but as motor-buses are now piercing and tapping the length and breadth of Bengal, even the peasants, who in most parts of Bengal sit idle for nine months in the year and whose sole subsistence depends upon the aman rice crop, refuse to walk much. They go in also for every article of luxury but not of utility. If there is a bumper crop with good price ruling in the market, they get cash and recklessly squander it on bicycles, gramophones, handkerchief of imported artificial silk, on gaudy tinsel and gewgaws.[14]

Benoyendra was far from alone in splurging to buy and maintain a car. 'Not only the Zemindar, over head and ears in debt, but even the professor drawing rupees five hundred per month or less must indulge in this luxury,' Ray complained. 'The importers of motors and automobiles are plying a roaring trade.'[15] This was the India calling to Benoyendra. He paid no heed to salt marches, *lathi* charges, and political fasts. His India was a nation of smoky taverns, overdrawn accounts, risqué comedies, British sedans cutting through the Bengali night, black leather shoes draped in brilliant white spats. What could Pakur offer besides red dust, seasonal harvests, thieving underlings, and ceremonial *pujas*?

Benoy lived for the ride, and Taranath was overjoyed to come along. They were seen together drinking, watching plays, leafing through books and newspapers – and at the movies. Benoy was frequently found chortling at the silent bioscopes playing in Calcutta's fourteen movie halls, and he was entranced by the British and American talkies that reached the city in 1931. He visited the cinema every other day without fail, his driver would later recall – often alone.

There, in the dark, with the magic of light on silver playing before his eyes, Benoy could imagine himself bigger, satisfied, free.

4

As Meat is Dangerous
for the Child

It was only natural that Benoy was drawn to the transgressive glamour of the cinema hall. Where some saw the seeds of moral decay, he found inspiration.

The miracle of moving pictures was first revealed to the subcontinent in 1896, when the Lumière brothers dispatched a technician and a small projector from Paris to Watson's Hotel in Bombay. There, 200 European guests were treated to a dazzling programme of six short films. The *Times of India* called it 'almost the greatest scientific discovery of the age'.[1] Soon, film shorts were being incorporated into live theatrical matinees, and Indian directors were shooting their own silent bioscopes. By 1928, British India boasted 300 movie houses. The most popular films, with their broad physical comedy or red-blooded action, featured the shirtless heartthrob Douglas Fairbanks, the death-defying stunts of Harold Lloyd, and Charlie Chaplin, the Little Tramp. Fairbanks' 1924 swashbuckler, *The Thief of Bagdad*, was 'the most popular film ever shown in India', a government report said.

British films naturally found an early foothold, but they were subsumed by a flood of American pictures, whose roaring popularity unnerved colonial elites. Hollywood threatened chastity, the family – and white supremacy. Yankee films, an Anglican bishop warned, 'are of sensational and daring murders, crimes, and divorces, and, on the whole, degrade the white women in the eyes of the Indians'.

The Federation of British Industries, unable to compete with US output, warned that American cinema was 'detrimental to British prestige and prejudicial to the interests of the Empire, especially in the Dominions which contain large coloured populations'.

Any form of mass entertainment was potentially toxic to the morals and prospects of Indian youth. 'As meat is dangerous for the child who is only teething, so are novels, these theatres and cinemas to young minds that are only budding,'[2] the Calcutta prostitute Manada Devi lamented in her autobiography.

Cinema was by far the most powerful corruptor, and the essentially Victorian institutions of the empire struggled to blunt its dazzling influence. But there was no stopping the taboo-busting onslaught. Some 8,832 foreign films were shown in India between 1920 and 1927. Domestic studios, hobbled by poor investment and weak scripts, produced just 902. Homegrown movies simply had limited appeal; Bengali films, for example, were seen as too crass for fans of the more polished Western movies, while Hindi cinema was too bland for urban audiences.

Benoyendra imagined himself as a potential saviour of the Indian film business. He believed he could make homegrown movies popular and profitable while recasting himself as a modern maestro – as something more than just one of the thousands of hereditary rulers whose fiefs dappled the subcontinent. The raja believed his transformation would come through the production of sophisticated Indian films that satisfied big-city viewers while toning down the racy bits enough to avoid offending conservative audiences. 'Calcutta productions are mostly "all-Bengal" productions, and being disproportionately beguiled with sex are not workable on an "all-India" basis,' he explained.

Benoy was right that movies produced in Calcutta were considered too vulgar for upper-class Bengalis, who preferred foreign films, and for prudish audiences elsewhere in India.

In a 1982 essay, the legendary Bengali director Satyajit Ray recalled his titillating, accidental introduction to vernacular cinema, describing how an uncle brought him to see the 1930 film *Kaal Parinaya* (*The Doomed Marriage*) at the tatty Albion theatre.

'The hero and the heroine – or was it the vamp? – newly married, were in bed, and a close-up showed the woman's leg rubbing against the man's,' he wrote. 'I was nine then, but old enough to realise that I had strayed into forbidden territory.'[3]

Where Calcutta films were too fleshy, early Hindi movies were too bland. 'We want better stories either taken from the ancient books or good modern authors,' said Ruby Myers, an Indian Jew who performed under the name Sulochana and was one of the highest-paid film actors of her day. Benoy would have agreed. 'Bombay produces extensively, and on an 'all-India' basis; but the backgrounds being almost invariably either religion or epic stories, are found deficient by the intelligentsia,' he later said. The Indian middle class was 'practically alien to Indian cinema,' he observed. Benoy's dream was 'to work out a production that would suit the Bengal intelligentsia and yet not be divorced from [*sic*] when tested on an "all-India" basis'.

For perhaps the only time in his life, Benoyendra's interests appear to have aligned with those of the government. Whether he knew it or not, Benoy was echoing the concerns of the Indian Cinematograph Committee, which had spent two years searching for ways to help local studios compete with American imports. If the British government agreed with the committee's call for financial support to the domestic film industry and Benoy could find the cinematic sweet spot in stories that satisfied both the snobs and the rubes, he could become a modern mogul.

But the committee was also deeply preoccupied with moral aspects of the industry, and here Benoyendra gave not a damn.

Egged on by reformers like the English eugenicist Sybil Neville-Rolfe (whose statements were later found to be riddled with lies), members of the Cinematograph Committee were keen to excavate testimony confirming their assumptions linking foreign films with India's advancing moral decay, but the results were both apocryphal and disappointing.

Mrs S.A. Stanley, a former London policewoman, testified before the committee that the Calcutta Vigilance Association 'had some evidence that some of the Jackie Coogan films which were shown a short time ago are definitely responsible for one or two small boys who are now incarcerated in the juvenile jail'. (Coogan, America's original child film star, became famous stealing scenes from Charlie Chaplin in the 1921 comedy-drama *The Kid*.) Similarly, the head of the Punjab censor board claimed to know of a youth arrested for theft who 'said he learnt the method of stealing the bicycle from the cinema'.

Other witnesses, including those more familiar with real-life crime and punishment, were quick to join the film industry in shooting down these suggestions. 'If, and where, crime is on the increase … it is largely attributable to the present-day struggle for existence due to extensive unemployment, and the modern resources of civilization, such as, fire-arms, Motor-cars, and so on, easily available to a would-be criminal,' the Bombay Cinema and Theatres Trade Association said. Sir Charles Tegart, the much-admired (and loathed) police commissioner of Calcutta, barely concealed his impatience. 'I can only say,' he told the committee, 'that I have had no case in which I could definitively say that the crime had been committed under the influence of the cinema.'

'I do not think crime in the Madras Presidency has anything to do with films,' testified B. Venkapatiraju, a prominent lawyer. Most criminal suspects, he noted, had never even seen a motion picture. Pressed as to whether he thought depictions of killers, gamblers, and strong-arm men might inspire real-life villainy, Venkapatiraju was dismissive. 'There is nothing of that,' he replied.

'For instance,' the lawyer added, clueless to what the future held, 'we see these Sherlock Holmes films.'

5

The Viper's Tooth

Ah, Holmes.

The upstairs tenant at 221b Baker Street had long towered over the subcontinent's English-language book trade. Indian readers were first introduced to Sherlock Holmes through Arthur Conan Doyle's *A Study in Scarlet* in 1892, the start of a love affair that's lasted more than 130 years.

Within months of Conan Doyle's novels reaching Indian shores, private detectives were touting their Holmesian prowess while advertising in the *Times of India*. Holmes quickly became a cultural touchstone. In 1907, the *Bengalee* newspaper mocked the Comilla civil surgeon for demanding a police investigation that 'Sherlock Holmes might have envied' following a petty dispute with a group of students on a commuter train.[1] Conan Doyle's hero inspired generations of fiction featuring Bengali- Urdu- and Hindi-language sleuths, some following plots inspired by the Baker Street case files. Sherlock Holmes has been translated into more than a dozen Indian languages, including Hindi, Urdu, Punjabi, and Assamese, with a Sindhi edition appearing as early as 1911. But the first language of the subcontinent to take to Sherlock Holmes was surely Bengali, owing to Calcutta's status as the literary, business, and political capital of British India. In 1905, author Pachkari Dey published the novel *Gobindaram*, which he described as a *chhayaoblombon*, or adaptation, of *A Study in Scarlet*.

In 1917, the Holmes anthology *His Last Bow* reached India. The fifth mystery in that collection, 'The Adventure of the Dying Detective', concerns a death by pinprick that bears an uncanny resemblance to the murder of Amarendra Pandey.

Culverton Smith, a greedy colonial planter and amateur bacteriologist, kills his nephew Victor Savage in London to inherit the younger man's estate. Holmes 'is an amateur of crime, as I am of disease', Smith brags to Holmes' compatriot Dr John Watson. 'For him the villain, for me the microbe. These are my prisons,' he says, gesturing to a row of bottles and jars in his office. 'Among those gelatine cultivations some of the very worst offenders in the world are doing time.' The story's murder weapon is an unnamed germ, a sample of which Smith has cultured and carried home from Sumatra. Victor Savage is infected by the pointed tip of a steel spring coiled, 'like a viper's tooth', inside a small, decorative ivory box with a sliding lid, his flesh pierced when he opens the 'gift' from his uncle.[2] The young heir dies in agony four days later. While investigating the case, Holmes receives a similar box and pretends to have been felled in the same manner so that Smith will confess his crime.

The *London Daily News* raved about the 'thrilling'[3] tale when it was first published in the *Strand Magazine*, and the *New York Times* wrote that, of all the Holmes stories, 'sure not the one among them was stranger than that recounted in the episode called *The Adventure of the Dying Detective*'.[4]

The story of Victor Savage's death was both inventive and timely. Conan Doyle, a trained physician, wrote 'The Adventure of the Dying Detective' just as newspapers and felons around the world began to take note of a promising new manner of homicide: the germ murder.

It was an era of sometimes breakneck discovery. Scientists had created the new field of immunology and found the means to prevent or treat maladies that had haunted humanity for centuries. Amid the development of vaccines for diseases like cholera, typhoid, and rabies, and therapies for malaria, yellow fever, and syphilis, numerous academics and amateurs became obsessed with the habits of deadly pathogens and the tools by which humanity might thwart them. This flourishing of investigation meant that samples of deadly bacilli were at times all too available to the public.

As early as 1895, the French bacteriologist Paul Gibier stunned a meeting of the Medico-Legal Society in New York by revealing that a stranger had come to him enquiring about the ease with which bacilli could be detected in human remains. Gibier said his 'suspicions were at once directed toward the possibility that would-be murderers might resort to bacteriology with deadly effect … In many instances death could be caused by such injection, and the evidence would be hardly discoverable.'[5]

That same month, an American chemist, W.H. Birchmore, published an article describing three unusual deaths that he suspected were really germ murders, and predicted that future killers 'will no longer have recourse to such vulgar poisons as "rough on rats," and the like, but they will purchase any one of the seventeen invariably fatal diseases that they can produce in the human subject at will'.[6]

In 1910, Patrick O'Brien de Lacy, a Polish count of Irish descent, was accused of murdering his Russian brother-in-law with an injection of diphtheria toxin. The count was assisted by a highly strung doctor, Vladimir Pantchenko, who was reduced to hysterics during the trial and claimed to be a victim of mind control.[7] That same year, a doctor in Kansas City was convicted of killing four members of his millionaire wife's family with cocktails of typhus, strychnine, and cyanide. (The verdict was later overturned.)[8] In France, an insurance broker named Henri Girard was found guilty of killing a friend with an injection of typhus he'd cultured at home, and of murdering his wife's hatmaker through a drink laced with poisonous mushrooms. The victims had purchased life insurance policies for which Girard had named himself beneficiary.[9]

Count de Lacy and the handsome Monsieur Girard appear to have been outdone by a German fencing master, Karl Hopf. Hopf, a former London chemist who spent time in Morocco and India, was accused of attempting to kill his third wife by spiking her food with cholera and typhus, and of murdering his first two wives, his father, and his two children using the poisoner's age-old friend, arsenic, along with typhus bacilli and tuberculosis. Hopf had even complained to a German laboratory that the cholera germs they'd sent him were insufficiently virulent. Could they not provide heartier samples collected, say, from the wartime trenches of Bulgaria?[10] (He was beheaded in 1914.[11])

Something was catching on, among both the criminal class and the bellicose nation states. In 1916, German agents established a secret laboratory in the suburbs outside Washington, DC to culture colonies of anthrax and glanders they used to infect horses and mules bound for wartime France. A similar effort saw 5,400 anthrax-infected mules shipped from Argentinian breeders to Indian Army troops fighting the Ottoman Turks in Mesopotamia.[12]

America was as susceptible to German germ scares as to actual bio-warfare. The country went into a brief tizzy over a far-fetched claim that the Kaiser was impregnating bandages with tetanus bacilli. Herbert O. Yardley, the retired head of the American 'Black Chamber' cryptography department, went so far as to claim he'd intercepted a message naming President Woodrow Wilson as the target of a germ conspiracy at the Paris peace conference after the conclusion of the First World War. 'I have no way of knowing whether this plot had any truth in fact, and if it had, whether it succeeded,' Yardley wrote. 'But there are these undeniable facts: President Wilson's first signs of illness occurred while he was in Paris, and he was soon to die a lingering death.'[13] (Critics said Yardley was just hyping his memoirs.[14])

In 1925, a Chicago lawyer, William Shepherd, was unaccountably acquitted of slaying his millionaire client Billy McClintock with typhus in another life insurance scam – this despite testimony by three separate doctors that he had tried to acquire from them samples of *Salmonella typhi*. In a newspaper interview, the pioneering neuro-immunologist Felix Plaut worried that 'the publicity given the Shepherd–McClintock case may be expected to give rise to a number of germ poisonings'.

Plaut spoke from experience. He'd been a consultant to the Munich police in the case of a student who tried to kill his former fiancée and her wealthy parents. His weapon was the bacteria for a hall-of-fame disease, one mentioned by Hippocrates around 400 BC, called *Erysipelas*. German authorities suppressed news of the attempted murder for fear of inspiring new bio-crimes. 'There are more criminal minds below the surface than above,' Plaut said. 'They need only to be stirred to be brought into action.'[15]

India's English-language press devoted a few column inches each week to tawdry foreign crimes, especially those involving heiresses, playboys, and other gilded unfortunates. Both the Karl Hopf and the Shepherd–McClintock germ murder trials received small mentions.[16,17] There's even a chance that Benoyendra, then in his early 20s, took notice of the Chicago germ case (and its – for the killer at least – happy conclusion).

Benoy also enjoyed fiction; it's likely he was among the many thousands of Indians who read 'The Adventure of the Dying Detective' as a short story. The tale may well have made a lasting impression: the symptoms of the 'obscure Asiatic fever' suffered by Victor Savage on his deathbed, and imitated by Holmes, closely resemble those of septicaemic plague.[18]

Just as probable is that Benoy's introduction to bio-crime was made in the flickering dark of a movie hall.

A series of forty-eight Sherlock Holmes silent films, each starring the English stage actor Eille Norwood, were released by Stoll Pictures, of Cricklewood, London, in the early 1920s. ('His wonderful impersonation of Holmes has amazed me,' Arthur Conan Doyle remarked.) Films from the Norwood series circulated throughout the empire over the next decade. The most popular among Indian viewers was probably *The Hound of the Baskervilles*, which saw a months-long run. An early entrant in the Norwood series, however, was *The Dying Detective*.

In this, the first of two Holmes films portraying murder by pinprick, Holmes is shown using forceps to force open Smith's booby-trapped box, revealing the inoculated metal spike. Unlike Conan Doyle's readers, who are strung along in suspense to the very end, film audiences were in on Holmes' feigned illness from the start.

Benoyendra was a young man when *The Dying Detective* was first released. In 1931, as Amarendra Pandey was attaining his majority – and with it, rights to equal proceeds of the Pakur Raj – a full-length American talkie, *The Return of Sherlock Holmes*, made its Indian debut.[19] Incorporating elements of two Holmes short stories, 'The Adventure of the Dying Detective' and 'His Last Bow', the film takes place on a modern-day ocean liner and is the first to feature the catchphrase, 'Elementary, my dear Watson.' It too portrays murder by pinprick. In the course of a transatlantic battle of wits, Holmes leads his arch-enemy Dr Moriarty to believe he's been fatally wounded by a booby-trapped cigarette case bearing a spring-loaded syringe.

The needle is 'filled with poison – a deadly alkaloid', Moriarty gloats to the 'dying' Holmes.

'A little device of my own.'[20, 21]

6

Savour of Self-Interest

In May 1929, as Jawaharlal Nehru was occupied with putting down a revolt by a group of partymen from Tamil Nadu, Mohandas Gandhi pushed for a nationwide boycott of foreign-made cloth, and police in Bengal prepared to arrest the publisher of a seditious new book called *India in Bondage*, the Pandey clan of Pakur sat vigil for a beloved giant.

The head of the family, Protapendra Chandra Pandey, was dying a lingering and painful death. The 50-year-old zamindar had been bedridden in his upstairs flat at Basanta Mansions near Calcutta's busy Hazra Crossing for days, his face vandalised by a raised, crimson rash that spilled across both cheeks, the sores on his legs turning septic under an unstoppable bacterial assault. Protapendra, Raja of Pakur, was suffering from the inflammation and infected skin ulcers of *erysipelas*, known as *vispara* in Sanskrit and in Europe as St Anthony's Fire. *Erysipelas* had been the attempted murder weapon in the hushed-up germ case revealed by Felix Plaut four years earlier. Over the centuries it had killed Pope Gregory XVI; Queen Anne, the last of Britain's Stuart monarchs; and the philosopher John Stewart Mill. It would soon take the raja as well.

Amid his suffering, there came good news. As he rested in his darkened bedroom, attended by friends and doctors, Protapendra learned that his younger son Amarendra had won admission to the elite Patna College, known then as 'the Oxford of the East'. On his deathbed, Protapendra knew he could leave the world satisfied that his two daughters had been married to honourable, educated men, and that his sons would inherit a thriving estate. His wealth would be split equally between the half-brothers, and they would – he was sure – work together to strengthen their ancestral holdings as generations had before them. At 26, Benoyendra was more than capable of running the family's affairs, despite his many distractions.

The dying raja was equally certain that Benoy could count on Amarendra's assistance once the boy completed his studies. In anticipation of his selection, Protapendra had arranged for a rented house in Patna, the capital of Bihar, where Amar could pursue his schoolwork in comfort. Protapendra had planned on living there with him. He had high hopes for his second son and had selected an up-and-coming historian to serve as Amar's tutor. Kalikinkar Datta was himself a native of Pakur, a former student at the Pakur Raj High School. The school was a source of pride for the Pandey family; it had been founded in 1859 by one of Protapendra's liberal-minded predecessors just two years after the establishment of the University of Calcutta. Now Kalikinkar would guide Protapendra's son through the paces of higher education – a fitting demonstration of the Pakur Raj's legacy. Beyond his support for the high school, Protapendra had served as a member of the Bihar legislative council, but other parts of his political life were less well known: he had once played a small role in India's violent struggle for independence by bankrolling a Bengali revolutionary who was under police surveillance.[1]

Protapendra left a fortune to his sons. In addition to his land-holdings, he was a moneylender and had an interest in businesses producing lac, a resin used in varnish and cosmetics. A cousin who watched as Benoy prised open his father's locked chests following his death said they were stuffed with 'ornaments and bags of money'.

It wasn't long after Protapendra's passing that Benoy showed he had new ideas about how to run things. Amarendra would still attend Patna College to study at the site of an eighteenth-century opium warehouse, but a private home with servants was out of the question. Benoy took the lease for himself, and the orphaned princeling was dumped into a hostel. Benoyendra stopped paying Amar's expenses – Rani Surjabati made up the difference in his room and board. Amarendra hated asking Surjabati for money almost as much as he loathed his brother's cupidity. 'I can leave all others to the care of God, but you are the only person of whose welfare I am personally anxious to know,' he wrote her. 'How much happier would I have been had there not been the savour of self-interest?'

Benoy pleaded poverty, but not convincingly. 'Since father's death I have relied totally on you regarding all matters, and from my quarters there had been no dearth of either respect or love towards you,' Amarendra wrote. 'Whenever two bodies are moving slight collisions are inevitable and always pardonable … It is my pride that you can scarcely cite any instance where I have disobeyed you. What more can you ask from your younger brother? I know that the time is hard. But my want is more cruel.'

Amar, still a minor, was left to stew while his brother splurged on entertainment in Calcutta and the Himalayan foothills of Darjeeling, and disappeared on a three-week holiday with Balika Bala to faraway Kashmir. Benoy cast a greedy eye over estates owned by his kinfolk and began preparing a lawsuit against Surjabati to grab the fat properties she'd inherited from his uncle.

After two years of humiliation, Amarendra turned 18, with rights to a direct share of the family income. He abandoned the hostel for a small rented house in Patna, collected a pair of servants from Pakur – and grew increasingly frustrated. Officially he was now entitled to half the money their properties generated, but Benoyendra still controlled the estate; the staff answered to him, and the raja held the ledgers. Amar was 240 miles away.

As he prepared for exams, Amar plotted his future while keeping abreast of India's sizzling political scene. In a letter to an uncle, Rabindranath Pandey (actually the son of Amar's grandfather's nephew), he mourned the recent death of the independence leader Motilal Nehru, father of Jawaharlal. 'It is not only good but it is one's duty to show some respect to such a great patriotic and self-sacrificing man,' Rabindranath replied approvingly. In a veiled reference to Benoy, he continued: 'At all times it is the students who perform their duties towards the country because they have not learnt to be selfish.'

By the spring of 1932 Amarendra's complaints were growing louder. Benoy tried to persuade him that they were under the gun – a property in which they owned a quarter share had fallen into tax arrears, and the government was preparing to sell it off. Benoyendra said he was scrounging for money, and he eventually had to borrow funds to regain the property at auction. 'I am extremely anxious for collecting the dues that have got to be paid' by the tenants, he wrote. Why couldn't Amarendra be patient? Yes, Benoy admitted, Amar was entitled to money, but he implored his brother to postpone his demands until their obligations were met.

'If, however, you think that your necessity cannot wait waiting [*sic*], you are, of course at liberty to take your own course and draw half the amount, or sell, mortgage or give away your properties, in the way that you think best,' he wrote. 'And in doing so you will be exercising your very legitimate rights. That would require no sanction from me.' This was Benoyendra's method: charm and conciliation, followed by aggression.

The profligate Benoy then went on the attack, suggesting that Amarendra was the family's true financial drain. 'In fact, it is hardly a little over one month that you have left Pakur, and you have already drawn about 600 rupees, and you are in want again. Add to that your tuition charges, medical expenses, traveling, servants' pay, emergency, ceremonies, poojas and whatnot, and the figure goes up to 1,000 rupees a month.'

Amarendra smouldered – and then produced a small flame of resistance.

7

A Specially Virulent Strain

Two very related things occurred on 13 May 1932.

In Pakur, Amarendra Chandra Pandey executed a power of attorney, appointing a manager working for Rani Surjabati and two local lawyers to look after his interests in the Pakur Raj, a move that would help him document Benoyendra's mismanagement and theft. The legal declaration, known as an *am-muktearnama*, ran for three dense pages of archaic legal boilerplate, invoking officials and worthies starting with the Privy Council in London and all the high courts of India down to minor 'Canungoes, Inspectors, all officers of settlement' and more.

'I do,' Amarandra affirmed, 'out of my own free will and while in a sound state of body and mind, execute this *am-muktearnama*. *Finis*.' Little brother was finally asserting himself in a manner that Benoyendra couldn't ignore.

At quarter past one that same afternoon in Calcutta, Taranath Bhattacharjee dashed off an express telegram to the headquarters of the Haffkine Institute for Plague Research in Bombay requesting a tube of one of history's great killers. His enquiry was brief:

Please do supply v.p. post earliest convenience specimen of virulent B. Pestis Culture laboratory work wire T.N. Bhattacharya [*sic*] MB DTM

Late Pathologist Medical College Hospital
7 Baishnab Sett Street

The Haffkine Institute was the country's premier centre for plague science. It was named for Waldemar Haffkine, a Ukrainian Jew who had created the first vaccines for cholera and plague, and who had served for years successfully fighting both diseases in India before he was falsely blamed for the deaths of several men during a vaccination drive and forced out by resentful British medical officers.[1] It took three years of exile for Haffkine, with the help of luminaries including the Nobel laureate Sir Ronald Ross, to clear his name and resume his duties in India. In 1925, ten years after Haffkine's retirement, Bombay's Plague Research Laboratory was renamed in honour of its founder. By 1932, the institute was India's sole producer of plague vaccine and a source of plague culture for researchers around the world.

The institute replied to Taranath on 14 May in a terse wire directing the physician to make his request in writing and to state his purpose. This was a foot in the door, and Taranath wasted no time:

Dear Sir,
With reference to your telegram, I have the greatest pleasure in requesting you send ... at your earliest convenience [a] specimen of B Pestis culture (virulent strain) and oblige. I require the same for experimental animal inoculation in laboratory.

But the institute was not persuaded by Taranath's brevity, nor by the out-of-the-blue suggestion that he had anything to add to the current research. While India was still enduring the long, deadly tail of the Third Plague Pandemic, which killed more than 12 million people on the subcontinent, the disease had been studied thoroughly by some of the world's top researchers. Who was this nobody in Calcutta? It was left to the director, Lieutenant Colonel John Taylor of the Indian Medical Service, to see him off. 'I have to state that under the instructions of the Local Government the supply of cultures, etc., by this Institute is made to Government

Institutes, and Officers only,' Taylor wrote. Private researchers could receive cultures on rare occasions, he allowed, but under stringent conditions: 'I shall be able to supply you the required plague culture if you will obtain the approval of the Surgeon-General of the Government of Bengal.'

This was an impossibility – both Taylor and Taranath knew it. Taranath tried one last direct gambit, wiring the institute as if he had never received the director's reply:

LETTER DESPATCHED CULTURE WHEN EXPECTED READY

But Taylor wouldn't entertain him. The foot in the door turned out to be a kiss-off:

PLEASE REFER MY LETTER EIGHTEENTH INSTANT WILL SUPPLY CULTURE ON RECEIVING REQUISITE PERMIT

Taranath 'has not made out a case, request should be refused', Major S.S. Sokhey, a biochemist who was the institute's deputy director, wrote to his colleagues. 'I am not sending culture.' Turned away at the front door, Taranath now went around the back. If the Haffkine Institute refused to supply plague culture to an unknown figure like himself, perhaps its officers would respond more favourably to a name-brand scientist. In late May, Taranath brought a patient to consult with Dr A.C. Ukil, a noted pulmonologist, director of tuberculosis research at the India Research Fund Association, and a former lecturer at the Pasteur Institute in Paris. He reminded Ukil they'd met before; the senior doctor had administered Taranath's exams when he was studying at the University of Calcutta. Further, Taranath exaggerated, they had another connection: he was a nephew of the well-known Dr Lalit Banerji, head surgeon at the Medical College Hospital.

The ground softened, Taranath began to dig. 'He told me he was working in a private laboratory and had found out a cure for plague of which he wished to test the efficacy with plague cultures,' Ukil would later recall. 'He told me he would have great difficulty in getting a culture of plague bacillus and requested me if I could give him an opportunity to get it. I said it would be very difficult, rather dangerous, to work with plague bacilli unless one had the requisite experience and knowledge of technique.'

Ukil, whose research had been published in English, French, and German scientific journals, had worked with plague in Paris and knew its risks. Plague investigations required facilities with an isolation chamber and dedicated autoclaves and incubators. Taranath had none of these, so Ukil generously offered to provide facilities from his lab at the All-India Institute of Hygiene – a government institution.

'I believed in his bona fides because of his references,' Ukil would later say. 'I took him for a keen worker and I wanted to help him.'

On 31 May, Ukil dashed off a two-line wire to Dr B.P.B. Naidu, the head of plague research at the Haffkine Institute. Naidu was away in Europe; Taylor, the director, quickly approved Ukil's request. 'I know him,' he told a colleague. The culture arrived by post on 10 June, a glass vessel of dread nestled in a smooth tin case, packed inside a wooden box. There was a note from Taylor: 'I forward herewith a good strain of *B pestis*[2] as requested. Will you please keep it in your own charge for use in your laboratory as it is a specially virulent strain.' Taranath had already visited the lab once to check if the culture had arrived. Now that it had, Ukil directed his senior assistant to make subcultures – to take cells from the original sample and place them in a growth medium to create colonies of new cells that could be used in Taranath's experiments.

The assistant was Sudhir Thakurta, a former classmate of Taranath's. He prepared the subcultures as directed, allowing Taranath to observe his work without touching the samples. 'I was not prepared to allow a worker who was not properly trained to handle the strain because it would have been dangerous both to himself and to onlookers,' Ukil said. Despite the risks associated with *pestis*, the process for creating a subculture was both exacting and basic – a normal part of bacteriology.

Over the next week Taranath returned twice to monitor the subcultures. But the cells refused to multiply. Thakurta tried again, and still produced nothing. 'Attempts were made I think twice or thrice to subculture it,' Ukil said, but 'there was no growth'. Ukil and Thakurta would later say that they determined the sample sent from Bombay was anything but virulent; they believed the cells had been dead on arrival. They destroyed the original sample and the subcultures using pressurised steam.

Taranath was eager to try again, but the chest doctor begged off. Fewer than three weeks had passed since Ukil had first readily agreed to help, but he now demonstrated a near-complete change of heart. 'I was not actually working on plague research,' he later explained, 'and it would be too much of a bother for me to write and ask for another strain as I was not working on it.' As curious as Ukil's sudden turnabout was the mystery of the unviable bacilli. The Haffkine Institute regularly posted virulent plague cultures to laboratories as far away as London. No one had ever heard of a researcher receiving an inert sample.

A year later, Taranath brought Ukil another patient with suspected tuberculosis. After the examination, he asked if Ukil would mind writing him a letter of introduction to Dr Naidu at the Haffkine Institute. Testifying under oath, Ukil would say he couldn't recall whether he had or not.

★★★

The Pandey brothers bickered through the spring and summer. Benoy resented the fact that Amarendra hadn't done enough to help him reacquire the property that had been put up for auction, and he seethed at the power of attorney appointing Amar's own representatives to monitor the estate; the presence of Rani Surjabati's retainer – a maternal uncle of their father's – was especially intolerable. Amarendra meanwhile demanded an immediate payment of 2,000 rupees, an amount Benoy said bordered on fantasy. He told Amarendra he was heading to Calcutta for medical treatment. Amar was welcome to drop his studies and take the reins in Pakur.

'It is a practical test of the situation,' Benoy wrote. 'If you come back from College to-day and want to manage affairs with your own hands, I will most certainly withdraw in your favour and will not mind any mistakes so long as you do not mean to play unfairly. If you think that the management is not up to your liking you can certainly propose an arrangement that you may think proper and if after full understanding we disagree, you may affect a partition and make your own arrangement. There can be no objection to that.'

The recent *am-muktearnama*, however, was another matter. 'But to thrust behind my back an arrangement that I do not approve of on the whole of the property would be trying an impossibility which would most certainly end in broken bones.' At this, Amarendra appears to have flinched. He replied that the new power of attorney wasn't *really* about contesting his brother's control, but was meant to facilitate the transfer of funds to help win back their delinquent parcels.

By mid-June, around the same time that A.C. Ukil had received Taranath's plague culture from Bombay, Benoy again chastised Amarendra over his legal moves. 'Such mistakes are palpable,' he wrote. 'I really never thought you could commit such mistakes.' Soon enough, he promised, it would be clear why they needed to stick together. 'Darkness causes suspicion and trouble,' he cautioned, adding, 'Please do not unnecessarily write to me for money before we have met and understood each other on all matters common.'

Having threatened to close the tap fully, Benoy ended on a friendly note, suggesting they provide a financial grant to Amar's tutor so that he might dedicate his new book to their late father. 'I am glad that you have at least written that I could count [on] your help more than anybody else's,' he told Amar. 'Minus your advisors, I really do count on you ...'

At some point in June, Amarendra agreed to reverse the power of attorney in exchange for 1,000 rupees from his brother, but their correspondence became rancourous when Amar insisted on having the money up front. In early July, Benoyendra denounced Amar's close relationship with Surjabati. Earlier in the year he had demanded that Amar separate himself from Surjabati, and the boy had resisted. Now Benoy pressed the point. 'Do not expect any brotherly dealings with me if you have decided to cast your lot with Surjabati,' he thundered. 'She never means any good to this family. She cannot mean it … She has already driven a wedge between us, and you mean to confirm it.'

'You simply want money,' Benoy said bitterly. 'Well, it is there that I must draw the boundary line. Please let me know if you really mean to undo those *am-muktearnamas* and are prepared to thrash out with me an arrangement.'

It was now or never. 'You are constantly harping on one half of the proposal and shelving the other half. Why don't you do it if you mean it? If you mean business, proceed in a businesslike way … and by God I would like to see where we stand.'

When Amarendra finally caved in on 7 July, Benoy gave him only 500 of the promised 1,000 rupees. He'd won the round. Amar was furious, and again powerless. 'Unnecessarily harsh expressions only wound feelings and does nothing else,' Benoyendra taunted him. 'What do you advise me to do? … Money is being sent to you as soon as it is coming in.'

Within a month of cancelling the power of attorney, Amarendra was again pleading for maintenance. 'When I find that in spite of my wants you are spending a lot of money in charities I think it is hardly necessary for me to give you an idea of my mental condition,' he wrote. Amar said that if Benoy didn't send money soon then, 'I shall have to make my own arrangement'. But his threats were empty. By late August Amar was thanking Benoy for a relatively paltry 100 rupees with a promise of 150 more in the future. 'I never write you for money unless my bare necessities suffer. If you find anything wrong with my previous letter, please excuse me. When you help me in time I am your servant.'

Amarendra did his best to hold on. While friends and family were gathering for a weekend of fun at Deoghar, a holiday destination in the hills of Bihar, he elected to stay at school. 'I thought I too would swell the crowd there,' he wrote Surjabati, 'but I gave up the idea for the sake of studies.'

Using a joint certificate of succession dating to when Amarendra was still a minor, Benoyendra had raided 13,000 rupees from an account of their father's at Allahabad Bank. He now had designs on 17,000 rupees that had been deposited in another account in partial settlement of a debt to their father. Amarendra fretted over how to keep that fortune out of Benoy's hands.

He had his future to consider. For some months Surjabati had been making inquiries about finding a bride for Amarendra but he was ambivalent about the options. A once-prospective father-in-law, Uma Kanto, had written to invite Amar to stay with his family in the holy city of Benares; he and his wife sent their respectful regards to Surjabati as well. 'Is this *asirbad* [blessing] in connection with a *pakadekha* [betrothal] ceremony?' he asked her. 'But why after such a long time?'

Amarendra attempted a diplomatic reply, telling the girl's father that Surjabati was 'proud to know your wife' and that he would 'always be happy to find myself in your midst'. Less diplomatically, he added that Surjabati was of the opinion that Kanto's daughter was still too young for marriage. 'On the whole I have put it nicely,' he wrote Surjabati. 'What do you think? The girl is of short stature. I have told them this plainly.'

If Amarendra relied on Surjabati's support and advice, he was also sharply aware of his duty to her. 'I was going to Muzzafarpur to-day to play football,' he wrote. 'But then I thought that I was the only son of my mother and lest I should suffer an injury it would be better that I should stay behind.'

'How are you keeping? Don't stop taking walks. Your lethargy and indifference to everything get on my nerves,' he scolded. 'God is displeased if one is indifferent to or dissatisfied with everything. So long as your life lasts you must take care of your health without any objection and be cheerful. Don't rashly place yourself under the treatment of any ordinary doctor. Send for me whenever necessary.'

It was a tragic exchange. Hard as Amarendra tried to watch out for Surjabati, he would soon enough find himself under her care.

8

Taut

One evening in October 1932, while Amarendra was staying at Surjabati's country home in Deoghar for the annual Durga Puja holidays, Benoyendra arrived by car in the company of Manmatha Bakshi, the estate's compounder. Compounders prepared basic medicines for the thousands of dispensaries serving small villages and plantations across India. The profession was considered essential, if barely skilled, labour, and compounders were sometimes accused of harming their illiterate patients through quackery and error.[1] These rough practitioners, with only elementary instruction in pharmacy, were often the first and only source of medical care available to communities of poor farmers and labourers. Why Benoy's compounder was in Deoghar this autumn evening, 80 miles west of home, he never did explain.

While his employee waited by the car, Benoyendra invited Amar for a private stroll among the *bel* trees a short way from Surjabati's house. Their hour-long conversation concluded on a bizarre note.

The brothers were walking in the cool air of the retreating monsoon when, Amar later told his relatives, Benoyendra offered him the unexpected gift of a pince-nez – the then-fashionable eyeglasses that sat perched on the wearer's nose. Amarendra had recently taken to wearing dark glasses during the daytime – he seemed to think they lent him a touch of the debonair. He tried on the new spectacles before handing them back. They're too small, he said. Nonsense, replied Benoyendra, who then clamped the pince-nez onto the bridge of Amarendra's nose with such power that, Amar recalled, 'It felt as if a vein in my head had burst'. The force was enough, maybe, to have broken the younger man's skin. He later told his sister Banabala that he felt moisture on his nose immediately after removing the pince-nez. Given the cool weather and the steady evening breeze, Amar doubted the sheen was from perspiration.

Benoyendra took supper with the family and left with his compounder for the regional centre of Dumka, where he had legal business. Four days after the uninvited pince-nez fitting, Amarendra began experiencing fever and aches across his body; he complained of pain in the muscles of his face and eyelids and he had trouble controlling them. Amar closed the shutters and took to bed as his eyes became unusually sensitive to sunlight. By the third day he had difficulty chewing, and was biting his tongue with involuntary snaps. Soon, his lips were twisted into a tortured rictus, his neck was painful and stiff as iron, his nose disfigured, mouth bleeding, jaws locked tight.

Infection by tetanus, from the Greek *tetanos*, or 'taut', is today rare thanks to widespread vaccination. But in the 1930s it was among a raft of deadly everyday infections. Tetanus bacteria lives in the soil and is introduced through even the smallest of flesh-breaking wounds. It takes hold among the dead, crushed cells of that injury, where its spores produce a powerful neurotoxin that puts the host at the mercy of sometimes bone-snapping contractions.

It killed both the rich and the poor. John Roebling, designer of the Brooklyn Bridge, died in 1869 amid a frenzy of tetanus seizures after his foot was crushed by a docking East River ferry.[2] It took just three days for tetanus to kill the eighteenth-century naturalist George Montagu after he stepped on a rusty nail during renovations at his eight-bedroom home in Devon.[3] Tetanus-related heart attacks were once common. 'Tetanus in all its varieties is a spasm of an exceedingly painful nature, very swift to prove fatal, and neither easy to be removed. An inhuman calamity!' wrote Arteaus, a physician and chronicler of first-century Cappadocia.[4] Nineteen hundred years later, little had changed with regard to tetanus, save for the development of an anti-toxin serum that, when administered, was effective in only 30 to 50 per cent of cases.

After first suspecting exposure to the cold and then rabies, a local doctor diagnosed tetanus as Amarendra's symptoms worsened. Surjabati telegraphed Benoy to send the family's long-time physician up from Pakur. He arrived instead from the more distant Calcutta with a slight, nicely dressed young man no one had seen before: Taranath Bhattacharjee. Benoyendra sat with Amar in the low light of his quarters, where they communicated through written notes – Amar couldn't speak. 'My teeth are set in a lock jaw but there is hardly any pain to speak of,' he scrawled on the back of an envelope. 'I cannot open my mouth but I do not feel so much pain today as felt yesterday.' Eating and drinking were impossible. 'I fear suffocation when I swallow,' he wrote. Comparing himself with a runner who had just completed an hour-long race, Amarendra explained that 'after taking one sip of water I also have hard breathing – this and the feeding do not go harmoniously'.

Benoyendra made sympathetic noises. 'Do not be nervous,' the boy answered. 'Consult the doctor carefully. If there is no chance of alleviation of pain within 2 to 3 days then of course you will have to remove me to Calcutta. And if there is a chance of its abating, what is the use of hurry? I think I shall easily be able to pass 2 to 3 days without taking food.' Amarendra was putting on a brave face, but the discomfort was severe. He requested medicine to quench his thirst and asked his brother, 'What do you think of calling in a big doctor?'

Taranath was 'well known in Calcutta', Benoy assured him. The local doctor, Sourendra Mukherji, had already been fighting Amar's infection with large doses of tetanus serum for a day and half when Taranath, flashing his metropolitan bona fides, suggested a different approach: what about morphine? That alone would do the trick. Taranath said he doubted the efficacy of serum, and implied that Mukherji was behind the times for thinking otherwise.

Morphia was known to ease the spasms and demonically clenched tendons that accompanied tetanus. But without serum the disease was a death sentence. Taranath's opiate-only regime would have left Amarendra insensible while giving the tetanus terminal control over his nervous system. This confirmed to Mukherji that Taranath was, as he later recalled, a 'raw junior'. Mukherji ignored his supposed reputation and insisted on continuing the serum; the two men compromised with an agreement to administer both serum and opiates. Injections of Eukodal, an oxycodone-based narcotic that would later become a favourite of Adolf Hitler's,[5] did more than relax Amarendra's muscles – they pushed him into a stupor. Benoy suggested Taranath stay on to act as Mukherji's assistant, but Mukherji had no use for him, and the pair left that night. With regular serum injections, Amarendra slowly returned from his prison of immobility, but his heart was notably weaker from the struggle.

On the day Amar became well enough to take solid food again, his brother reappeared at Deoghar, this time with a new Calcutta doctor. Unlike Taranath, he was no slouch. Durga Ratan Dhar was a certified member of the medical elite. A native of Jessore in eastern Bengal, he'd studied in London and Calcutta, and was a fellow of the Royal College of Physicians. When Amarendra asked from his sickbed the name of this new physician, he laughed at Benoy's answer and pulled a magazine from under the pillow. It was an issue of the Bengali monthly *Bichitra*. Inside was an essay, '*Ora O Amra*', or 'We and They', written by none other than Durga Ratan Dhar, about his experiences as a medical student in London. Dhar had been deeply influenced by his time in England and by what he saw as the fundamental fairness of British society. He returned home convinced that India, even amid its freedom struggle, had much to learn from the United Kingdom.

In the essay, Dhar described his admiration for the English habit of self-reliance. 'One winter evening I went to see a retired high official of the Medical Department of the Government of Bengal,' he recalled. As the two men sat in conversation and the flames in the hearth became low, Dhar was taken aback when the esteemed host 'himself got up and brought in shovelfuls of coal to feed the fire ... Nobody in that country is ashamed of doing his own work himself.' Even upper-class women, he marvelled, carried large parcels while running for the train as if it were not cause for humiliation. Dhar seemed to attribute this self-sufficiency to Britain's status as an independent nation, rather than economic or cultural factors. 'In a free country this does not mean a loss of prestige, whereas in our country people hang down their heads in utter shame if they have to depend on their own selves,' he wrote.

England's charity hospitals, often funded through public appeals, also made a strong impression. Despite their being 'a race of merchants', Dhar noted, 'these materialistic English people give away vast sums in charity,' while, he suggested, rich Indians were only in it for themselves. 'There are many millionaires in our country where religion is dear to the people as their lives, but how many of them spend money for the poor and suffering of humanity?' More impressive was that British doctors, even very senior ones, appeared to treat their patients like honoured guests. 'I can hardly describe how very courteous and gentle they are in their behaviour towards the patients. This appeals to me very much because in our country the behaviour of newly passed young doctors, and very often of these superiors, towards these patients is extremely reprehensible.'

Dhar noted the occurrence of political violence in London, the pitched throw-downs between British socialists and fascists; it wasn't all rosy across the dark waters. But there was one last comparison he couldn't help making: that between the English and Indian constabularies. 'The thing that struck me as very strange was the courtesy and efficiency of the police in that country,' Dhar wrote. London police appeared uniformly strong, competent, and polite in their dealings with the public, while 'the police in our country are like so many bloated officials whose very name and sight strike terror in our hearts'. This frank assessment may later have come back to haunt him.

Though Amarendra was clearly recovering, the muscles of his face continued to spasm and his neck remained stiff. Dhar recommended more serum to neutralise any toxin remaining in his bloodstream. Mukherji objected at first; Amar's progress was good, and he had already received a rather large volume of tetanus immunoglobulin – a total of 125,000 units. This was true, Dhar agreed, but he assured his colleague that while a small dose or two would at first bring back the symptoms, it would also protect Amarendra from long-term damage. While Mukherji had personally treated more cases of tetanus, Dhar was by far better educated and was more up to date on the scientific literature. 'Knowledge,' he told Mukherji, 'is better than experience.'

Was it? At the turn of the century, in the early years after tetanus anti-toxin was first developed, highly educated physicians in France and Switzerland were convinced that the most effective delivery of tetanus immunoglobulin must be directly into the patient's brain following removal of a small piece of skull. After all, tetanus was a disease of the central nervous system – where better to inject the serum? This method was employed on numerous occasions in France, Switzerland, the UK, and Brazil. Experience later showed that a simple subcutaneous prick to the arm or the bottom produced superior results – and fewer dead patients – than intracerebral injection.[6, 7]

Nevertheless, Mukherji agreed to a single extra dose of anti-toxin. While Surjabati waited nervously in the next room, Dhar 'took out a phial of serum from his bag and his own syringe with it', a member of the family later recalled. There was a parley over where to administer the injection before they settled on Dhar's preference: the muscle of Amarendra's right buttock. All Mukherji's previous serum injections had been jabs into the flesh of Amar's flank or back. An intramuscular shot was sure to cause greater pain, but Dhar said it would prove more effective. Amar was by now well enough, and wary enough, to request that Mukherji drive it home.

'I had certainly no suspicion in my mind at that time that something untoward was being done,' Mukherji recalled. Dhar prepared the injection, filling his syringe from a rubber-topped vial of Parke-Davis serum he'd brought up from Calcutta. After Dhar sterilised the needle, Mukherji swabbed Amarendra's exposed flesh with alcohol, took the syringe in hand, and delivered the injection deep into his gluteals. It burned.

Benoyendra and Dhar left that evening. (Dhar would later recall that he had the sense, as he and Benoy made their journey north to Deoghar and back again, that the raja was subtly probing his character for a sense of his appetites and limits.) Within hours of their departure, Amar's old clamping returned, accompanied by fever. Amarendra's stomach became distended. Dr Mukherji was by now away from Deoghar and the family summoned Dhar back from Calcutta. He arrived the following day with Benoyendra. The spasms were treated with Eukodal. Rabindranath, an ayurvedic physician, gave the injections, but there was no immediate benefit. Amar was confined to his bed, the stuffy room lit by a single candle. Dhar advised the family to open the doors and windows and allow the drugs time to work. In a few days the symptoms fully receded, as Dhar had predicted.

Days later, Benoy returned in the company of both Dhar and a third Calcutta physician, Sivapada Bhattacharjee, to examine Amarendra's damaged heart.

Sivapada, at least, was a known quantity: an eminent doctor with a substantial practice, holding the coveted position of assistant professor at the Calcutta School of Tropical Medicine. Sivapada had attended to the boys' father Protapendra during the late raja's final days and was frequently called by members of their social circle for expert advice. Taranath had been one of his students, and Sivapada was a paid member on the advisory board of the Medical Supply Concern where Taranath worked. (The board was a marketing exercise; it had never met.) Sivapada examined Amar, prescribed some heart tonics, and left. Dhar was in town to see a different patient and had come as a courtesy. A week later Benoy was again in Deoghar, this time bearing fresh fruit and the medicines from Calcutta that Sivapada had prescribed. These were left untouched.

Amarendra was walking, talking, and eating almost normally after two months confined to his bed, but soon another problem developed. His leg had started aching, and pus began to ooze from the site of that last serum injection. He suffered panic attacks and a racing pulse when Dr Mukherji recommended an operation to drain the abscess; the infection was left to fester over fears for

Amarendra's weakened heart and fragile emotional state. Amar had seen enough of needles and medical men, but Mukherji was once again called to the house after the Doljatra holiday when he 'suffered a severe attack of palpitation of the heart lasting for several hours that frightened the whole family', the doctor recalled. Benoyendra had come earlier that day with his wife and children to pay their respects on the last festival of the Bengali calendar.

The cardiac episode was, Mukherji said, 'a result of a conversation with Benoyendra over their private affairs'.

Amar saw a cardiologist in Calcutta, and the family moved south to the warmer climes of Orissa for two months of pilgrimage and a change of scenery, but there was no escaping his compromised health. While bathing in the reputedly healing spring waters of a Bhubaneshwar temple, a large quantity of pus discharged from the flesh of Amar's right haunch. He had the spot lanced and drained, but it wasn't enough. Soon he complained of pain near his pelvic bone; X-rays revealed a putrescent cavity, or sinus, lodged deep within his gluteal muscle. Lalit Banerji, a respected Calcutta surgeon (and a distant relative of Taranath) described it as the size of a large orange. He performed three operations over the next four months to clean out the site and finally kill off the infection. Benoyendra paid a small portion of the medical bills, leaving Surjabati to cover the bulk.

Amarendra was 'suffering for seven or eight months' after the tetanus infection and 'got nervous in consequence', showing 'mental weakness', Rabindra later recalled. 'I saw him getting frightened at small trifles. The fright would not last long.'

9

I Will See You, Doctor

In late November 1932, as Amarendra submitted to a series of operations to clean out the dangerous infection in his backside, Benoy opened a months-long gambit to raid a small fortune from their late father's accounts at the Allahabad Bank. The funds were held in trust for both heirs, but Benoyendra and a local lawyer were chipping away at the bank's intransigence. Soon the cash would be transferred to the custody of courts near Pakur, where Benoy had outsized influence. Even as Amar begged for help with his medical bills, Benoy partied at the Calcutta Hotel. In January, Amar made another abject plea. His faithful housekeeper hadn't been paid for nearly a year, his college tutor Kalikinkar Datta was owed his monthly salary, and there was an important puja to be performed. 'You know that I am totally friendless,' he wrote.

Certain current and day to day expenditures are unavoidably necessary and require immediate payment. The Saraswati puja can't be duly performed with less than Rs. 250 and I should get it as early as possible. Jotra, the servant, has not received his wages for the last 8/10 months. He is in real need now and has been serving well. Please pay him up. The money should be sent to his house. Lastly I beg to remind you that the remaining amount should be paid to Kali Babu. I am improving. Hoping you are all right.

PS: Please remember that I have to undergo untold difficulties if you make delay in sending me the Rs. 150.

In March, Amar was eager to show that he was pinching paise. 'Following your advice I am practising rigidest economy,' he wrote. 'In spite of this I don't find my purse sufficient and reliable.' The infection was still playing havoc with his finances; he'd taken out loans to cover part of the shortfall. 'Once I am well, expenses are expected to be reduced naturally. But it would be unsupportably unjust if you don't supply me with legitimate necessary money now.'

By April it was clear that, having beaten tetanus against the odds, Amarendra was now recovering from his nasty pelvic infection as well. It had seemed a terrific stroke of luck for Benoy when Surjabati first decided to favour religious pilgrimage over medical attention for Amar's wound, but now medicine had made up for lost time, the scalpel and iodine achieving what sacred temple waters could not. Dr Lalit Banerji was paying Amar daily visits in Calcutta to monitor his progress.

The boy wasn't going anywhere, and as his health improved the confidence of youth, coupled with his grasping resentments, would return like angry, entitled weeds, Benoy was convinced. How long before, under the influence of their satanic foster mother, Amarendra was again challenging his control?

What's more, Surjabati had put Amarendra on the market. If she were able to make a match, Amar could soon have an heir who would be another claimant to the brothers' joint property, and to Surjabati's estate as well. For Benoy, this was unthinkable.

The time had come to resurrect Dr Battacharya's plague cure.

Sometime that spring, Taranath brought a new patient to see Dr A.C. Ukil at the Medical College Hospital in Calcutta. Ukil, who had ordered a tube of plague bacilli for Taranath the previous year before abruptly changing course, ran a large department at the hospital where general practitioners brought tricky chest infections. During the examination, Taranath's patient, who appeared to be a man of no great wealth, offered to pay Ukil a cash reward if his condition were cured. Ukil replied that, while it would be inappropriate for him to receive a bonus for simply doing his job, there was nothing improper about accepting donations on behalf of the city's tuberculosis research fund. At the end of the appointment, Ukil had a new patient, and Taranath had in his hands a letter of introduction from the esteemed pulmonologist to Dr B.P.B Naidu, head of plague research at the Haffkine Institute.

Taranath then called on Sivapada Bhattacharjee, his former professor at the School of Tropical Medicine. 'Dr Taranath told me that he would be going to Bombay in connection with [a] certain patent food business with a Marwari friend of his and wanted to utilise the opportunity to visit the Parel Laboratory,' he later told police. Sivapada wrote a general letter of introduction, vouching for Taranath as a former 'student of mine and a practitioner in Calcutta'.

'I will add that there was no question of [a] plague work visit by the said Dr Taranath in the letter of recommendation,' Sivapada later emphasised.

Despite his success in acquiring introductions from two of the city's leading medical men, Taranath was anything but a commanding presence. Could he close a sale? Small-boned, short of stature, a nervous figure with neatly trimmed moustaches on either side of his nose, he'd done well enough in getting Ukil and Sivapada on his side. But how would he perform in Bombay without the benefit of his Calcutta old boy connections? For the next phase of their plan, Benoy left his sidekick in Bengal and, letters in hand, hopped on the Calcutta Mail to Bombay, ostensibly for meetings with people in the film business.

Instead of cadging lunch with movie producers, Benoy set his sights on B.P.B. Naidu. Naidu was a heavyweight scientist, with advanced degrees from universities in Edinburgh and Liverpool. He had served as a bacteriologist with Indian Army troops along the Euphrates River during the Great War, and he had the distinction of being the first Indian admitted to the Pathological Society of Great Britain and Ireland. While entry to the elite Indian Medical Service had been obtained through colour-blind examinations since 1855, for decades native medical officers had typically found themselves assigned to the field and seldom to the laboratory. Naidu was part of a new generation of Indian scientists who rose in the 1920s and '30s to challenge long-standing European dominance of medical research on the subcontinent.[1]

On 1 May, Benoy appeared at Naidu's flat near the stately Whiteaway & Laidlaw buildings in south Bombay, a stone's throw from the Arabian Sea. The scientist had only recently moved into this new flat, and he was caught off guard by Benoy's unusual pitch: a Calcutta doctor needed facilities to test a new cure for plague. He was bearing a letter of introduction from Calcutta. 'I told the gentleman to write to the director of the Haffkine Institute for permission,' Naidu recalled, not realising that the institute had just the year before given Taranath the brush-off, or that Ukil had been provided plague germs for this very same doctor while Naidu was away in Europe. Benoy left empty handed for Calcutta that night, a journey of 1,340 miles and thirty-seven hours. He made another trip to Bombay two months later, checking into the Sea View Hotel, where he listed his address as 7 Tagore Castle Street – Taranath's residence.

One afternoon, he came knocking at the home of E.R. Nagarajan, a veterinary surgeon who worked under Naidu at the plague department. 'He told me he wanted a tube of plague culture,' Nagarajan recalled. 'I told him I could not give it without the permission of my superior officer.' Nagarajan was baffled by Benoyendra's approach. Why come all this way? Couldn't Benoy's doctor friend get the necessary sample from the Calcutta School of Tropical Medicine? Nagarajan was on his way out, and he walked Benoyendra to his taxi where a driver and a guide were waiting. They said they were off to see the sights, and Benoy invited Nagarajan to join them on an excursion to the exquisite

Shiva temples located on Elephanta Island in Bombay Harbor. Nagarajan passed on the day trip, accepted a ride to his tram stop, and carried on with his day.

He was surprised the following morning to find Benoyendra, hat in hand, once again at his doorstep in Bombay's leafy Matunga suburbs, again asking for plague germs, and refused him a second time. Benoy pressed Nagarajan on a third occasion, catching him unawares on the white-columned portico of the Haffkine Institute, originally a seventeenth-century Jesuit chapel, situated on the heights of the Parel neighbourhood.[2] At each meeting, Benoy 'offered me some reward to procure plague culture', the surgeon said. All the badgering wasn't fruitless. Nagarajan refused to come up with the germs but he did provide some useful intelligence: Nagarajan told Benoy the names of other institutions in the city where he might find plague culture, including the infectious disease hospital on Arthur Road.

Nagarajan nervously confided in his fellow veterinary surgeon at the Institute, Ram Chandra Sathe, about Benoy's visits, only to learn that the zamindar had approached Sathe as well, also offering cash for bacilli. Neither man's address was public information, but Benoy had managed to find each one at home. He had made two visits to Sathe's residence before finally catching him there to make the same hard deal. 'He induced me and said, "I will see you, doctor, I will see you,"' Sathe later recalled. 'Even then I refused.' Neither man gave in – and neither, strangely, thought to alert his superiors, colleagues, or staff members at local hospitals about the single-minded Bengali zamindar determined to bribe his way into a colony of killer bacteria.

After making no headway at the Haffkine Institute, Benoy finally scored with the superintendent of the Arthur Road Infectious Disease Hospital. P.T. Patel was an MD from London University, a DTM from Canterbury, author of a handbook on tropical disease and fevers, dean of the medical school at Bombay University, and had recently helmed the reorganisation of two city hospitals 'on modern lines'. For all his experience and accomplishments, Patel was a soft touch. He readily agreed to help.

'He said he had a doctor friend who had a remedy for plague and he wanted to test it,' Patel later said. The superintendent even made the disturbing suggestion that Taranath might try his novel 'cure' on unsuspecting plague sufferers at the hospital. 'I told him to let the doctor come and then let him try [it] on some animals first, and then I should see about trying it on patients,' he said. But Benoyendra first needed to seal the deal, to transform an apparent goodwill offer into an explicit quid pro quo. The next day, Patel received a message at his clinic on Queen's Road summoning him to a hotel that catered to Indian tourists and businessmen. The manager said a visitor was in grave distress. A taxi arrived to carry him there.

Patel was surprised that, 'When I reached the Sea View Hotel, I found my patient to be the same Mr Pandey'. Benoy explained that he was suffering from chest pains after over-exerting himself on the 2-mile trail leading to the Elephanta caves. Upon examination, however, 'I found no objective signs,' Patel recalled. 'As he said he had pain, I prescribed some medicine for him. I got my fees.' Benoy settled the bill for 35 rupees and wired his bank to send 500 more. In the following days, he visited Patel's clinic for at least two more consultations over this phantom malady. The doctor prescribed 'light treatment'.

Benoy relaxed, shirtless in dark glasses, under the salubrious rays of an ultraviolet lamp.

He paid cash.

10

Cito, Longe, Tarde

There are plagues, and then there's plague.

For as long as people have gathered in settlements, kept live-stock, traded and warred, disease has been along for the ride. The first-century AD Antonine Plague killed an estimated 25 million people after victorious Roman centurions carried home smallpox from Mesopotamia. The Spanish Influenza of 1918 (likely born in Kansas)[1, 2] killed as many as 50 million in the terrifying space of a year. Covid-19 left at least 7 million dead worldwide (though experts say the official toll is a gross undercount).

But plague, now known as *Yersinus pestis*, has devastated like no other malady during three great global outbreaks.

Plague is generally said to have originated among wild, marmot-like rodents on the steppes of Central Asia. Fur traders carried the disease to China, from where it followed the Silk Road to Europe after infected fleas jumped from their wild hosts to populations of urbanised black rats.[3]

The rat flea *Xenopsylla cheopis* is plague's tormented vector, an insect driven mad by plague-induced starvation. Each infected flea develops a blood clot in its gullet that stops food from reaching the stomach. Insatiable hunger drives the flea to bite incessantly, each desperate nip a new stab at transmission. When the rats die, human beings are next in line.[4]

The first two plague pandemics were relatively Western affairs that cut down generations. Justinian's Plague claimed as many as 5,000 people a day at its peak in sixth-century Constantinople, killing 40 per cent of the population of the eastern Mediterranean region. This was followed by the fourteenth-century Black Death, which took between 75 million and 200 million lives – more than half of Europe.[5]

The third plague pandemic belonged to Asia, especially India. While it touched every continent, pandemic deaths in India and China reached into the millions, while cities elsewhere saw mortality in the tens and hundreds. Plague reached Hong Kong from mainland China in 1894. Within a decade, cities from Sydney to Buenos Aires to Glasgow were affected. Most contained their outbreaks. Bombay, so important to Benoyendra's plans, was an exception.

In 1896, Bombay was the most populous city of British India, with 850,000 densely packed souls, and one of the empire's busiest ports. The island city crackled with trade, scholarship, and the labour of millhands, sweepers, dock workers and others living crammed in airless tenement *chawls*.[6]

It was spring when the city's traditional *vaids* and *hakims* first began receiving patients suffering from 'a peculiar fever which entirely puzzled them and usually ended fatally', a government servant later reported.[7] By August people across the city bore the swollen, froglike buboes that are the telltale sign of plague. On 18 September, an Indian physician, Dr Acacio Gabriel Viegas, attended a poor, middle-aged woman suffering from high fever, exhaustion, pounding headaches, nausea, and a painful bubo at her right inner thigh. He then saw a young man from a prosperous family with similar symptoms. Both patients were dead within a day. 'The rapidity of the course of the disease and the fatal termination both struck me,' Viegas recalled.[8]

Viegas examined the patients' blood and compared what he found with an image of plague bacteria published the previous year in the medical journal *The Lancet*. They looked alarmingly similar. In addition to his medical duties, Viegas served as president of the

Bombay Municipal Corporation; at a meeting of its standing committee two days later, participants reported mass die-offs of black rats in slum-like neighbourhoods adjoining Bombay's docklands. European and Indian doctors alike reported seeing patients with similar symptoms. They all agreed: this had to be plague. Bombay faced a tsunami of disease.[9]

Colonial officials responded with denial and character assassination. After all, the initial diagnosis of plague was by a 'native' MD, one of those 'qualified (or otherwise) local practitioners', as one European medical officer put it.[10] Captain John Hext, director of the Royal Indian Marine, India's navy, assured his government contacts that the doctors raising the alarm were 'mostly charlatans'.[11] Viegas and his colleagues were 'a group of doctors beating their own tom toms in this city with more zeal than discretion',[12] the *Bombay Gazette* said. The 'glandular fever' in the district of Mandvi, home to more than 150,000 people, was probably due to the vegetarian Bania trading community dealing in, and eating, poorly stored commodities, the newspaper concluded.

Still, word was getting out. A top civil servant, John Hewett, telegraphed bacteriologist Waldemar Haffkine to drop his work on cholera inoculations in Bengal and make haste for Bombay. But the surgeon-general of Bombay, James Cleghorn, called him off, cabling that there was no need for Haffkine's services because there was, in fact, no plague.

This government deflection didn't survive the week. On 29 September, Cleghorn's subordinate, Arthur Dimmock, announced that bacteria he had personally drawn from the bubo of a victim of the so-called glandular fever was identical to the short bacilli with rounded ends that Alexandre Yersin and Kitasato Shibasaburō had first identified as plague in Hong Kong two years before. With a white man's confirmation, the government now invited Haffkine to depart for Bombay 'at once'.[13]

Soon, hundreds were dying every day. 'The Bubonic Plague which devastated Hong Kong two years ago is steadily gaining on the doctors of Bombay and a rigorous quarantine will probably be enforced,' Winston Churchill, then a lieutenant with the

4th Queen's Own Hussars, wrote to his mother from Bangalore (now Bengaluru) that October.[14] Bombay lost nearly half its population to an exodus of residents unknowingly heeding the advice of the sixteenth-century 'Sicilian Hippocrates', Giovanni Ingrassia. The only cure for plague, Ingrassia wrote, was 'pills made of three ingredients: *cito, longe,* and *tarde*'. (Run swiftly, go far, and return slowly.)[15]

'Plague appears in a place, sweeps off anything from one-tenth to one-third of the population in a few months, and then disappears,' a mystified medical officer reported. The flight helped carry plague to Poona (now Pune), Karachi, and points across India. 'Bombay concealed its first cases, then minimized them, and now it is face to face with a severe epidemic, its trade ruined, and by its flying population it is likely to spread the disease far and wide,' the *Indian Medical Gazette* said.[16] Western India was in the grip of famine while plague ravaged Bombay. Relief shipments carried it to new locales. The rat flea *X. cheopis*, it turned out, was 'best bred in the debris of cereal grains'.[17]

Authorities began an at times brutal public health regime characterised by a militant absence of doubt.[18] While the connection between rats and plague had been known for centuries, the prevailing wisdom held that rats and humans were both victims of plague, not that the rat was a source of the disease. (Viegas and other local doctors were ignored when they suggested rats were vital to the chain of transmission.) Experts held that plague spread through rotting waste, the scouring sun, and tropical humidity. Unsanitary gases, usually emanating from the haunts of the unwashed poor, brought sickness and death. Disease could thus be conquered with a firm hand: clearing slums, flushing sewers, collecting garbage, educating natives.

The rat flea's confirmation as the source of plague was fourteen long years away when infected specimens of *Rattus-rattus* first made landfall in Bombay. Scientists, many competing for bragging rights, were flying blind and, in some cases, wilfully misleading one another – and the world – in their quest to learn the causes and cures.

In 1898, the French researcher Paul-Louis Simond reported in *Annales de l'Institut Pasteur* that, through small, seemingly intuitive experiments, he had made a powerful breakthrough, observing that plague transmission appeared impossible without the presence of fleas. 'That day, 2 June 1898,' he wrote, 'I felt an emotion that was inexpressible in the face of the thought that I had uncovered a secret that had tortured man since the appearance of plague in the world.'[19]

But Simond's findings met with scepticism. The early doubts now appear to have been appropriate. Simond was right about rats, fleas, and plague, but new scholarship indicates he never proved it. In 2022, researcher Christos Lynteris examined Simond's original notebooks and found that his experiments had actually been failures – the fleas had escaped. To cover his tracks, Simond had committed 'experimental perjury',[20] claiming a result that never happened. (His 'inexpressible emotion' may have been the galvanising fear of discovery.)

Even as officials asserted the plague in Bombay was 'mild'[21] and 'not of the severest form',[22] a vast machinery of sanitation and coercion was engaged. Mandvi was 'cleansed of its filth, its sewers flushed with torrents of salt water, and the roads and gullies drenched with disinfectants', a witness wrote with satisfaction.[23] Sanitation was one prong of the anti-plague effort. It meant inspections of private residences, torching the belongings of plague victims, tearing the roofs from affected homes to allow in purifying sunlight, washing walls in lime solution, destroying slum housing. The second prong was segregation: on 6 October the municipal corporation made hospitalisation mandatory for plague patients. Healthy residents of plague-affected homes were to be moved to segregation camps far from the affected neighbourhoods.

The forced separation of families; the fear of pell-mell mixing of high-caste patients with low; worries over whose dietary laws – if anyone's – would be respected in the new plague infirmaries, all combined to produce dread and resistance.[24] These concerns fell on deaf ears. Indians 'have not the faintest conception of the meaning or value of sanitary precautions, and attribute every calamity to the direct intervention of some supernal power', the *Gazette* complained.[25] 'They secretly resent any endeavour to change the even tenor of their ways as an attempt to tamper with their religious convictions.'[26]

In late October hundreds of millhands stoned the new Arthur Road Hospital, later home to the obliging Dr P.T. Patel, and attacked members of its staff over rumours that one of their own had been dragged there against his will.[27] In Calcutta, the *Hitavada* newspaper had condemned Bombay's measures as nothing more than an 'opportunity for the officers, big and small, to extort bribes from the people and a cause for anxiety'.[28] So it was on the streets of Bombay, where con men impersonating health officials squeezed mill workers for cash to keep them out of hospital where, it was said, the inmates were given 'some sort of poison, and that before death ensues; his body is mercilessly dissected for experimental purposes'.[29] These outlandish stories were made credible by the agonised cries, heard by passers-by on the street, of patients dying within the thatch-roofed wards.[30]

British credibility was further pulverised by the plain, tragic fact that hospitals hadn't saved anyone. There was no cure for plague – you got better or you didn't. (Antibiotic therapy wouldn't emerge until the 1940s.) Bombay's plague mortality reached a staggering 85 per cent in the pandemic's first year. Rumours flourished: the hospitals were charnel-houses meant to cull an unruly population; a mystical life-giving oil known as *momiai* (from the Persian for 'mummy') was being rendered from patients' bodies and used to protect Europeans from infection; plague was a creation of the English. The gulf between the rulers and the ruled was too wide to support something so weighty as trust.

When it came to assigning blame for the plague pandemic Indian society was an outlier in that – unlike elsewhere – it refrained from scapegoating vulnerable communities. So it was that ethnic Chinese were imagined responsible for outbreaks in Sydney, Honolulu, and San Francisco. In Cape Town 'raw Africans' and 'dirty Jews' were blamed. When authorities in

Buenos Aires were forced to admit a long-denied outbreak, they pointed the finger at indigenous people. In Glasgow, Irish Catholics were found at fault.[31] After the disease reached Los Angeles, city fathers razed[32] 2,500 homes of poor Mexican–Americans; they took no similar action when plague-infected rats were found in wealthy Beverly Hills.[33]

Haffkine rolled his eyes at the Indian government's infatuation with segregation, demolition, and carbolic acid. He considered immunisation 'the only rational first line of defence against contagion'.[34] On 10 January 1897, in secrecy, Haffkine became the first test subject for his new plague vaccine – just as, years before, he had tested the first-ever cholera vaccine on himself. With the director of the Grant Medical College looking on, Dr Nusserwanji Farkirji Surveyor injected 10 cubic centimetres – four times the expected public dose – into Haffkine's thighs. The fever and headache disappeared within twenty-four hours, and swelling subsided five days later.[35] The vaccine was later shown to be 50 per cent effective at preventing plague. The breakthrough came after three months of furious effort that drove two assistants to quit and one to suffer a nervous breakdown.[36] Thirty-six years later, the lab was still India's centre for plague investigations – and Benoyendra's first stop on his quest for a colony of his own.

While some plague-hit communities clamoured for vaccination – Haffkine's lab couldn't keep up with demand – the jab was elsewhere met with paranoia. The public's visceral response to the government's plague regime is echoed today in the deeply felt fever dreams of Covid-19 conspiracy theorists and those profiting off them.

T.K. Gajjar, a professor of chemistry at Wilson College, swore that, far from curing the disease, Haffkine's vaccine was in fact its leading agent of transmission.[37] The vaccine, he asserted, contained live but dormant bacteria that were awakened after injection, causing Indians who received the jab to unwittingly infect the unvaccinated. 'Whenever inoculations were done, the mortality, which was on the decrease, jumped up,' he told the Indian Plague Commission. 'The increase of the total mortality increased with the number of inoculations.' Anticipating the global mania for false Covid-19 cures like hydroxychloroquine and the antiparasitic drug ivermectin, Gajjar asserted that iodine terchloride, an inexpensive antiseptic, was the most effective therapy for plague.[38]

Thirty-six years later, T.K. Gajjar's iodine cure would resurface in a Calcutta courtroom as part of the high-stakes defence of Benoyendra Pandey and Taranath Bhattacharjee.

The disease continued its march across India, but British deaths were relatively few, as Churchill noted to his mother. 'The Plague of which I heard plenty coming up is here unnoticeable,' he wrote from Bangalore in December 1898. 'We have about 60 deaths a day – but nobody cares a rap & you never hear a word about it.'[39]

Plague was officially declared at Calcutta in April 1898, after Haffkine confirmed *B. pestis* in the remains of Issur Chunder Dey, a strapping young ghee seller who'd complained of fever one morning and was dead the following night. Calcuttans recalled the violations and restrictions experienced in Bombay and bolted from the city in a stampede of 100,000 people, 'though it was plague measures rather than plague they fled from', health officer J. Nield Cook reported.

Those who remained paralysed the city. On the streets where Benoyendra and Balika Bala would later enjoy the city's plentiful nightlife, mobs attacked ambulances as if they were little more than murder-mobiles. Plague vaccine was considered death in an ampoule. An Austrian visitor drowned fleeing a gang that mistook his handbag for a vaccination kit. A British doctor was forced to shoot dead two members of a group that had stormed his patient's residence.[40] As the anti-vaccine fever broke, Dr M.M. Traill Christie, a young woman on Cook's staff of harried vaccinators, remarked that, 'It is quite a pleasant change to go out without the expectation of being killed.'[41]

By the time of Amarendra Pandey's death, bubonic plague was in what passed for a lull. Some 43,000 Indians would die of plague in 1933, 'not nearly so high as in some years', the journal *Nature* remarked.

Only one fell in Calcutta.[42]

11

Squirming Rats

If it was movies he wanted, Benoyendra was spoiled for choice in Bombay. For comedy there was *What! No Beer?* with Buster Keaton and Jimmy Durante at the Capitol. If he fancied adventure, a few paise would get him Douglas Fairbanks in *Mr. Robinson Crusoe* at the Wellington Talkies, paired with a Technicolour 'Silly Symphonies' cartoon. Fans of the Gallic charmer Maurice Chevalier were doubly in luck. He was starring in both *Love Me Tonight* at the Pathé and *Love Parade* at the Palace in Byculla. But the closest Benoy, the movie-mad would-be studio boss, got to the cinema that sultry July was Ratan Salaria.

The silver-haired Salaria had once worked as a handsome bit player in Bombay silents before giving up movies for tourism. Now he worked as a guide and managed a few mid-range hotels including the Sea View and a property called the Royal Punjab. Salaria had accompanied Benoy on his April visit to B.P.B. Naidu, wholly believing that he was looking to test a cure for plague. Benoyendra had even promised Salaria a concession on the therapy once it went to market. Drawn in by the promise of an exclusive business opportunity, Salaria escorted Benoy around the city free of charge.

After concluding his wholesome ultraviolet treatments, Benoy met P.T. Patel for a last time on Arthur Road, and Patel finally directed his staff to provide facilities to Taranath. The lab was

50 yards down the road from the main hospital building. Benoy visited Patel's assistant J.M. Mehta there to ensure he was prepared. 'He told me he had seen Dr Patel and that he was bringing a doctor from Calcutta who was to do work on plague,' Mehta said. 'He asked me to keep living plague culture ready for him.'

One afternoon before Taranath's arrival, Salaria escorted Benoy to the sprawling cast-iron and glass Crawford Market, where wholesale meat and produce were supplied to the city's restaurants and grocers. Not far from the market's pyramids of mangoes and its ranks of hanging goat and mutton was a strip of five shops specialising in live birds. There, among the Muscovy ducks and parakeets and mynahs, they met Jan Mahammad, a 26-year-old former seller of hand-rolled *beedi* cigarettes. Mahammad had recently joined the animal trade; it was known around the market that he sometimes had white rats for sale. There was no stock just then, he told the well-dressed visitors, but if Benoy and Salaria returned in the morning, he would have what they needed. The next day, they received two white rats in a new wire cage, paying 5 rupees, no questions asked. (Mahammad had himself bought the rats the night before off a rich European's driver, collecting them from the boot of a polished Ford Lincoln, surely without the owner's knowledge that his car was being used to traffic laboratory mammals. Mahammad paid just 2 rupees for the rats and took home a nice profit.)

At the Sea View Hotel, Benoy instructed manager Ali Abbas to store the rodents in the cloak room, and 'to take care that they be not eaten by cats'. Abbas was in no mood for rat-sitting. Just a few days earlier, the hotel had been known as the Nizamiya, catering to Muslim travellers. It had rebranded overnight as a vegetarian establishment now targeting a Hindu clientele. The extra work of the changeover – replacing Urdu signage with Hindi, swapping posters of Sufi saints for those of Hindu deities, scrubbing out the lingering aroma of mutton – had been exhausting. Abbas refused Benoy's rats. The pushy guest could keep them in his own spacious room. If Benoyendra was worried about feline predators, Abbas said, the solution was simple: keep the door shut.

Mehta had a month-old sample of plague culture on hand at Arthur Road, but he wasn't sure if the germs were still viable. He prepared a subculture, using a platinum ring to collect the bacilli from a sealed tube before depositing them in agar growth medium, a thick gel of carbohydrates derived from red algae. The germs could take as long as forty-eight hours to grow – time would tell if they were active. As a hedge, Mehta filled out a form in triplicate requesting, or indenting for, a new tube of virulent plague from the Haffkine Institute. It arrived on 7 July, just as Taranath reached Bombay.

Arthur Road was by now the only hospital in Bombay author-ised to treat plague patients. It had been decades since fearful, frenzied mobs had hurled stones over its walls and attacked the staff. The hospital regularly sent *B. pestis* cultures to the Haffkine Institute, where they were utilised in the preparation of large quantities of Haffkine's plague vaccine for use in India and around the world. The institute in turn supplied plague culture to researchers in Europe and Africa. When a suspected plague patient arrived on the wards at Arthur Road, a doctor would draw fluid from the bubo into a sterilised syringe, placing a single drop onto a glass slide, where it was dried, fixed, stained, and examined under a microscope. The remaining fluid was deposited into a test tube lined with agar growth medium, cultured, and eventually sent to the Haffkine lab in Parel.

It's possible Patel – medical superintendent of both the City Isolation Hospitals at Arthur Road and the Maratha Plague Hospital; Honorary Physician at the King Edward VII Memorial Hospital; clinical professor of infectious diseases at Bombay Medical College; and, briefly, consulting physician to Benoyendra Chandra Pandey, Raja of Pakur – was a scrupulous man whom nature had created so deeply incurious that he never thought to inquire after the substance of Taranath's cure. It's more likely, however, that Patel heard Taranath's cover story about trying iodine against plague and, not realising Benoy and Taranath's true intent, was happy to have his palm greased in return for allowing this no-account doctor to waste time on experiments that were destined to fail.

Patel knew that better than anyone, for his own 1929 book, *Infectious Diseases and Other Fevers in India*, details the comprehensive uselessness of iodine and other disinfectants against plague. Patel believed he was fleecing a pair of greenhorns, taking harmless money in return for opening his lab. He would soon enough learn the consequences – though they would never accrue to him.

On 8 July, Taranath arrived at the laboratory carrying a small black satchel and the white rats in a cage. The subcultures were not ready – they hadn't yet grown. Mehta showed him around the lab and its equipment, and Taranath set to work, hunched over a table, creating his own cultures from both the Arthur Road and Haffkine Institute plague samples, turning a handful of germs into many. The rats were set loose in a chicken wire outbuilding adjacent to the lab. The next morning, Taranath retrieved a squirming white rat from the shed, secured it to a bench, and shaved its abdomen. Using forceps and a cotton swab, he rubbed Mehta's plague subculture onto the animal's bared flesh, in a process called scarification. While plague can't be transmitted through the unbroken skin of a human being, the flesh of rats is fatally, sufficiently porous to receive infection. The rat was placed in a cage on a shelf of the outbuilding, separate from the others. It died, curled and shivering, within twenty-four hours.

The morning of 10 July, Mehta looked on as Taranath performed a post-mortem. Taranath took samples from the dead rat's spleen, liver, and neck glands. These were stained and examined on glass slides under a microscope. 'They showed plague bacilli,' Mehta said. That same morning, Taranath, again using scarification, applied the Haffkine Institute's culture to the belly of a second white rat. Late the night of the 11th, he visited the outbuilding to check on its progress. The rat was dead. He called up to Mehta, whose private residence was above the lab. Mehta came down and unlocked the laboratory, where Taranath began a new post-mortem. Smears from the spleen, liver, and neck all revealed plague. The cultures were virulent.

Taranath removed the animal's spleen and rubbed the cut end of the diseased organ onto the exposed flesh of a third rat that Benoy had purchased at Crawford Market. That night, as their guide Ratan Salaria approached Benoy and Taranath's shared room at the Sea View, he came within earshot of them discussing the results. 'I heard Dr Taranath say to B.C. Pandey as I was outside that the doses had been given to the rats but the rats died,' Salaria said, still under the impression they were treating rodents with Taranath's cure. They changed the subject as he came nearer. The last animal died three days later, by which time Taranath and Benoy had abandoned Bombay.

The gullible crew at Arthur Road never saw them again. On the evening of 12 July, Taranath told Mehta that a family emergency had called him home; he would be in touch. There was no need to learn the fate of the third rat. They were ready. The pair departed the Sea View the following morning. Manager Ali Abbas charged for the full day when they missed the eight o'clock checkout time. Benoy didn't even complain.

Fourteen months later, in a stuffy Calcutta courtroom, Sessions Judge T.H. Ellis interrupted Dr Patel's testimony to remark on the convivial ease with which the hospital's director had placed a pathogen responsible for scores of millions of deaths into the hands of an untested stranger:

> You were approached by a man of whom you knew nothing, on behalf of another man of whom you knew nothing, for facilities for work in your laboratory... When that man arrived, you did not verify his credentials, you did not enquire of his address and that of the first man, you have no record of their visit except for the notes kept by Dr Mehta ... Do you consider that this was a proper exercise of your responsibility?

Benoyendra had one last piece of business before he and Taranath hot-footed it back to Calcutta. It was a meeting at the Bombay Mutual Life Assurance Society inside the ornamented, wedding cake Whiteaway & Laidlaw building in south Bombay to discuss a policy for Amarendra. He wished to insure himself for 23,000 rupees, and Amarendra for 51,000, but there'd been a hitch. Benoy's Calcutta insurance agents were keen to get this business – they explained in a letter to Bombay Mutual that, while Benoy was on the heavy side, 'we believe that this excess weight is due to solid bones and fully developed muscles of the applicant'. If Benoyendra could receive favourable terms despite being technically overweight, they wrote, 'we have a bright chance to capture his entire family'. But the company had baulked at a provision Benoy had insisted on for Amarendra's policy: in the event of the boy's untimely demise, he wanted the full claim paid immediately to Amar's 'legal heirs, successors, assigns, executors, or administrators' – in other words, his elder brother – without an investigation. Benoy spent two hours in Bombay trying without luck to persuade the society's secretary, Jose Mignal Cordeiro. Cordeiro assured him that Bombay Mutual policies always paid out, 'except on grounds of fraud or wilful misrepresentation'.

'Mr Pandey was not very keen to pay the premium on his own policy but he was particular in insuring his brother,' Cordeiro reported. 'I asked the reason and he told me his brother was to be married shortly.' This was, of course, untrue. Cordeiro wore Benoyendra down, and Benoy finally agreed to drop his demand for instant payment on any claim related to Amarendra's life and to complete the purchase of a policy for himself. He'd issued a cheque for 325 rupees to pay Amarendra's first quarterly premium. Cordeiro was ecstatic at landing the big fish. 'After a discussion of two solid hours the gentleman has agreed to accept our usual conditions, and he went away fully satisfied,' he wrote to the Calcutta agents. 'I think after a hard work for two hours I should deserve some remuneration on this case. Do you agree?' But Cordeiro's work was for nothing. The cheque bounced.

It is a maxim among American police detectives that the three essential elements of a homicide are means, mode, and opportunity. The means for Amarendra's murder was now sealed behind glass, carefully sequestered within Taranath's back leather handbag. The motive had been simmering inside Benoyendra's resentful heart since childhood. All he needed was an opportunity.

12

The Poisoned Spear

Benoy returned home to yet another battle.

Rani Jyotirmoyee Devi, a wealthy member of the Pakur Raj clan and the widow of Benoy's father's cousin, had been holding weekly *hatis*, or markets, in a part of the Pakur subdivision over which Benoy now claimed to hold rights. She was taking money from his pocket, and those of his employees – or so he said. In fact, Benoy had been the one to set up an illegal rival market while banning his tenants from patronising hers. Benoyendra then escalated matters by sending goons to physically force the sellers attending Rani Jyotirmoyee's *hati* to relocate to Benoy's, held nearby inside the mango orchard of a local widow. The local administration banned public assembly, and a local judge warned that both parties were 'expected to be law abiding' and to 'obey orders quietly and sit quiet till the matter has been heard and decided by the court'. The town simmered. Police were curiously slow in producing a report for the court, perhaps because the results would have been unfavourable to their friend Benoyendra – and, by extension, his one-time mistress Chanchala.

Two weeks later, Benoy backed down and closed his market, and he and Jyotirmoyee withdrew their mutual legal complaints. Benoyendra's lawyer assured the judge that the raja 'never did anything which might lead to any breach of the peace or any disturbance of public tranquillity. He is always respectful to the authority and law abiding.' While this de-escalation removed the judiciary from their dispute, tensions remained high.

'There is a great agitation going on in Pakur about social affairs,' Kananbala's husband, Ashutosh Chakravarty, wrote to a friend in early August. 'There have been two factions in the village and between them quarrels and disputes are frequently taking place. It has been a matter of great inconvenience for an outsider to go to Pakur and live there at this time.' He was reluctant to describe the *daladali* in writing. 'When I meet you I shall tell you everything in detail.'

Amarendra, meanwhile, was still starved for cash, and chastised Benoy over his spending. 'I did not purchase the gramophone,' Benoy replied. 'It was presented to me ... My trip to Nagpur, Warda, Bombay, etc., was in connection with the production of a film, and the costs were paid by the company to a rupee.' He told Amarendra to ask Surjabati to cover his recent operations and convalescence. 'Let her bear a portion of the Calcutta expenses. There is nothing wrong in it.'

'I will send you money in one week's time, sure. Do not get vexed,' he added affably.

Taranath had crossed India from west to east carrying tubes of death itself inside his black handbag. Now he needed somewhere to keep it. It would have been impossible to culture plague in the laboratory at the Medical Supply Concern. There was no privacy – a half-sized saloon-style swinging door separated the laboratory from the front office – and he didn't have after-hours access. Taranath had closed his small dental practice months before; he lacked a dedicated bench or workspace in which to feed the bacilli and keep them near the optimal temperature for growth.

Years later it was suggested by one official that Taranath had built a laboratory far from prying eyes at the Gokulpur Palace in Pakur. There, he could labour without interruption or interrogation while Benoy kept him fed and entertained. There was little evidence for this. A city boy to his neurasthenic core, Taranath could not have survived confinement in a village, whatever the rewards.

Every great endeavour calls for sacrifice, but Taranath could not have survived a spell in Pakur. Later that summer, a Calcutta homeowner named Jotindra Mohan Dutta of Meherali Mondal Street, a short walk from the sessions court at Alipore, began letting his garage at 12 rupees a month to a new tenant. The receipts listed him as a bookkeeper named Bhola Nath Bhattacharjee, but the real occupant was his brother Taranath, who experimented on rats and other small animals behind the garage's bolted door. The doctor often had company in the makeshift laboratory: a dark-complexioned taxi driver who took Taranath around in an old Ford.

Benoy and Taranath were on to something only imagined in literature and cinema. Did they see themselves as criminal innovators, or merely as happy warriors in the service of greed? The conspiracy against Amarendra shone with a modern finish, born of scientific advances by Pasteur, Haffkine, Kitasato, and Yersin, while inspired by the pen of Arthur Conan Doyle and the alchemy of the Lumières. But the concept of homicide-by-germ was older than they may have supposed. It was older than the microscope.

The medieval period is rich in claims of attempted germ warfare; most come from uncorroborated but tantalising accounts, from the use of dead animals as intentional vectors of disease at Thyne Levesque during the Hundred Years War, to the Golden Horde's decision to catapult its plague fatalities into the Genoan outpost of Cafa, on the Black Sea, in 1346.[1]

In India, the Rajput prince Prithi Singh was said to have 'expired in great torture' of smallpox after donning 'a poisoned dress presented by the Mughal emperor Aurangzeb'.[2] Poisoned garments causing fever, heat, and death feature in several legends derived from the many Rajput wars of succession.[3]

Poisoning was an ancient practice, one possibly first used by southern African hunters who applied ricin-infused beeswax to their spearheads some 40,000 years ago.[4] Kautilya, in his classic turn-of-the-first-millennium manual of statecraft, the *Arthashastra*, includes poison alongside potable water and plentiful grain as one of the pillars of a successful empire. Kautilya held that the poisoning of a single rival king was preferable to a destructive war between realms. But poison wasn't reserved for the odd obnoxious suzerain. Poisoned food could be employed against enemy troops when they visited eating houses operated by secret agents of the emperor, and on enemy parties while they worshipped at temples. Poisoned alcohol was prescribed against robber bands, to instigate conflict between rivals, and to disable enemy troops when the capital was under siege. Insiders who abetted rebellion, disgruntled princes, malcontented ministers – all faced death by poison when they least expected it.

In April 1932, as Amarendra was mustering the courage to appoint his own representatives to monitor affairs at the Pakur Raj, the members of a puzzled High Court bench in Nagpur, about 500 miles from Bombay, set free two brothers who'd been found guilty of murdering their pregnant sister. The wealthy landlords Kasherao and Ruprao had killed their sibling Lilavati after her husband abandoned her over suspicions she was carrying another man's child. Rather than live with the disgrace, they paid a local doctor named Balkrishna to inject her with a fatal dose of strychnine.[5] (The convictions were overturned after all the prosecution witnesses, including the doctor, recanted.)[6,7] While Benoy packed for his successful visit to Bombay, a Brahmin engineer was in the process of murdering his wife and two young daughters with cyanide and leaving their bodies to burn atop a charcoal heap on the kitchen floor of his rented home not far from the Sea View Hotel. There was a woman at the office with whom he was infatuated; they could never be together so long as he was married.[8]

Benoyendra and Taranath were inheritors of a tradition as old as humankind and as fresh as tomorrow's newspaper. In a way, they too were smearing poison onto a spearpoint, praying their tribe would profit from the kill.

13

When a Man Becomes Desperate

Even as Taranath tended his flock of plague germs, infectious disease continued to haunt the Pandey family – even without human intervention.

It had been the habit of Amarendra and other family members to stay at the home of his sister Kananbala and her husband Ashutosh in the quiet Bhowanipur neighbourhood when they visited Calcutta. It was here that Kananbala became ill that September, and where she died nine days later of an apparent attack of the measles, with her husband, daughter, and siblings – save Benoyendra – by her side. (While the disease typically affected children, that month had seen a wave of adult measles cases in the city.) Within days of Kananbala's passing the family abandoned the house for a new residence that Surjabati had rented on Jatin Das Road near Kalighat. No one returned to the old house, least of all Ashutosh. They had to get away from the spectre of death.

While the family mourned their loss, Amar's patience with his elder brother reached its end. On 11 September, Benoy had written another note heavy with excuses and light on cash:

My Dear Amarendra, Rs50 only has been sent to you to-day for out of pocket expenses. 80 per cent of the local population is down with malarial fever and the collection of *astam* money has been a trial. I will send you further money as soon as the *astam* money is collected and sent ... The peons, officers and all are down with fever, and work has become very difficult.

Now Amarendra began consulting lawyers and friends, looking for a painless, or the least painful, path to a division of the properties. His advisors were his uncle Rabindranath; Rabindra's attorney cousin, Baidyanath; and Sakhilal Upadhya, his father's uncle and a long-time employee of Surjabati's. They had referred him to the private practice of Rai Bahadur Ranjit Singh, an experienced government advocate in the district seat of Bhagalpur. The plans came together slowly, hampered by the outside commitments of Amar's advisors, an illness that was going around, and Amarendra's insistence on absolute secrecy.

On 18 October he wrote to Baidyanath, 'Your fever has complicated matters a little. However, please let me know how you feel.' He asked if Baidyanath had been wearing his customary protective amulet when he became ill, and recommended he see the family doctor in Pakur. Baidyanath was more than a decade his senior, but Amar still chastised him for a recent indiscretion at the Pakur telegraph office:

It would, perhaps, have been better if no mention had been made of Ranjit Babu's name in the wire that you had sent. *Dada*'s spies are very sharp ... Things that have been told by Ranjit Babu cannot be communicated to you in details by letters.

A week later, it was Amar who was too ill for a trip to see Ranjit Singh. He tried to push the errand back onto Baidyanath. 'One thing more,' he added. 'Please don't let anybody know that you are going to Bhagalpur solely for the purpose of seeing Ranjit Babu – not even to the respected *barakaka*,' by whom he meant their great uncle Sakhilal. Rani Surjabati was also down sick. 'Mother has begun to take injection and is well,' he wrote. 'Unless one or two more injections are given the result will not be definitely known.'

On 22 October, Benoy announced that the estate was in financial crisis. Crop failure had left the tenants in poverty and unable to pay their rents. 'This is to tell you that famine has already started here,' he wrote. 'I have just now finished with the *rayats* of Anjua and Nawada, where roughly we have Rs. 30,000 lying and after alternately hammering and coaxing them for more than two hours, I have failed to realise one hundred rupees. They are really prostrate. Their faces speak that beyond doubt. It is really famine and not a year of scarcity and we must get ready to face it as best we can. The expenses here would be curtailed, in consultation with mother, to a rupee within two or three days.'

Collections were down to nearly zero 'in spite of the hardest haggling', he said. 'I have failed to send you the promised money because the definite promises on which I counted have completely failed and not even small parts have turned up.' It was impossible for Amarendra and Surjabati to comprehend this from the comfort of Calcutta, Benoy said. 'Those who are somewhat away from the place may not realise the gravity of the situation now, but they would certainly realise it two months hence when Rs. 3,000 will not be collected out of Rs 16,000 due.' (Later testimony would show there was no famine at Pakur that year.)

It isn't clear if Amarendra believed the crisis was real. He finally went to see the advocate in Bhalgalpur on 26 October and returned to Calcutta. The next day he received a letter from Baidyanath, who fretted about Amar's illness – and over his safety. 'You and Nabu [Rabindranath] must be very careful about your movements in Calcutta because when a man becomes desperate, there is nothing in this world which he cannot do,' he warned. 'I consider it to be more necessary [than ever] for you to come to Pakur as soon as possible and to live amongst your relatives.'

In these, his last weeks, Amar worked with focus and determination. It always seemed that things were happening to him. Now, by fighting for his destiny, Amarendra was the one driving events.

It was taxing and stressful; it felt good. Amar had left a note with another advisor, Charu Chandra Bose, a pleader who had once worked with his father, exploring the different ways the partition might play out. Was there any way to keep the matter out of the courts and avoid expensive litigation if Benoy refused a friendly split? One idea of Amarendra's was to send agents to claim his share of the monthly rents directly from the local collectors. They would then 'hand the sum over to me', he wrote. But he feared that being too assertive on the ground could hurt his interests before the law. It was crucial that Benoy be made to answer for his wasteful and fraudulent spending. 'As I have not so far interfered with the affairs of the estate my co-sharer as the *karti* of the family is liable to me for account,' he wrote. If Amarendra tried collecting his shares directly, 'Would these proceedings in any way free him from these liabilities?'

In the event Amar somehow succeeded in collecting his share of the revenues up front, 'in what points would it differ from … [a] partition effected by the court? In other words, would it be regarded by the law as a partition *de jure*?' Amarendra would be at a disadvantage in any civil case, with Benoy holding most of the cards, including cash flow, the loyalty of the Pakur Raj's top employees, access to the books, and his innate ruthlessness. There was much to consider.

Amarendra understood he couldn't play fair against his rogue brother. In early November he learned Benoy had successfully persuaded a judge to let him withdraw 13,000 rupees from their father's account at Allahabad Bank on grounds the money was needed to resolve Amar's medical bills. (Amarendra, meanwhile, had gone into debt to pay his surgeon.) Amar turned to their father's maternal uncle, Sakhilal Upadhya, whom he had named as a representative in his short-lived power of attorney the year before. The uncle's presence on the document had infuriated Benoy, who soon took petty revenge: Sakhilal had for decades lived in a house owned by the Pakur Raj. After Amarendra reversed the power of attorney, Benoy evicted Sakhilal under the pretence of renovating the property.

Sakhilal was now acting as Amarendra's all-but-secret agent. Writing from Calcutta, Amar piled instructions onto the loyal kinsman. For the first time in his long contest with Benoyendra, he was playing to win. He wanted copies of recent suits Benoy had filed against other landlords, an accounting of how much the estate was earning, from where, and what properties he actually had claim to. He directed his aged uncle to pay for this knowledge wherever it was available.

'You shall have to prepare a list of immovable properties as will be required for the purpose of an amicable partition,' Amar told him. 'It is here that you can show your experience and ability. You possibly remember the names of the *mehals*. But that's not [enough]. You have to state accurately what is the income derived from each of the *mehals* and what is the amount of rent payable there for [*sic*]. But how?'

'It will be easier for you than me to find out the means in regard to this matter,' Amar wrote. After decades of working for his father and aunt, Sakhilal would have an intimate familiarity with the different parcels. He would have access to some of the recent rent receipts, and to those tardy collectors who hadn't yet submitted theirs. 'Those papers or copies thereof will have to be obtained from those who have not filed them,' Amar wrote. 'If 2 or 4 rupees have to be spent for this purpose in particular cases you should not hesitate to do so.'

Amarendra also needed account books showing where, and on whom, money was being spent. For these, he told Sakhilal to see Benoy's lawyer, Kalipada Ojha. He would do anything for money. 'Kali Ojha of the other party is willing to work in mother's office,' away from prying eyes, he wrote. 'You shall be able to get some work out of him by inducement and bribes. But you must remember one thing very particularly ... that he should not be told anything which, if communicated to *Dada*, may be prejudicial' to the partition plan.

'In short, we must achieve our object by having recourse to tricks or artifices,' he said. Benoy's dependence on corrupt deputies would now be used against him. 'It is my belief that there is no such officer in *Dada*'s office who will not let you examine the papers of the office in return for some extra gain. See that not even a word of the fact that I am doing these things in order to become separate is disclosed.'

In addition to bribes, Amar encouraged Sakhilal to use misdirection. 'If it be absolutely necessary, you may spread this rumour, that litigation is imminent between mother and *Dada* and that you are doing all these things on behalf of mother,' he wrote.

Benoy was anything but idle during Amar's weeks of plotting. On 9 November, he moved a subordinate judge at Pakur for permission to collect the entire 17,000-rupee deposit that had been held in trust for him and Amarendra, but the judge refused because the matter had already been calendared for the following week. Having failed to pre-emptively capture the windfall for himself, Benoy wrote to Amarendra with more cash and upbeat promises of an equal distribution. Soon, he told Amar cheerfully, 'We will be in a position to withdraw the money on any Treasury day we like.' He enclosed 50 rupees. It was too little, too late.

On Tuesday the 14th, Amarendra returned to Pakur. The next morning, he and Rabindranath raced by taxi to the town of Amrapoara, 32 miles away, where the judge was sitting that day, and filed an objection to Benoyendra's joint succession certificate. 'Your petitioner has come to learn that ... B.C. Pandey, has already filed a petition for withdrawal of the said amount ... without knowledge and instruction of this petitioner,' their plea read. 'The petitioner submits that the sole intention of Babu B.C. Pandey is to deprive him of his legal and legitimate share in the said amount of Rs. 17,000.'

'Your petitioner has lost all faith in Babu Benoyendra Chandra Pandey,' Amar swore in his affidavit. The Pakur Raj's legal servants, he added, 'are absolutely under his control and as such are his creatures'. The manoeuvre worked: the court barred withdrawal pending a hearing. As they drove home to Pakur, Amar and Rabindranath crossed paths with a car heading in the opposite direction. Inside were Benoy and two of his advisors on their way to see the judge, where he asserted his rights as *karti* to withdraw funds for any family purpose he saw fit. In this case, Benoy affirmed, the money was needed to pay the 'personal debts of Amarendra Chandra Pandey'.

It was too late. Benoy – for once – had been foxed. The funds were frozen.

Amarendra returned to Pakur and carried on preparing a case for partition with the help of his uncles – snooping, strategising, hoping. At 3.05 p.m. on the afternoon of 18 November, an express inland telegram was sent from Calcutta to Pakur at a cost of 2 rupees, 5 annas:

Amarendra Chandra Pandey
Harindanga, Pakur
Come Calcutta after court hours do not anything without
consulting me.
Surjabati.

14

Boro Ghori

Rani Surjabati Devi reclined without rest in the sitting room of her rented home on Jatin Das Road in Calcutta.

The quiet of Bollygunge, the post-monsoon sun through the windows, the riot of growth in the garden outside brought no comfort. Surjabati felt depleted, depressed, unwell. She'd been low since before Amarendra took sick with tetanus, but the trials of the past year had truly drained her. The emotional and financial burden of Amar's health scares had been made worse by her conviction that Benoy and his carousel of doctors were somehow complicit in both Amar's tetanus and the subsequent crippling infection. She was ever-worried for Amarendra – and ever-wary of his brother. How far had he really gone to harm Amar? How far would he go? Already she had insisted that Amarendra never travel alone; one of her servants accompanied the boy whenever he left Pakur. What more could she do? Surjabati never knew what to make of Amarendra's story of the pince-nez. Could spectacles cause disease? She herself hadn't seen any marks or cuts on his nose. She'd witnessed a lot in her time, but the tale was too strange. And Amarendra had complained of a blister on his toe two weeks before the tetanus. He'd popped the blister with a sewing needle.

None of it made sense.

Whatever the source of Amarendra's sickness, Surjabati had no doubt that Taranath, the first of Benoy's uninvited doctors, had been something of a joke. She knew a weak, dishonest man when she saw one; they were everywhere. Dr Sivapada was more of a puzzle. He was well known, and he had treated her brother-in-law Protapendra, and many others in their wealthy community. Then again, Protapendra had died under Sivapada's care. But people died all the time. (Average life expectancy in India was barely twenty-eight years.) Still, the very fact that Sivapada had come to Deoghar at Benoyendra's behest made him suspect. Who knew what these Calcutta doctors were all about? Benoy's mania for *kamini kanchan*, women and gold, tainted all his associations. Dr Dhar may have been educated in England, but Amar's terrible abscess was a direct result of the serum injection he had demanded. Dhar had brought the immunoglobulin from the city in his own bag. It was anyone's guess what poison he could have slipped inside, or what Benoy might have paid him to do so.

More than two decades had passed since the death of her husband, Satyendra, Protapendra's elder brother, and she had made the most of things within the constraints of her gender and childlessness. Unlike many women, she had been allowed to inherit her husband's valuable holdings, and she controlled her own money – 30,000 a year – chose her own managers, and hired and fired as she liked. Through the tragic deaths of Protapendra's two wives, she had received the gift of motherhood. His four children had brought Surjabati tremendous joy and provided both a wellspring of unconditional love and a purpose beyond the dry management of property and profit. Even foul Benoyendra, she had to admit, had once been a little beauty.

The rani had been married as a young teenager to a man in his 20s, absorbed into her husband's joint household to fight for survival and, if possible, thrive. The days had revolved around keeping house, *zenana* gossip, and tending her spouse. Only through her own initiative (and, sometimes, if blessed with a supportive husband) would a bride in young Surjabati's position find a life of the mind. The Bengali writer Jyotirmoyee Devi* described the limited opportunities and intellectual expectations that countless girls faced as they became young wives. Recalling 'the education of a bygone age', she lamented how 'we had no opportunity to experience [literature's] depth, its sweeping realms'.

'Five books by Vidyasagar – from Part I to *Bodhoday* – comprised all our learning. And, we heard the *Ramayana*, the *Mahabharata* and the *Puranas*. Learning began around the age of five and was over by the age of ten or eleven. That marked the entry into domestic life – married life,' wrote Devi, who was married at age 10 and widowed at 25. 'Sometimes, very rarely, we were taught the First English primer or the alphabet: so that we might be able to address letters!'[1] Literature was beyond the pale. 'Most women would have been heartily ashamed of an accusation that they were hankering after these very elementals of knowledge, and hotly resented it,' wrote Frieda Hauswirth, a Swiss artist who lived for nine years in Calcutta with her Bengali husband.[2]

The process of widowhood would have been even more traumatic to the thousands of teenage girls who lost their husbands each year, some before they had reached puberty. The grieving woman-child would be stripped of her jewellery, made to smash her bangles. Her wrists would remain bare for the rest of her life. She would wash from her forehead the red vermillion *sindur* that her husband first placed there on the wedding day as a symbol of her married state. Until death, she was to remain cold, inert, banished from desire. The new widow would remove her warm, colourful sari and exchange it for one of plain white cotton.[3] Her hair was cut off.

The Indian census of 1931 counted twenty-five widows under the age of 15 for every 1,000 women.[4,5] (In 1929 the legal age of marriage for girls was set at 14; that same year, Britain raised its legal age from 12 to 16.) Widows were forbidden to remarry in the Hindu tradition, and a common sentiment held that a woman outlived her spouse only by dint of her own sins. The remainder

---

★   Not to be confused with the brothers' aunt of the same name, Rani Jyotirmoyee Devi of the Pakur Raj Estate.

of a widow's life was meant to be penance for this most terrible of crimes, though her deprivation could be mitigated if she were lucky enough to birth a son before her husband's death. Whether a widow was treated as a detested servant or as a beloved family member, the rules of her station were usually ironclad. In many households, she could not eat or even touch savoury foods; she was prevented from attending festivals and celebrations.[6] While reformers had pushed for the remarriage of young widows, they failed to make an impact. The prevailing conservatism appears in Nirad Chaudhuri's memoir of 1930s India, *Thy Hand, Great Anarch!* Chaudhuri recalls his grandfather's horror when, following the funeral of a fellow clerk, someone insinuates that a member of their party might marry the dead scribe's wife, whom he had loved since childhood:

'Widow re-marriage?' cried out Grandfather, shocked and scandalized.

'Why not? The law allows that,' replied the man who had made the suggestion.

'But whose law?' asked Grandfather quickly, turning on the speaker.

'The law which the English have made, is it not? The English and chastity? Oh, Oh! Marriage of widows is adultery.'[7]

Surjabati was in her early 20s when her husband died. Even in the relatively forgiving setting of the Gokulpur Palace, living under the protection of her brother-in-law, caring for his children, enjoying a large personal income, the rani still inhabited a world of obnoxious boundaries. 'Those were times when, let alone mixing with others outside of the home, even conversation with one's near relatives within the home was governed by outlandish rules and regulations,' author Jyotirmoyee Devi recalled. 'It was forbidden to talk to one's husband's father, elder brother or uncle, and the older women were not allowed to speak with their sons-in-law and other male relatives by marriage.'[8]

Many widows relied on the care of their fathers or their sons. Surjabati expected nothing but antipathy from Benoyendra, while Amar's devotion was clear. She wished to see her boy secure, married, unafraid. The ordeal at Deoghar, followed by Kananbala's death, had been overwhelming. It was both reassuring and a reason for apprehension that Amarendra was now taking the fight to Benoy. There would be nothing but vexation until their dispute was settled – if it could be settled. And Surjabati knew that, even if Benoy somehow conceded to a decent peace with Amarendra, she would forever remain in his gunsights. He wanted her money and he wanted her gone. It was something she'd grown used to, like monsoon flooding and seasonal dengue.

Surjabati didn't raise her head at the sound of the bell, but she shot bolt upright when Amarendra walked in. 'Why did you come?' she asked. He showed her the telegram. Benoy again, she seethed. Amar settled into a guestroom. His sister Banabala was staying at Jatin Das Road, as were Kananbala's husband Ashutosh and their daughter Anima. Having made the journey down, Amarendra agreed to stay the week and travel back to Pakur with Surjabati and the rest of the gang. It would give him time to consider what Benoy was planning, and to visit his Calcutta lawyers. And to maybe have a little fun.

Benoyendra came to visit the next day and the brothers spoke alone for more than an hour. Amarendra absorbed what Benoy had to say about the financial shortfall in Pakur, and then told him of his intention to seek a permanent division of the estate. Benoyendra was unusually magnanimous, and the meeting ended on a cordial note. 'If you want a partition, let us do it amicably,' he told Amar. 'If we fail, then go to court.'

Amarendra spent the next few days in Calcutta among his friends and relations. On Tuesday, the 21st, Surjabati dictated and signed a letter to Amar's great-uncle Sakhilal in Pakur; soon they would all be safe at home. Surjabati instructed him to rent a cottage owned by a local attorney for her son-in-law Ashutosh to live in. She went on to write:

Hearing about the telegram ... I think that ... [Benoyendra] may, at any moment, send a wire in my name to any one of you for paying money or for having something contrary to my wishes done. In the circumstances if you get any such wire please have it verified and if you have the least doubt please write to me to ascertain the truth or otherwise of it.

Benoyendra was staying a twenty-minute drive from Surjabati's with his wife, children, and his paternal grandmother. Surjabati and Amarendra visited so she could pay her respects to her aged mother-in-law, and the brothers again discussed a potential framework for their legal divorce. It was here that Benoyendra learned of their plans to return to Pakur the following Sunday.

That Friday night, Amar, his sister Banabala, and Anima drove from Jatin Das Road to the Purna Theatre for a night's entertainment with Rani Jyotirmoyee Devi, their elder aunt from the Pakur Raj. Surjabati and Jyotirmoyee were estranged. Despite their common experience as affluent, childless widows of the same vaunted clan – each targeted by Benoyendra, no less – there was some ancient injury or antipathy that neither woman cared to discuss. Jyotirmoyee was wealthier than Surjabati's wing, with a considerable income of 150,000 rupees a year. Unlike Surjabati, she had received a full education; she lived a public life. Jyotirmoyee was active in educational causes, and would, after independence, serve as deputy health minister in the Bihar state government.[9, 10] Surjabati's late husband had boycotted her wedding to his cousin, a maths prodigy; she in turn never paid social calls on Surjabati.

No one had any quarrel with the children, however. The Purna was neutral territory, and the night was young. The art deco theatre on Russa Road served second-run foreign and local productions to an educated audience of lawyers, clerks, teachers, and students. The movie hall occasionally ran what the censors referred to as 'sex films' – pictures that included passionate kissing on the face, neck, and shoulders – but few women attended. Ladies came out in force for Bengali productions based on Hindu mythology or popular novels. On those nights, 'We get a very large percentage of *zenana* audience', the manager reported. 'In fact, I might say the *zenana* audience then is more than the male audience … and it is sometimes difficult to control the rush.'

This night's entertainment featured neither borderline smut nor the pious adventure of the *Ramayana*. Instead, the family had come out for the thrills of *King of the Jungle*, a Tarzan knock-off starring the hunky former Olympic swimmer Buster Crabbe. It was a setting that Surjabati would have found unthinkable. Jyotirmoyee and a few friends arrived ahead of the 6 p.m. show; she told her driver, Ramjas, to direct Amarendra's party upstairs where she was waiting. A short time later, they pulled up to the portico and made their way to join her on the mezzanine.

As Ramjas idled outside the hall, chatting with Surjabati's driver inside his employer's car, he saw a third vehicle arrive with a Punjabi wheelman and two passengers: Benoyendra and 'a man of dark complexion, neither tall nor long, with an ordinary shirt on', whom Ramjas had never seen before. He watched as Benoy first entered the theatre, and emerged a moment later. Benoyendra called over to the stranger and brought him inside. After five minutes they exited again and loitered outside the Purna, moving from an outdoor snack bar to a betel-nut stall until thirty minutes before the theatre let out, when they finally drove off. Idly, Ramjas and the other driver wondered what Benoy was doing, but it was soon time to take their charges home and the matter was forgotten.

At around 9.30 the following evening, a businessman named Tulsi Charan Bose and some friends stopped into Kellner's Refreshment Room at Howrah railway station for bottles of lemonade while they waited for two members of their group to leave on a 10.20 train. Nearby, on the right, he spied a man he knew. Bose owned a stone quarry and a coal business in Pakur, and he recognised Benoyendra right away, though he didn't know the man who shared the slouching raja's table. The stranger was, like himself, on the darker side, a man 'short of stature', wearing a homespun cotton shirt. Bose pegged him for 30 or 32 years old. 'Just as one man notices another man, so I noticed the colour, stature, dress,' he said. 'I did so as one notices a man sitting beside him.' Benoy either didn't see or chose to ignore the quarry owner; he and his drinking partner left a few minutes later, having each put away a glass of Exshaw #1 brandy and two White Label whiskies. The bill was 7 rupees, 10 paise, and the saloon 5 miles and a river away from Benoy's rented house on Bondel Road.

The next morning, Sunday the 26th, Benoyendra stopped at Surjabati's house to confirm their departure on the 1.30 Pakur Express and said he would come after lunch. Around noon, Surjabati sent a taxi bearing her cook, two servants, and part of the household's baggage ahead with Ashutosh Chakravarty. Shortly after reaching the station, Ashutosh spotted Benoyendra standing near the first-class booking office and approached him. Benoy told his brother-in-law he had come early in case the train left ahead of schedule. Calcutta friends and family always assembled at the station to see off Surjabati's brood, but Benoyendra had never once been among them. Sometime later, Surjabati, Amarendra, Banabala, and Anima boarded a second taxi with still more luggage. (Surjabati's own car, purchased the month before, had been loaded onto a morning train and would be waiting when they arrived in Pakur.) The taxi wove a path through Calcutta's thick lifeblood of plodding oxcarts, horse-drawn tongas, diesel lorries, electric tramcars, and man-pulled rickshaws. It carried them over the muddy Hooghly River and made a series of tight turns into the queue at the Howrah Station entrance. Howrah was the biggest train station in India, its façade a glazed redbrick jumble striped with layers of arched grilles and windows facing downtown Calcutta across the river.

As they waited for another car to unload ahead of them, Anima spied her uncle standing beneath one of the eight symmetrical red towers that gave the junction the air of an escape-proof penitentiary. She watched with interest as 'Benoy made a signal by a nod of the head', she recalled. 'I cannot say to whom he made the signal. He looked towards our taxi.' Banabala noticed it, too. 'At first I saw Benoy making a signal with his eyes,' she said. 'Next, I saw him raising his hand. When he made the signal, he was looking right at us.' Like her niece, she couldn't tell who her brother's cue was meant for. When they finally pulled up at the entrance, Benoy came forward, called for some porters, and had their bags removed from the taxi. He was in a gay mood, charming, almost affectionate.

Amarendra, wearing a grey flannel kurta and vest with a cotton shawl, got down first and went ahead to see if Ashutosh had purchased their tickets. He returned to the taxi a few minutes later, tickets in hand, and beckoned the women to join him. They passed first through the public booking hall: Amarendra, followed by Anima, then Banabala, and Rani Surjabati about 3 yards behind her; Benoy brought up the rear. Just as Amarendra passed the 'No Exit' gate dividing the booking hall and the passenger-only station hall, within sight of the station's two-faced *Boro Ghori*, or Big Clock, he felt a blow and a sharp pain to his right shoulder as someone barrelled into him and wheeled away, swallowed by the nebula of travellers.

Amar stood in the dim hall between dust-heavy bolts of sunlight and pushed up his sleeve to examine the wound. There was a clear liquid like ghee on his shirtsleeve, and his bare skin bore a single crimson dot ringed with a shining, translucent corona.

They made their way to the carriage on Platform Three, where Amarendra's cousin, Kamala Prosad Pande, and a friend, Ashoke Prokash Mitra, waited to see him off. It was clear Amar was upset, and before they could ask, he described what had happened, gesturing to the mark on his arm. '*Futu-da*,' he said, using Kamala's nickname, 'just see what the matter is.' Kamala leaned in for a better look and saw a red pinprick with 'something dried up and glazed around it'.

Amarendra became ashen, his youth evaporating. 'I asked Babu why he was so much afraid, and he said that when the *murtiman* [ogre] had come to show his love for him, he was very suspicious,' Kamala recalled.

Right away, Kamala told him to forget about the train and stay back in Calcutta to have his blood examined. The cousins were on opposing sides of a legal dispute over property in Pakur, but these matters never got in the way of their affection. Having already heard Amar's account of the pince-nez and the tetanus, Kamala was instantly deeply alarmed. Benoy reached the group and asked what the trouble was. '*Dada*, someone has pricked me,' Amar replied. The elder brother 'said it was nothing', Banabala recalled. 'He said it without examining *Babu*'s arm.' As Amarendra pointed to the tiny wound, Benoy pushed forward for a first look, led Amar from the platform into the carriage, and rubbed the spot with his bare left thumb. He scoffed, and pressed Amar over his urgent business in Pakur. Didn't he remember? They had an estate to divide.

Amarendra asked his cousin to see if he could squeeze anything out of the pinprick, and a little blood was produced. The glaze Kamala had first noticed was now gone; Benoy had rubbed it away. Amar's loose sleeve had been pushed up under his armpit; he allowed it to fall and, as it did, a single drop of oily liquid was seen to glide down the flannel fabric.

'I insisted on Babu's not going by that train,' Kamala said, but Benoy 'got annoyed and rebuked us, saying we were making a mountain out of a molehill and asked why we were detaining him as he had lots of work to do. He said we had no sense. He asked Babu to leave and, in a way, forced him into the compartment.' No one yet said the word *poison*, but it was already twisting and flowering within the group.

After Benoyendra's outburst, Amarendra's friend Ashoke refrained from speaking up; to do so meant violating the rules of propriety. They had met just six months before during the family's stay in Bhubaneshwar, and the two were now loyal friends and confidants. Even in the face of the strange assault, Benoyendra's reputation for treachery, and the events at Deoghar, neither Ashoke, nor his cousin Kamala, nor the wounded Amarendra himself would contemplate upsetting the customary chain of command. 'I could not dare to ask Babu to stay on in Calcutta, as Kamala Prosad was being taken to task,' Ashoke explained. 'We were asking him to stay and his own brother was telling him to go on.' Rather than openly challenge Benoyendra, Ashoke advised his friend *sotto voce*. 'I said something to Babu, whispering in his ear: I told him he would do better to stay, but first cut the portion and let the blood flow.' There was no argument; no one spoke up. 'Kamala did not rebuke

Sadhan, Sadhan was rebuking him,' Ashoke said. 'He was the elder brother. How could Kamala rebuke him?'

With the practice of decades, Benoy had muscled Amarendra onto the train without the slightest shove. With the practice of decades, Amar did as he was told. He bent low and 'took the dust' from his brother's feet, and then his nemesis and his champions got down from the train and their lives went on, while his approached its end.

The ladies had by now taken their seats in the compartment and Ashutosh had finished stowing the luggage. As they settled in, Amarendra showed no sign of pain, but he was 'anxious and of disturbed mind', his brother-in-law recalled. He asked for a knife to cut away the wound as Ashoke had suggested, but none was available. Banabala doused the spot in iodine and asked him, 'Did you see the man? Was he a *bhadralog*?' – a gentleman? Was he *one of us*? He wasn't, Amar replied, describing what he could recall of the small, dark-complexioned enigma wearing handloomed cotton who had slapped into him and vanished.

It was a grim journey home. Anima, who'd lost her mother just two months before, shared a cushioned bench with Amar. Ashutosh was on the next bench, with Banabala and Surjabati facing them, the rani lying back, a hand draped over her eyes.

15

Like Something Out of a Foreign Novel

They spoke little about the strange events at Howrah. Those who learned of them were alarmed. Amarendra was frank with his uncles. 'You know my brother well,' he told Rabindranath. It wasn't the pinprick alone that occupied him, but Benoyendra's presence at the station. When Sakhilal rebuked him for returning to Pakur instead of seeking medical attention in Calcutta, Amarendra responded with fatalism. 'My brother is determined to take my life,' he said. 'What precaution can I take?'

Anima and Banabala appear to have said nothing about Benoyendra's strange behaviour outside at the station. They hadn't yet connected their observations with Amarendra's predicament. Three days passed without action. Whether it was due to fear or simple inertia, Amar's defenders were paralysed while the microbes in his blood were anything but. Already *B. pestis* was colonising Amarendra's lymph nodes. Plague endotoxins had begun their assault on his lungs and other organs. Yet he still felt fit. Amar tried to put the incident out of his mind and focus on work – ledgers, receipts, land records, the details he believed would make or break his future.

On 27 November Kamala Prosad Pande wrote, imploring Amarendra to return to Calcutta. He had told his elder brother Rama about the incident, and both siblings felt it was imperative

Amarendra get himself back to the city. Kamala sealed the letter in an envelope, handed it to a servant, and hoped for the best:

> Dear Babu, hope you have all reached Pakur safely. On seeing the state of things, the anxiety in my mind, as also in the mind of that friend of yours [Ashoke], has increased all the more after your departure. I would have done better if I could compel you not to go. Ramudada has become very suspicious on hearing [of the events at Howrah]. Of course, our surmises may be entirely false and pray to god that they may be so. But when the thing has happened it is better to come to Calcutta sharp and to get your blood examined … The thing may or may not be injurious, but it is his very presence that is to be the most dreaded … Write to me about your welfare as early as possible. Accept my blessings. Finis.

Kamala's letter seems to have stirred Amarendra. On Tuesday the 28th, two weeks after he and Rabindra had thwarted Benoy's designs on the 17,000 rupees, Amar and Rabi caught a southbound train to Calcutta. Amarendra went straight to the house on Jatin Das Road, but Rabindra taxied first to the home of Dr Nalini Ranjan Sen Gupta, one of the city's top physicians, and left a note asking him to visit as soon as possible. Sen Gupta made a house call at 2 p.m. the next day, but his examination of Amarendra revealed nothing beyond the heart damage left behind by tetanus. Sen Gupta was sceptical when Amarendra told him the story of the mysterious jab at Howrah, but on closer look, 'I found the mark of prick on his right upper arm, the right deltoid – something like the mark of a hypodermic needle.' Amar had no fever, felt no discomfort, but 'was very anxious about this prick', Sen Gupta said. Amar told the doctor 'that his brother had been trying to kill him for some time past'.

Amar 'inquired from me whether he was going to get anything serious', Sen Gupta said. 'In order to cheer him up, I said it was nothing … I gave him some medicines against bacterial poisons, accepting his story, to prevent some possible sepsis.' Later, when asked to define sepsis, Sen Gupta replied, 'sepsis means a poison producing putrefaction in the system ... In ordinary meaning it means blood poisoning.' Prescriptions in hand, Amarendra was keen to get back to Pakur, but 'after some hesitation' Sen Gupta recommended he stay back another day.

Late the next morning, Sen Gupta found Amarendra with a fever of 38.9°C and pain in the right armpit. He quickly scribbled a note and asked Rabindra to deliver it to his nephew, Dr Santosh Gupta, an assistant researcher at the School of Tropical Medicine. He requested tests that would indicate Amar's white blood cell count, his red blood cell count, and the presence of malaria parasites:

My Dear Sontosh [*sic*], I want you to come and take the blood of a patient of mine ... Please treat this as v. important and urgent. If you can't come, please send Dr Kali Banerjee or Dr Panja or Dr B.M. Das Gupta and L.M. Ghosh.

An hour later, Rabindra Pandey knocked at the door of Santosh Gupta's laboratory at the School of Tropical Medicine on Central Avenue. The school had been established by the pioneering bacteriologist Leonard Rogers (he and his new wife drew up the plans during their honeymoon in Shillong[1]) and was a critical centre of research on diseases including malaria, kala-azar, and cholera. Santosh read his uncle's note and gathered his gear. He carried a glass flask of glucose broth, a sterilised syringe, glass slides, alcohol, and cotton, all of it wrapped in a parcel of sterilised paper. They left together at 1 p.m.

At Jatin Das Road, Santosh recorded Amarendra's pulse, noted the young man's fever, and drew 5 cubic centimetres of blood. Santosh was meticulous. He took the flask from the paper wrapping, removed the stopper, and ran a flame over the lip before ejecting Amar's drawn blood into the broth. He burned the cork to destroy possible contaminants and plugged the flask tight. There was a small amount of blood remaining in the syringe. This he deposited onto a glass slide; from there he drew it into two thin, glass pipettes for determining white and red cell counts. The last of the remaining blood he divided between three slides on which he prepared dried smears for examination. He wrote the patient's name and the date on each of these with a grease pencil.

On the 2-mile taxi ride to the laboratory with Rabindranath, Santosh Gupta held the flask upright in his hand to prevent the broth from sloshing and making contact with the stopper. Once there, he placed it in an incubator set to 37°C where, over time, any bacteria present would feed on the glucose, multiply, and reveal themselves. Following his uncle's instructions, he looked for, but found no sign of malaria; there was a slightly elevated white blood cell count indicating infection or inflammation. As Santosh closed the lab and headed for home, Amarendra's blood sample was snug and warm in the incubator. The coming days would tell which, if any, bacilli were running riot in his veins. Rabindranath called him daily hoping for word of a breakthrough.

That evening, as Amar's condition worsened, Surjabati received a wire from Rabindra: 'Babu got high fever. Case seems complicated. Send servant and money.' Amarendra was still breathing without difficulty, though a throbbing ache under the arm preyed on his mind. Surjabati gathered the family and made for Calcutta the next day.

On Friday, 1 December, Dr Sen Gupta brought over Amarendra's former surgeon L.M. Banerji. Banerji knew Amarenda well, having treated his infection and return to health, but Nalini also wanted him present as a witness in case the mysterious illness became a police matter. 'I acted as if I believed the story to be true,' Banerji said, 'but the story seemed so incredible that I did not accept it altogether.' Amarenda's fever had risen to 40°C. The right axilla was swollen with enlarged glands that were tender to the touch. The injection site, with its raised weal, was now producing some discharge. With the stethoscope to his damp chest they heard something more than Amarendra's enlarged heart. Pneumonia was creeping in.

'We were altogether in the dark as to what might have been injected,' Sen Gupta recalled. 'We were like blind men.' He had business in Allahabad the next day and left Amar in Banerji's care, but the case continued to trouble him. Before heading off the next morning on the Bombay Mail, Sen Gupta asked his nephew if anything had turned up in the blood culture. It was wishful thinking – he knew twenty-four hours was insufficient. Santosh hadn't even left home for work. 'How can you get a result so early?' he asked his uncle. When he reached the lab, Santosh briefly removed the flask from the incubator and held it to the light. As expected, there were no signs of growth; the broth was clear.

Surjabati, Ashutosh, Banabala, and Anima were by now back in Calcutta to watch over Amar. On Saturday, 2 December, L.M. Banerji returned in the company of another doctor, Bidhan Roy. Banerji asked about Amarendra's story of the pinprick at Howrah. If it was true, he told Surjabati, she had to inform the authorities. 'Rani Surjabati replied that as she had not seen anything herself, what could she say to the police?' Either out of concern for Amarendra's feeble health or from reluctance to risk the clan's reputation on an investigation – or both – no detectives were called. 'As Amarendra had grown nervous, the inmates [of the house] did not like to summon the police for fear that he should be upset by their arrival,' Banerji recalled.

As desperation set in, the family called for still more doctors. That afternoon they summoned Sivapada Bhattacharjee, who had examined Amar at Deoghar, and Girija Sankar Chatterji. Sivapada listened to the story, examined Amarendra, and said that some bacterial agent must have been injected. 'Is this not the work of B.C. Pandey?' he exclaimed.

'How do you suspect this?' Rabindra asked. No one had mentioned Benoyendra's presence at the train station.

'I know the chap very well,' Sivapada replied. Still, he said, he was optimistic that whatever was causing Amar's sickness would pass with antiseptic treatment. Rabindra was not convinced.

At nine that evening, they were joined by Chatterji, who had been Rabindranath's teacher at Ashtanga Ayurvedic College. He lived just a short walk away – it was two minutes from his back door to Surjabati's. The doctors of Western and Eastern medicine had a brief conference. 'We together examined the right upper arm – the site of the puncture,' Chatterji said. 'I found a red, dark area about the size of a rupee [coin] over the deltoid emitting a discharge at its centre. The area was enflamed.' Sivapada told Chatterji he had found a pneumonic patch in the lungs, and as they examined the weal he wondered if it couldn't be a case of anthrax they were observing. Anthrax might produce malignant pustules at the site of the injection. And, while the inhalation of anthrax spores was closely associated with pneumonia, infections of the flesh were also known to sometimes reach the lungs. But anthrax in Asia was considered less virulent than in Europe.

As the two stepped out of the room to wash their hands, Sivapada told Chatterji in Bengali, '*Je rakam Bilati novele pora jay*.' The case, he marvelled, was 'like something out of a foreign novel'.

Still, Chatterji said, 'I did not myself believe the story at the time.'

By now Amarendra was surrounded by family. Benoy wasn't among the visitors, though Kalikinkar Misra, his *dewan* from Pakur, did come to enquire about Amar's worsening health. At Sivapada's direction, the family had hired an oxygen tank. Sivapada and an assistant administered the oxygen in shifts. Throughout, the family said, he assured them Amarendra would recover. 'I never heard Sivapada say that the patient was getting worse,' Ashutosh reported. 'I asked him every time he visited what his condition was. I last asked him at 8.30 or 9 p.m. on Sunday night. We could see that his condition was getting worse from Sunday evening.'

Whether he acknowledged it or not, the doctor clearly did know Amarendra was deteriorating. Working the phones from his home office, he scoured the city for a supply of Felton's serum, an intravenous therapy made of concentrated antibodies that was known to reduce certain pneumonia fatalities by half.[2] He persuaded the owner of a dispensary to open up after hours and sent an aide with one of Surjabati's servants to collect the serum that evening.

The family wired Nalini Sen Gupta in Allahabad, 500 miles away, that things had become dire, and he cut short his business and booked a ticket to Calcutta. The gaunt Amarendra was still speaking until 10 p.m., when he faded into a private struggle to survive. Ever since Amar had taken to his bed, his rasping speech had one constant refrain: that 'for his property, which he would have given away for the mere asking, his *dada* did not scruple to take his life'. Everyone heard him say so.

Around midnight Rabindranath looked in on Amarendra and found him struggling while Sivapada's assistant R.D. Ghose rested between oxygen sessions in the next room. The house didn't have a telephone. Rabindra woke Ghose and sent him to summon Sivapada, who lived near College Street 5 miles away. He returned alone; Sivapada never came. Amarendra died around 3.50 a.m. on the morning of 4 December 1933, seven and a half days after boarding the train from Howrah.

Dr Ghose was reluctant to sign a death certificate – other physicians had examined Amar, while his own role had been limited to administering oxygen and intravenous medicine. He drove Provash Misra, an employee of Surjabati's, to Sivapada's residence. They pulled up in front of the white, three-storey house and called out from the car into the marble courtyard, waking Sivapada's servant, who had been sleeping on a mat just inside the front door. He opened the gate, spoke with Ghose, and went back in. After some time, Misra was summoned inside and told to take a seat in the front room. After ten minutes, the servant came down from Sivapada's quarters and handed him the signed certificate. He read and folded the document and placed it in his shirt pocket. It named septic pneumonia as the cause of death. When Misra left the house with the night sky just beginning to lighten, he was surprised to find that Dr Ghose – and his Austin 7 motorcar – had left without him. It was the last they saw of Ghose. Misra hoofed it to Cornwallis Street and found a taxi back to Jatin Das Road.

When dawn came, Ashutosh and Rabindranath started the grim work of preparing for Amarendra's funeral while attending to the desolate women of the household. Surjabati was 'almost out of her mind' with grief. Ashutosh and Provash Misra drove to Benoy's house to inform him of Amar's death and to request he join them and take his customary role in performing cremation duties for his brother. Benoy exploded at Ashu and asked why he'd been kept in the dark – this despite the fact his top lieutenant Kalikinkar Misra had visited the house two days before, when it was clear Amar was in bad shape.

'I was shocked to hear what they said, and I demanded to know why I had not been informed that Amarendra had been so seriously ill,' Benoy later recalled. In light of the insult, he said he would boycott the funeral procession and meet them at the cremation ground. He sent his corrupt aide, K.K. Misra, and his cook back with Ashutosh to help carry Amarendra's body.

At half-past seven that morning, a hastily assembled group of Brahmin pall-bearers lifted a bamboo litter holding Amarendra's body and set out for the Keoratola cremation ghat on the nearby Tolly Canal. Rabindranath and Ashutosh stayed behind to attend to the grief-stricken women; this duty saved them from having to look upon the victorious Benoyendra. A party of six barefoot men, including Surjabati's cook and two volunteers from the neighbourhood, trudged the long mile through a waking city, past men and women bathing at public taps, overtaken by trundling rickshaws, the smell of breakfast wafting from the houses and food stalls – puri, dal, woodsmoke. Four men carried the body at a time, with the others providing relief.

Midway to the burning ground, at the junction of Rash Behari Avenue and Russa Road, not far from the Purna Theatre, they saw a taxi approaching in the opposite direction. The car stopped, the driver opened a rear door, and Benoy stepped out. Heel on the footboard, he took in the advancing procession and beamed like he'd won the Calcutta Sweep. 'I saw him in a very jolly mood, laughing and chewing betel nut,' said Amiya Chatterjee, a teenager from the neighbourhood who had offered to help carry the body. He couldn't make out what Benoy and his driver were saying but, while minding the burden on his shoulder, he watched as Benoyendra 'pointed out the dead body with his hand … His look was quite jolly.' Benoyendra removed his shoes, crossed the street, and joined the procession.

When the funeral party reached Keoratola, Benoyendra took the death certificate from Provash Misra and complained again that he hadn't been told of Amarendra's illness. He requested the names of the different doctors who had treated Amar and then he and a companion walked to the registration office while Misra stayed with the body. Amiya Chatterjee, the young pall-bearer, watched as Benoy and his men left to perform the necessary paperwork and purchase wood for the cremation. He then asked to take his leave. The boy's mother had died the month before and he was scandalised at Benoyendra's gaiety. 'Sorrow was a stranger to him,' Amiya said. 'Even I was more upset than he was.'

Beni Madhab Dutt, an employee of Surjabati's landlord, learned of Amarendra's death and helped to round up neighbours to carry the bier. (As a member of a lesser caste, he was prohibited from polluting the dead body of a brahmin with his living touch and thus could not serve as a pall-bearer.) He reached the ghat after the funeral procession. As he stood under a banyan tree near the cremation ground's administrative office, Dutt saw Benoy and another man conferring with the registrar.

'After some talk, they came down,' he said. 'I saw Benoyendra take some money from his pocket and hand it over to the dark-complexioned man with him ... Benoy handed the notes to his companion behind his back ... I was behind them when I saw it.' He followed the group to the ghat, where the registrar removed part of Amarendra's shroud and surveyed his body. They then made for the north gate to buy wood from the out-caste *doms* who would perform the cremation. The registrar instructed them to select quality pieces of dry timber, so as to spare Benoyendra the inconvenience of an overlong immolation. Benoy was still chewing his *paan*. This would be the last known sighting of the dark-complexioned stranger who had haunted Amar's final days.

The body of Amarendra Chandra Pandey, 21, was consumed atop a cordwood pyre. When it was done, the *doms* pushed his smouldering ashes into the canal. Following custom, the pall-bearers bathed in the water at the completion of the ceremony.

Benoy remained dry and carried on with his day.

16

Hello!

The Belvedere Ball was the hottest ticket of the frantic Calcutta social calendar, with thousands of upper-crust Indians eager to rub elbows with the viceroy, Lord Willingdon, and just a few lucky hundreds allowed in. Rejected elites were sometimes slow to accept their fate; Willingdon's military secretary had the unappealing duty of fielding the aggrieved, imploring letters of those business executives, nobles, and other eminences who hadn't made the cut. 'It is needless to mention the fact that almost all our relations have got the privilege of getting the invitations in the said function, and I do not understand the reason why my sister and my wife have been omitted when we stand English etiquette thoroughly well, and we have been brought up in a thorough European manner in every respect, and being the first cousins of the late Dowager Maharanee of Cooch Bihar ...' one scorned aristocrat complained.[1]

Somewhere among the happy hundreds getting tipsy on the viceroy's punch that night were Deputy Commissioner Henry Le Brocq, commanding officer of the city's port police and Willingdon's personal bodyguard during his stay in Calcutta; Police Commissioner Lionel Colson; and the Manchester-born Thomas Hobart Ellis, a judge of the sessions court who had recently been targeted for assassination for his role overseeing the trials of several Bengali militants. All would soon become embroiled in the still-obscure death of Amarendra Pandey – none more than Le Brocq.

Henry worked and played hard. A Channel Island native of Jersey, he had arrived in India at age 20 as a greenhorn assistant district superintendent and was soon promoted up the chain of command. By 1930, Henry was a senior officer, one of several lawmen to shoot it out with armed militants during a raid on a safe house in Chandernagore (now Chandannagar), north of Calcutta. Henry was an avid sportsman and accompanied his new wife Betty, the daughter of a prominent lawyer, to dances at the Saturday Club, swimming and polo at the Tollygunge, and hot jazz at the Grand Hotel. It was a charmed, interesting life. 'I loved Calcutta, you could play any game you liked,' recalled Isabel Colson, the police commissioner's wife, in an unpublished memoir.[2]

In winter the calendar was thick with engagements, with balls and dinners sponsored by the Calcutta Light Horse, the Calcutta Scottish, the Knights of Caledonia, the Golightly Club – a group of wealthy businessmen who wore formal uniforms of ruffles, silk knee breeches, stockings and ruffled pumps – and the *Vingt-et-Un*, twenty-one British bachelors who would each invite five people for dinner at their own headquarters before carrying on to the Tollygunge for dancing.[3, 4]

Benoyendra wasn't partying just yet. The day after Amarendra's death he paid a visit to Dr Sen Gupta's house to learn who it was that collected the blood sample. Sen Gupta's assistant, Dr A.K. Sen, replied it was Santosh, and that, as far as he knew, nothing had turned up in the culture. As a further courtesy he also provided Santosh's home address. At the last moment, as Benoy readied to drive off, it occurred to the assistant that he should enquire about the name of this visitor, and thus discovered he was the brother of the deceased.

Santosh had maintained something of a vigil over Amarendra's blood culture. On 2 December, there was no hint of a colony in the flask, but on the following day he saw some 'definite growth' floating atop the broth. He wrote Amarendra's name in grease pencil on the lids of three shallow glass plates, or petri dishes, containing different gelatine growth mediums, and sterilised a loop of platinum wire in flame.

The researcher began a long, detailed process of elimination, heeding, whether he was familiar with it or not, the Sherlock Holmes adage that 'when you have excluded the impossible, whatever remains, however improbable, must be the truth'.[5]

Removing the flask from the incubator, he sterilised its mouth, collected the visible bacteria, and used the platinum instrument to draw criss-crossing patterns across the three plates. Then he burned the cork, stoppered the flask, and returned it and the agar plates to the incubator. He burned the platinum loop once more, leaving it sterile. Each growth medium would tell Santosh something about the unidentified germs. Blood agar, typically made from sheep, would rule out organisms that could not grow in blood. MacConkey's plates would show to what degree the germ might contain a certain lactose.

When he reached the lab the morning of 4 December, hours after Amarendra's death, Santosh 'found a very faint but definite growth on all the three of the plates'. Now one step closer to knowing the culprit pathogen, Santosh took these growths and distributed them in lightning-bolt scrawls among eight 'sugar' plates, each a different colour and holding a different medium – blue for lactose, pink for glucose, and so on. How the bacilli responded to each of these media would reveal additional clues. Everything went back into the incubator.

The next day, there was enough material on the initial three plates to place them under the microscope for a first look. 'I noticed non-motile Gram-negative rods,' he said – rectangular microorganisms lacking the ability to propel themselves, resistant to a violet stain used to classify bacteria. (Gram staining was typically the first step in the initial identification of a bacillus.) Santosh collected some of the bacteria from the plates and noted the growth had a slimy character – he added this to more agar medium and closed the lab for the night. His uncle, Nalini Sen Gupta, had reached Calcutta that morning and learned of his young patient's death. The two spoke that evening, and Santosh told him that 'something was showing in the culture', but he wasn't sure what it could be.

On 6 December, Santosh had new indicators: a number of the sugar plates had become acidic, suggesting the possibility of typhus or a strain of dysentery. Typhus was usually motile – it moved under its own power – but there were some exceptions, and Santosh now needed to disprove the possibility. More tests showed the pathogen was neither dysentery nor *Salmonella typhi*. Of the dozens of possibilities, two were now ruled out. He took a fresh look at the bacteria by creating another smear on a glass slide and staining it with more of the violet Gram's solution. Now, through the microscope, he saw clearly what he hadn't before: the stain hadn't adhered to the bacilli, *except at the very ends*, where the dye was now visible. This meant the bacteria were bipolar. Santosh believed and disbelieved his eyes.

'I saw suspicious, bipolar-stained, gram-negative rods,' he said.

'I thought it might be plague.'

Santosh called several of his seniors, including Captain C.L. Pasricha of the Indian Medical Service, a professor of bacteriology and pathology. Without sharing his suspicion, Santosh asked Pasricha to have a look at the stain. Pasricha, who had trained at St Barts Hospital in London (site of the fictional first meeting between Sherlock Holmes and Dr Watson), leaned in, focused the microscope's eyepiece and called out, 'Hello! That looks like plague.' They locked the slide into the school's 'museum microscope', closed the shades, and projected the image onto a wall of the darkened room. There was the killer, each cell enlarged to the size of a Cuban cigar. That evening, Santosh brought the stained bacteria for his uncle to examine, without telling him its origin. 'I saw the slide was full of plague bacilli,' Sen Gupta said.

'If there had not been the tragedy behind [it], it was what one would have called a beautiful specimen.'

Pasricha ordered additional steps to confirm the find, and Santosh began, in a way, recreating the experiments that Taranath had carried out on Arthur Road in Bombay four months before, using the very same culture and some of the same methods. By

13 December, 'I was definite it was plague,' Pasricha said. Four rats had been injected with the bacilli cultured from Amarendra's blood, and four rats had died. 'The post-mortem revealed plague everywhere,' Santosh recalled, with 'bipolar rods in the heart, spleen and site of inoculation'. He treated smears of the bacteria with two different stains, revealing 'Gram-negative bipolar rods and, with the Leishman stains, very beautiful bipolar rods'. It was the talk of the lab – no one could recall a case of plague in Calcutta for the last dozen years. Photos were taken of the smears from each rat. The school's director informed local health authorities.

With his uncle advising him on the language, Santosh wrote to Rabindranath Pandey in Pakur:

My Dear Mr Pandey.

I have the very melancholy duty of informing you that the Kumar[3] A.C. Pandey died of Plague. The blood culture has by inoculation into rats and by all other tests has been confirmed as one of pure Plague (Pasturella Pestis). The discovery of Plague infection in Bengal and under these unusual circumstances has led to widespread interest and all the leading bacteriologists of the School of Tropical Medicine have seen the culture, identified the organism and have taken great interest in the case. I am sending you this positive finding in case you require it.

We are now convinced that nothing could have saved the patient because the poor boy was a victim of one of the most deadly bacilli known.

My uncle Dr Sen Gupta was profoundly shocked and distressed when he learnt of the fatal termination after his return. My uncle requests you to see us when you come to Calcutta again. Kindly acknowledge receipt of this letter.

Yours sincerely,
Santosh K. Gupta

An earlier draft of the letter asserted that Amar had 'died of plague presumably introduced in the way Amarendra alleged', but an attorney relation of Sen Gupta's 'cautioned me with a lawyer's caution not to put it in writing'. He had the line replaced with a request that Rabindra come see him in Calcutta. In the face of a homicide, no one was taking chances with his own status or safety. None of the leading scientists who marvelled at the 'beautiful' plague germs cultured from Amarendra's blood made any move to contact the police.

Santosh burned his notes.

17

People of Position and Money

Surjabati and the others returned to Pakur the evening of Amar's death and settled down to virulent strains of guilt and despair. Their boy was dead and they'd been powerless to prevent it. Word began to spread about the strange passing of Amarendra Pandey, and who could have been behind it.

It was shortly after Amar's funeral that Benoyendra received a letter from his judgemental friend warning him to stop his womanising, to pay closer attention to his thieving underlings, and get right with God. 'If you continue keeping two women in this way you will lose your life someday through somebody's wrath,' he wrote. 'Besides that you drink. How long will you be able to stand such dissipation? Instead of indulging in dissipation any further you should turn your mind to religion from now and direct your attention to the estate's affairs.'

The friend added: 'You will suffer for the sin you have committed.' This was almost certainly a reference to Benoy's pleasure-seeking, rather than the fresh murder in Calcutta – but he wasn't wrong.

On 7 December, three days after Amarendra's death, a local attorney named Kalidas Gupta typed a confidential letter to Suresh Chandra Chaudhury, the government pleader and public prosecutor in Dumka, asking if they might speak in private about 'a very

serious matter'. Kalidas performed legal work for different members of the Pakur Raj clan; earlier that year he had been misled
into helping Benoyendra raid a bank account of 13,000 rupees that
was meant for both brothers to share. The lawyer was mortified
and angry to learn he'd unknowingly had a role in the theft – it
soured his opinion of Benoy. Now Kalidas was hearing chilling
reports about Amarendra's final days.

'I'm giving you some details for the present, just to enable
you to direct your attention to the legal points on which I want
a discussion ... preferably after court hours,' he wrote to the
prosecutor. Kalidas' own brother had sent him a note about the
case, and Amar's uncle Baidyanath Pandey had spoken with him
to provide more details about the feud between the half-brothers,
the incident at Howrah Station, and Amarendra's death one week
later, which he now conveyed to the prosecutor. Kalidas' letter
was a window into the fears now consuming Amar's family:

> ... It is also reported that Kananbala developed symptoms of
> the same poison.
>
> I am told that there [are] various rumours afloat at Pakur,
> but no step for any inquiry has yet been taken by anyone, as
> it is apprehended that people of position and money may be
> found involved.
>
> Whatever that may be, I feel there should be an inquiry as
> the circumstances related to the sudden death of the poor boy
> lead me to conclude that there was some foul play. But the
> question is, 'Has the Santhal Parganas police any jurisdiction
> over the matter ... being had to the facts that the injection
> and death took place in Calcutta?'
>
> As Babu suffered for a short time at Pakur, this I think may
> give the SP [Santhal Parganas] police jurisdiction to hold
> an enquiry. But there is none to come forward to lodge a
> formal information.

The two met in the bar library. Chaudhury said that without a witness on the record the law's hands were tied. It was as if a homicide

wasn't the state's business until and unless the victim's family or an eyewitness made a direct complaint. He wanted the case wrapped in a bow. Soon enough the authorities would have it.

Sometime around 15 December Rabindranath received Santosh Gupta's letter revealing plague as the cause of Amarendra's death, and learned of Kalidas Gupta's approach to the public prosecutor. Rabindra and Surjabati were relieved to learn that Kalidas was already working towards an investigation – and that they could trust him. On Christmas Day, Rabindra wrote to Kalidas asking him to formally take on the case. 'During Babu's illness Dr L.M. Banerji advised us to inform the police but at that time we were so busily engaged with his nursing and treatment that we had scarcely any other thought than Babu's life,' he explained. 'After he died, it was difficult for me to manage the bereaved family.'

'Now,' he wrote, 'Rani Surjabati Debi has collected herself a little and wants to get at the truth.'

Rabindranath travelled to Dumka to hand-deliver the letter to Kalidas, but the lawyer was away in Calcutta. He left the envelope with a servant. On New Year's Day 1934, Kalidas took a train north from Howrah to Rampurhat, where he caught an Auto Express Service bus for the last 40 miles to Dumka, reaching his home there around sunset. As the porters pulled his baggage from the coach's roof, Kalidas spotted Kamta Singh, Benoy's local driver, standing a short distance away. The driver 'came and *salaamed* and said his *malik* was [*sic*] come and was waiting in the car,' Kalidas recalled. He could see Benoy's sedan parked down the road near the courthouse gate. 'I asked him to fetch his master to my office.'

Kalidas called for a lamp, and Benoyendra joined him there. Benoy towered over the small, bespectacled lawyer, who had placed at the top of his class at Calcutta University. Tea and sweets were ordered. Kalidas took a seat behind the desk and expressed his condolences over Amarendra's passing. It had all happened so suddenly, Benoy replied. As Kalidas opened his mouth to say more in sympathy, Benoy broke in and 'asked me abruptly if Nabu [Rabindranath] had come to Dumka and seen me ... Then Sadhan [Benoy] enquired if anybody had come to me from Pakur with any letter from Nabu.' Kalidas said, truthfully, that he didn't know of any letter, nor had he seen Rabindranath, not for several years. Benoy chewed this over for a moment and replied that 'his informations were otherwise which may not be correct', Kalidas recalled. 'It appeared he wanted to tell me something which he suppressed on receipt of my answer.'

In the oil-lit room, the shutters open to the night, surrounded by lawbooks, they moved to careful small talk: Kalidas' visit to Calcutta, the current crop of 'talkie films', Kalidas' blood pressure.

Benoy passed on the sweets, finished a cup of tea, asked for more, and suggested that he might want to pay Kalidas a retainer for future legal work. Would he be amenable? The offer had potential – Benoyendra was a compulsive civil litigant. The lawyer was light on his feet, and played for time; the longer Benoy considered him an ally, the better. Kalidas declined a formal retainer agreement, while agreeing to accept a one-time payment in return for a non-competition arrangement in which he would not take any civil cases that placed him opposite the raja in the Dumka courthouse. 'If he would give me an understanding in writing then I would not accept any brief against him, but he would have to engage me in such cases and pay my usual fees,' Kalidas recalled. Benoy hadn't quite bought Kalidas, but it was the best he could do. A money order for 35 rupees would soon be on its way. He stood to leave, and Kalidas escorted him to the car. As they approached the vehicle, Kalidas saw the figure of an unknown man standing next to Benoy's driver and asked who it was. Benoy, not answering, 'said there were some ladies' inside the sedan, warning him off for reasons of propriety. 'Hence I did not go up to the car.' The stranger remained anonymous.

Kalidas walked back to his office, where a servant brought out the correspondence that had piled up in his absence. There, among the envelopes and telegrams, was Rabindranath's letter of 25 December revealing Amarendra had been killed by plague. The letter had been hand-delivered by Rabi himself to Kalidas' servant – who must have been bribed into showing it to the raja. Now he fully understood Benoyendra's pervasive, corrupting influence.

Infected

Amarendra Nath Pande, son of prominent Calcutta, India family, who was murdered with bubonic plague germs.

An image of the victim, Amarendra Chandra Pandey, from an article in the *New York Daily News*, dated 9 April 1939.

Accused And Wife

Benoyendra Nath Pande, the accused half-brother, and his wife, whom he was alleged in court to have neglected in favor of a dancing girl. It was when his brother moved for partition of estate, upon reaching his majority, that Benoyandra launched his murder scheme.

Right and overleaf: Newspaper cuttings from the *New York Daily News*, dated 9 April 1939, containing the only known images of the killer Benoyendra Chandra Pandey and his wife Pritilata. The article also includes a microscope image of the actual plague germs that were cultured from the murder victim's blood at the Calcutta School of Tropical Medicine.

Where Science Solved Mystery of Youth's Death

Two views of laboratory of the Calcutta School of Tropical Medicine, in which Dr. Santosh K. Gupka, research assistant, discovered bubonic plague germs in blood sample taken from body of Amarendra Nath Pande. This was the day after the youth's death. Discovery launched an investigation which uncovered fantastic murder plot. In lower foto a doctor is examining the germs used in the killing.

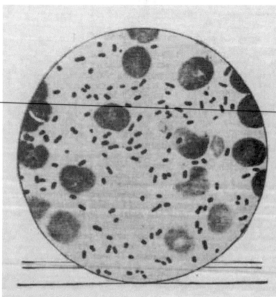

Murder Weapon

Microsopic photograph of bubonic plague germs used to kill Amar. The fatal germs were injected into the victim via a needle or pin as he was about to board train.

Seated, third from the right, in light suit and a tie: Murder-accused Dr Sivapada Bhattacharjee, a professor at the Calcutta School of Tropical Medicine. His reputation was ruined by the charges even after a jury found him not guilty.

Seated, fourth from right, in light suit and bow tie: Dr C.L. Pasricha, who helped identify the plague germs that had been cultured from victim Amarendra Pandey's blood. (Annual Report of the Calcutta School of Tropical Medicine, 1930)

Seated on the ground, left: Santosh K. Gupta found the plague germs in Amarendra's blood and was accused by the defence of faking his results. (Annual Report of the Calcutta School of Tropical Medicine, 1930)

Seated on chair, centre, in dark suit and tie: Murder-accused Dr Sivapada Bhattacharjee. (Annual Report of the Calcutta School of Tropical Medicine, 1932)

As a young boy, Emmanuel Marandi witnessed the deadly 1947 siege of Gokulpur Palace. Many residents took the fugitive raja's side. 'People are questioning in their mind, "Why are they going to kill this man?" Because he was good to them.' (Dan Morrison)

Burning the bedding of infected households, Bombay, 1897. Invasive plague remediation efforts, including forced hospitalisation and the use of segregation camps, provoked a furious backlash against British authorities. (The Bombay plague epidemic of 1896–1897: work of the Bombay Plague Committee. Photograph attributed to Capt. C. Moss, 1897. Wellcome Collection)

European 'Lady Doctors' inspect Bombay women for signs of plague, 1897. (The Bombay plague epidemic of 1896–1897: work of the Bombay Plague Committee. Photograph attributed to Capt. C. Moss, 1897. Wellcome Collection)

A European doctor grips the wrist of a young Bombay train passenger while inspecting him for signs of plague, 1897. Plague had a death rate of 85 per cent during the pandemic's first year. (The Bombay plague epidemic of 1896–1897: work of the Bombay Plague Committee. Photograph attributed to Capt. C. Moss, 1897. Wellcome Collection)

A Bombay man receives Waldemar Haffkine's plague vaccine from a foreign doctor, 1896–97. (The Bombay plague epidemic, 1896–1897: inoculation against plague. Photograph attributed to Clifton & Co. Wellcome Collection)

Karachi: A plague-affected home that was destroyed by civil authorities, 1897. The true cause of plague was still unknown when the Third Plague Pandemic reached India. Officials believed the miasma of unhealthy homes and neighbourhoods caused the disease. (Photograph, 1897. Wellcome Collection)

Waldemar Haffkine, creator of the first vaccines for cholera and plague, sometimes clashed with British Indian health authorities over their methods of plague remediation. (Wellcome Library)

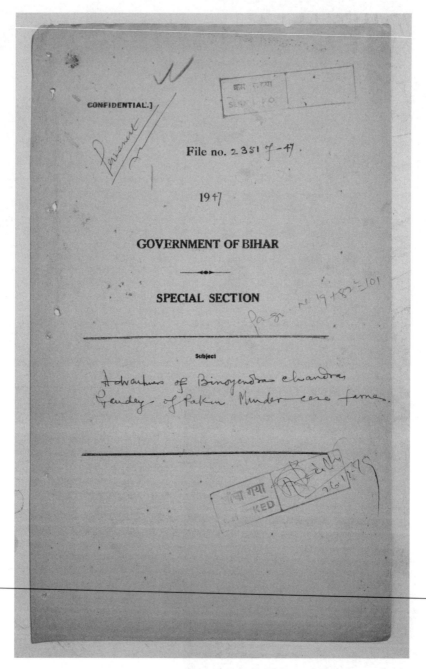

Cover page of the Bihar government's confidential file on Benoyendra's fatal 1947 standoff with police and the army.

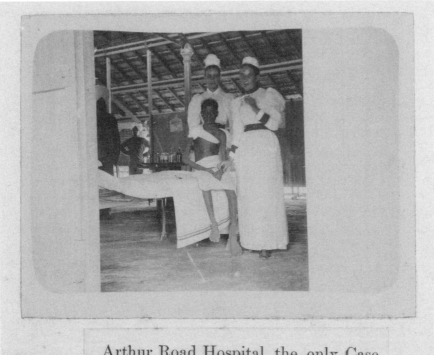

Arthur Road Hospital, the only Case of Black Plague which recovered.

A rare plague survivor at Arthur Road Hospital. Hundreds of millhands stoned the hospital and attacked staff in October 1896 over rumours that patients were being murdered within its walls. The wails of the sick and dying could be heard from the street. (Photograph attributed to Captain C. Moss, 1897. Wellcome Collection)

Rani Surjabati Devi, Amarendra's wealthy aunt and surrogate mother, tried to protect him from his elder brother's predations. (Courtesy of Meera Singh)

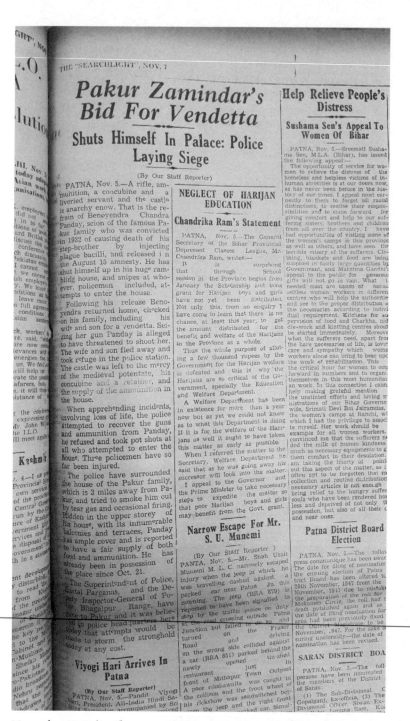

Pakur Zamindar's Bid For Vendetta

Shuts Himself In Palace: Police Laying Siege

(By Our Staff Reporter)

PATNA, Nov. 5.—A rifle, ammunition, a concubine and a liveried servant and the castle is anarchy enow. That is the refrain of Benoyendra Chandra Panday, scion of the famous Pakur family who was convicted in 1932 of causing death of his step-brother by injecting plague bacilli, and released i n the August 15 amnesty. He has shut himself up in his huge rambling house, and snipes at whoever, policemen included, attempts to enter the house.

Following his release Benoyendra returned home, checked on his family, including his wife and son for a vendetta. Seizing her gun Panday is alleged to have threatened to shoot her. The wife and son fled away and took refuge in the police station. The castle was left to the mercy of the medieval potentate, his concubine and a retainer, and the supply of the ammunition in the house.

When apprehending incidents, involving loss of life, the police attempted to recover the guns and ammunition from Panday, he refused and took pot shots at all who attempted to enter the house. Three policemen have so far been injured.

The police have surrounded the house of the Pakur family, which is 3 miles away from Pakur, and tried to smoke him out by tear gas and occasional firing. Hidden in the upper storey of his house, with its innumerable balconies and terraces, Panday has ample cover and is reported to have a fair supply of both food and ammunition. He has already been in possession of the place since Oct. 21.

The Superintendent of Police, Santal Parganas, and the Deputy Inspector-General of Police, Bhagalpur Range, have gone to Pakur and it was believed in police headquarters here today that attempts would be made to storm the stronghold today at any cost.

Viyogi Hari Arrives In Patna

(By Our Staff Reporter)

PATNA, Nov. 5.—Pandit Viyogi Hari, President, All-India Hindi Sahitya, accompanied by Sri

NEGLECT OF HARIJAN EDUCATION

Chandrika Ram's Statement

PATNA, Nov. 5.—The General Secretary of the Bihar Provincial Depressed Classes League, Mr. Chandrika Ram, writes:—

It is surprising that through School session in the Province begins from January the Scholarship and book grant for Harijan boys and girls have not yet been distributed. Not only this, from an enquiry I have come to learn that there is no chance, at least this year, to get the amount distributed for the benefit and welfare of the Harijans in the Province as a whole.

Thus the whole purpose of allotting a few thousand rupees by the Government for the Harijan welfare is defeated and this is why the Harijans are so critical of the Government, specially the Education and Welfare Department.

A Welfare Department has been in existence for more than a year now but as yet we could not know as to what this Department is doing. If it is for the welfare of the Harijans as well it ought to have taken this matter as early as possible.

When I referred the matter to the Secretary, Welfare Department he said that as he was going away his successor will look into the matter. I appeal to the Governor and the Prime Minister to take necessary steps to expedite the matter so that poor Harijan boys and girls may benefit from the Govt. grant.

Narrow Escape For Mr. S. U. Munemi

(By Our Staff Reporter)

PANTA, Nov. 5.—Mr. Shah Uzmir Munemi M. L. C. narrowly escaped injury when the jeep in which he was travelling dashed against a parked car near Patna Jn. this morning. The jeep (BRA 879) is reported to have been signalled to stop by the traffic police on duty at the road crossing outside Patna Junction but failed to do so and turned on the Fraser Road and driving on the wrong side collided against a car (BRA 851) parked behind the a car newly opened just tin-shed In restaurant Outpost in front of Mithapur Town A poor rikshawalla was caught in the collision and the front wheel of his rickshaw was sandwiched between the jeep and the right front marked car. Simul-

Help Relieve People's Distress

Sushama Sen's Appeal To Women Of Bihar

PATNA, Nov. 5.—Sreemati Sushama Sen, M.L.A. (Bihar), has issued the following appeal:—

The opportunity of service for women to relieve the distress of the homeless and helpless victims of inhuman atrocities is at our doors now, as has never been before in the history of our times. I appeal most earnestly to them to forget all racial distinctions, to realise their responsibilities and to come forward for giving comfort and help to our suffering sisters, brothers and children from all over the country. I have had opportunities of visiting some of the women's camps in this province as well as others, and have seen the terrible misery of the sufferers. Clothing, blankets and food are being supplied in fairly large quantities by Government, and Mahatma Gandhi's appeal to the public for generous gifts will not go in vain. What is needed most are bands of non-selfless women workers in different centres who will help the authorities and see to the proper distribution of the necessaries according to individual requirement. Kitchens for supervision of food and Charkha, and die-work and knitting centres should be started immediately. Moreover what the sufferers need, apart from the bare necessaries of life, is loving care and sympathy which women workers alone can bring to bear upon the work of rehabilitation. This is the critical hour for women to come forward in numbers and to organise themselves in this most humanitarian work. In this connection I cannot help making grateful mention of the unstinted efforts and loving ministrations of our Bihar Governor's wife, Srimati Devi Bai Jairamdas, the women's camps at Ranchi, which I had the privilege to associate myself. Her work should be example for all women workers. I am convinced one that the sufferers needed the milk of human kindness much as necessary equipments to give them comfort in their desolation. I am taking the liberty of pointing out this aspect of the matter, as I am often apt to be forgotten that mere collection and routine distribution of necessary articles is not enough to bring relief to the hungry suffering souls who have been rendered homeless and deprived of not only their possession, but also of all their dear and near ones.

Patna District Board Election

PATNA, Nov. 5.—The following press communique has been issued. The date for filing of nominations for the ensuing election of Patna district Board has been altered to 26th November, 1947 from the November, 1947 due to mistake the preparation of the roll for Mokameh Circle, the roll had to be re-draft published again and as the date of filing nomination for area had been previously fixed by the District Magistrate to be November, 1947. For the sake of securing uniformity—the date of nomination has been revised.

SARAN DISTRICT BOARD

PATNA, Nov. 5.—The following persons have been nominated as the members of the District Board of Saran:—

(1) The Sub-Divisional Gopalganj, Ex-officio, (2) The Divisional Officer, Siwan Ex-officio, Jamuna Ram, Kumar

The rooftop where Benoyendra was killed by soldiers from the Rajputana Rifles in November 1947. The Gokulpur Palace was built to withstand an indigenous peasant uprising. Benoyendra used it to hold off the police and army for more than three weeks. (Dan Morrison)

GERM MURDER CASES

DEATH OF PRESIDENT WILSON.

The "germ murder" cases in India recall that many Americans believe that the death of President Woodrow Wilson was caused by a similar diabolical method.

In "The American Black Chamber," by Major Herbert O. Yardley, appears the following statement:—

" . . . . ., the reader may well appreciate the shock I received as I deciphered a telegram which reported a plot to assassinate President Wilson, either by administering a slow poison or by giving him influenza in ice. Our informant, in whom we had the greatest confidence, begged the authorities for God's sake to warn the President.

GERM SLAYING CYCLE FEARED BY PROFESSOR

German Neurologist Cites Case of Bacteriology Student Who Inoculated Ex - Sweetheart

French bacteriologist Paul Gibier predicted the advent of 'germ murder' at a medical conference as early as 1895, and the early twentieth century saw high-profile cases in Europe and the United States involving typhus, cholera, diphtheria, and *erysipelas*. Herbert O. Yardley, the former head of America's 'Black Chamber' codebreaking unit, went so far as to claim in a memoir that President Woodrow Wilson was targeted with deadly bacilli. 'It is the most difficult thing to convict the germ slayer,' German neurologist Felix Plaut said. (*Dalby Herald*, 24 January 1936)

PAKUR MURDER CASE

Trial Commences At The Court Of Sessions

STORY OF PROSECUTION

" Well-planned Scientific Design Unparalleled In The Annals Of Crimes In India "

The Pakur case made headlines around the world. Defence attorneys complained that press coverage of the plague murder case would prejudice the jury. 'Whether it was a case of murder or of natural death is to be decided by the court,' one defence lawyer told the judge. (*Amrita Bazar Patrika*)

BENOY OF PAKUR KILLED BY MILITARY

Dramatic End Of A 'Rebel' After 28 Days' Single-Handed Fight

BY OUR STAFF REPORTER

PAKUR, Nov. 18.

Benoyendra Pande already made well-known by the Pakur murder case met with death from military fire on Monday last after he had again drawn the spotlight of public attention on himself by being engaged, soon after his release, in a solo fight with the forces of law and order which lasted 28 days in circumstances of moving drama.

Benoy's twenty-eight-day standoff still made news amid the many crises India faced in its first months of freedom. (*Amrita Bazar Patrika*, 20 November 1947)

Eille Norwood starred as Sherlock Holmes in a 1921 silent film adaptation of 'The Adventure of the Dying Detective', which features a germ murder by a disease bearing the hallmarks of a septicemic plague. (Sayre Collection of Theatrical Photographs, University of Washington)

'The Adventure of the Dying Detective' was first published in 1913. Sherlock Holmes solves the germ murder of Victor Savage by pretending to have been infected by the same culprit. The *New York Times* marvelled that, of all the Holmes stories, 'sure not the one among them was stranger than that recounted in the episode called *The Adventure of the Dying Detective*'. (Frederick Dorr Steele, *Collier's* magazine)

MISS BETTY BROWNE, daughter of Sir Philip Browne, and Mr. E. H. le Brocq, of the Indian Police, who were married at Liphook, Hampshire.

India's first prime minister, Jawaharlal Nehru, shared an address with Benoyendra Pandey in early 1934 – both were inmates at Alipore Central Jail. Nehru was serving time for sedition, while Benoy awaited trial for murder. (Library of Congress/Press Information Bureau, India)

Newspaper clipping from E. Henry Le Brocq's wedding to Betty Browne. As an officer of the Indian police, Le Brocq battled militants, chased smugglers and led the investigation of the Pakur murder case. (Courtesy of Philip Le Brocq)

Calcutta Police Inspector Luftar Rahman delivered withering testimony about Taranath Bhattcharjee's lies and evasions during a fraught and emotional interrogation. (Archives of Prof. M.M. Rahman of St Xavier's College)

Calcutta Police Commissioner Lionel Colson was at first sceptical that detectives had enough evidence to arrest the four suspects. (Courtesy of Richard Colson)

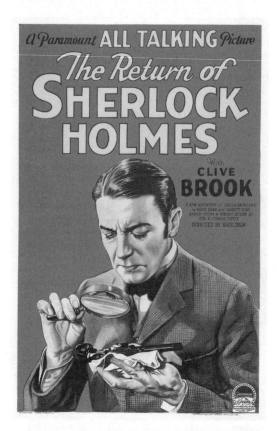

The Return of Sherlock Holmes, starring Clive Brook, debuted in India in 1932, as Amarendra Pandey began asserting his rights to the Pakur Raj. The story features a death by pinprick, and the attempted murder of Sherlock Homes with a syringe of poison. (Universal Art Archive / Alamy)

Justice John Lort-Williams of the Calcutta High Court found that Session Judge T.H. Ellis had, on several occasions, sided with the prosecution during the plague murder trial and also in his instructions to the jury. Yet he and Justice Nasim Ali held that the defendants were nevertheless guilty of slaying Amarendra. (Llyfrgell Genedlaethol Cymru – The National Library of Wales)

18

Forward Under Custody

Kalidas was back in court the next day, serving as defence attorney in an abduction case. Suresh Chandra Chaudhury was the prosecutor. When the proceedings were adjourned, they met again in the law library, where Kalidas showed him the letter from Rabindranath and a memorandum he'd written the night before describing Benoy's ominous visit. Chaudhury repeated that he was sure jurisdiction for Amarendra's case would lie in Calcutta; still, he said, there was a chance police in Dumka could begin some sort of preliminary inquiry.

On 10 January, while Benoyendra – citing his brother's tragic end – applied to a judge for possession of the full 17,000 rupees they had scrapped over, Rabindranath Pandey sat across the road with the police superintendent of the Santhal Parganas district for four and half hours, describing the chain of events leading to Amarendra's death. When the consultation was over, he walked to Kalidas' office, where the lawyer typed up a four-page official complaint that Rabindra left with a police inspector before returning to Pakur. The next week, on the day of a massive earthquake that devastated northern Bihar, Benoy's brother-in-law Ashutosh Chakravarty and Surjabati's employee Provash Misra drove to Dumka in Surjabati's car for police interviews. With three witnesses now on the record, Kalidas was finally given a written referral to the Calcutta police. 'I request that you will be so good as to grant him an interview after taking sufficient precautions about his identity,' the deputy commissioner wrote.

Kalidas travelled to Calcutta on 18 January and paid a late-night call at the home of Assistant Commissioner Saktipada Chakrabarty, second-in-command at the Calcutta detective department. He briefed Chakrabarty on the case and showed him Rabindranath's declaration, Amarendra's blood report, and other documents. Soon after, Kamala Prosad Pandey, Amar's cousin and a Calcutta resident, filed an official murder complaint containing more details and a list of more than forty potential witnesses. 'I have in my possession some documentary evidence and I am also prepared to lead oral evidence which combined would establish a set of circumstances that would prove beyond doubt that the death was due to a [*sic*] foul play and that it was not a natural death,' Kamala wrote. Emphasising the detective department's jurisdiction, he located the conspiracy in Calcutta, with 'the subtle inoculation of the deadly poison to which the death has been pronounced to be due, was done, at the Howrah station by a blackman [*sic*] in *khaddar*'.

The conspiracy was now clear as far as Kalidas and the Pakur clan were concerned. With help from the respected doctors Sivapada Bhattacharjee and Durga Ratan Dhar, and the 'rank junior' Taranath Bhattacharjee, Benoy had first infected his brother with tetanus. He brought in Taranath to block Amar's treatment with life-saving serum and to finish him off with excessive morphine. When that failed, Dhar had persuaded Amar's doctor to allow a last injection of serum that had been adulterated in some way, leading to the boy's debilitating infection. Sivapada, as one of the city's leading physicians, and a former professor of Taranath's, had provided essential advice. After all these efforts failed, and with a 17,000-rupee windfall on the line, Benoyendra sent the false telegram summoning his brother to Calcutta so he could be injected with plague at Howrah.

Despite all the treatments he administered the dying Amarendra at Jatin Das Road, Amar's defenders were adamant that Sivapada had known all along the boy was fatally infected. He had refused to come to the house during Amar's final hours – and had produced a fraudulent death certificate that made no mention of his own intimations of homicide. They now suspected Benoy's possible role in poor Kananbala's recent death as well – he was at that moment challenging his late sister's probate, trying to snatch her estate from Ashutosh and their daughter Anima. Some even wondered about the infection of *erysipelas* that had killed his father Protapendra.

Where did it end?

The Calcutta detective department was already running at full steam when Kalidas presented himself at Saktipada Chakrabarty's door. The city crackled with crime, scandal, and rebellion; the department was short-staffed by two inspectors. The week before, detectives had finally found an escaped Hindu brigand who had been living as a Muslim for nine months in a Bengali village. (The fugitive had worn a beard and fez and performed five daily prayers after tunnelling out of his jail cell and scaling a wall to freedom the year before.[1]) Chakrabarty's men were closing in on an elusive confidence man, Framroze D. Commissariat, who was wanted in Bombay for 102,000 rupees in missing government bonds.[2] They were soon to arrest a local lawyer in the matter of his forgery of a magistrate's signature in order to steal a large amount of escrow funds.[3] While the city had been free of revolutionary violence for some time, the police superintendent of Chittagong had recently been targeted with bombs, leading to the internment of hundreds of young men in eastern Bengal. Death sentences were confirmed in Calcutta for two revolutionaries over their 1930 attempt on the life of the then police commissioner Charles Tegart, and the Bengal legislature was in an uproar over a new terrorism law that critics said would further muzzle the free press.

As Kalidas made his presentation to the assistant commissioner, Jawaharlal Nehru had just completed the last of three speeches in Calcutta in which he expressed solidarity with the people of Midnapore, 90 miles west, who were suffering an obnoxious police presence following the assassinations of three British district magistrates there in as many years. Nehru's speeches, one delivered in

Urdu, would soon land him again in prison – each public event was attended by Special Branch investigators listening for intimations of sedition or mere disapproval of the colonial government. 'We in other provinces feel keenly the misfortunes of our countrymen in Bengal although the whole country at present is in the grip of the severest type of repression,' he told an interviewer.[4]

Twenty-seven murders had been recorded in Calcutta during 1933.[5] Saktipada Chakrabarty now began a confidential inquiry into what now appeared to be the twenty-eighth and assigned sub-inspector Sarat Chandra Mitra to lead it. He deputed Kalidas to assist Mitra's probe; in time the team would expand to more than half a dozen investigators. The detective department had over sixty Muslim and Hindu officers, men of diverse talents who were at home in any setting, from gambling den to lecture hall. The busy roster included writers and poets and a trained *maulvi*; their individual dress ranged from suit and bow tie to kurta and dhoti. Some of the bloodhounds went bareheaded, others wore *taqi-yah* or fez. A few were built like wrestlers, and some were thin as apprenticed clerks. In the variety of crimes he faced, the high and low cultures he inhabited, and the humid grandeurs of Calcutta, a detective at Lalbazar arguably held the best police job on earth – topping his counterparts in London, New York, Istanbul and even Bombay. Each man was a prince of the city, with unique freedom of movement and inquiry.

With the viceroy safely away, Henry Le Brocq resumed his duties at the Port Police, where his investigators were credited in the Bengal legislature for their numerous weapons seizures and 'the arrest of a number of terrorists in possession of firearms and the externment of 22 arms smugglers and brokers from Calcutta'.[6] On 7 February, the police commissioner abruptly handed Henry an additional, temporary, portfolio: he was now in charge of the detective department, replacing its commanding officer, who had gone on leave to England. Assistant Commissioner Chakravarty briefed his new boss on the strange and accelerating Pakur case. Henry, wide-eyed, dug in.[7]

The following week found Sivapada Bhattacharjee in the role of consulting physician at the Tollygunge home of Rani Jyotirmoyee's father, where one of her aged aunts was down sick. After Amarendra passed away, Jyotirmoyee's driver had told her the story of Benoy and his mysterious companion lurking outside the Purna Theatre. This information troubled the rani, but she was reluctant to get involved. Now, as Sivapada prepared to leave the family home after seeing the patient, she pressed him in Bengali over the cause of Amarendra's death. Sivapada, unaware of the still-secret investigation, replied in English: 'It was a pure case of murder.'

Jyotirmoyee had been expecting a medical diagnosis. 'I think I gave no reply as I was completely taken aback,' she later said.

Two nights after his candid chat with Jyotirmoyee, Sivapada was stunned to receive a visit at home from Sub-Inspector S.C. Mitra and Kalidas Gupta. They stayed until 10 p.m., questioning Sivapada about his entanglements with Benoy and Amarendra, his trip to Deoghar during the 1932 pujas, and his treatment of the patient on Jatin Das Road. The doctor refused Mitra's request to make a written statement and claimed to harbour no suspicions of malice in Amar's death. The next day, he appeared, annoyed and uninvited, at Jyotirmoyee's doorstep to ask if the rani had been talking to the police. She hadn't — in fact, she had twice refused to speak with Mitra. Sivapada insisted 'he had done nothing wrong, but the police were making trouble for him without justification', she recalled. He blamed Rabindranath Pandey and asked her to get a message to him so they might speak.

The inquiry was no longer confidential. On 13 February, as Sivapada was pressing Jyotirmoyee, Benoy came to Nalini Ranjan Sen Gupta demanding the names of the police investigators and lawyers probing Amar's death. 'I told him that it was a curious question to ask and what did he want the names for?' Sen Gupta said. 'He replied that they were trying to manufacture a case against him. I said, "If you are innocent, you should damn care about the name but if you are guilty do you think we would help you?"' Later that day, Benoy was seen speaking with Taranath outside his workplace at the Medical Supply Concern.

With word of the police investigation spreading, Le Brocq grew concerned about the danger of the suspects fleeing, destroying evidence, or buying and intimidating witnesses. The detectives had only a partial outline of the murder plot; with the suspects behind bars Henry's men would be free to proceed without fear of obstruction. In addition to Benoyendra, the detectives saw Sivapada Bhattacharjee and Durga Ratan Dhar as their key targets – the likely masterminds. Taranath, a small-timer with zero reputation, appeared less important. But the prestige of Sivapada and Dhar was an obstacle. It was one thing to haul up a factory worker or a dockhand for murder and quite another to start pinching members of Calcutta's medical elite. There could be consequences for bringing needless scandal on the city's upper crust.

Henry and Saktipada, the assistant commissioner, were in luck; Police Commissioner Lionel Colson was out of town. The stolid commissioner was likely to insist that the detectives use a light hand, while the deputy commissioner in charge of Lalbazar, Fred Bartley, didn't share Colson's social sensitivities and would, Henry was confident, defer to the investigators.[8] Still they hesitated, hoping for conclusive evidence.

Their hand was forced on 16 February by an urgent telegram from Howrah Station.

Kalidas Gupta had been hired for a piece of last-minute legal work in Bombay. He raced from his Calcutta office to the station that night and asked Ashutosh Chakravarty to collect a suitcase from Kalidas' city home and meet him there. A magistrate friend of Ashutosh's came along. Not for the last time, Kalidas found chance smiling on him.

Boarding the train, the lawyer saw he had been assigned an uncomfortable middle sleeping berth; there hadn't been time to reserve a better spot. He stowed his luggage and left Ashutosh and the friend behind to seek out a less claustrophobic bunk – and a better night's rest. Outside the next compartment, stuck to the reservations board, was a list of assigned places. Scanning it for an open seat, he felt a jolt: one of the berths was allotted to a 'Mr Pandey'. Kalidas grabbed a steward and asked if he knew the full name of the Mr Pandey or his destination. The passenger had reserved all the way to Victoria Terminus in Bombay, but his first name or initials weren't on the steward's paperwork. With a few minutes to departure, Kalidas bolted to the ticket office at the end of the platform and learned the passenger was indeed his adversary, B.C. Pandey, address Pakur. He ran for a phone and made panicked calls to police headquarters, working his way from S.C. Mitra to Saktipada to Henry Le Brocq to Commissioner Colson himself – none was available.

As the warning whistle blew, he raced to his original berth where Ashutosh and the friend waited. Ashutosh, unaware of where Kalidas had been, pulled him close and whispered that they had just now seen Benoy enter the next compartment. Kalidas agreed to stay on the train to keep an eye on Benoyendra while the other two got down. As the Bombay Mail steamed away, Ashutosh sent an emergency wire to Lalbazar. The telegram reached Sub-Inspector Mitra roughly thirty minutes later; he rounded up Henry and Saktipada, and they deliberated with Deputy Commissioner Bartley for more than an hour.

The detectives were 'in a very unhappy position', Henry recalled. 'We were by no means ready to make arrests when information was received that Benoyendra had suddenly left for Bombay ... I felt we could not take the risk that his object might well be to try to tamper with some of the witnesses.'[9] Finally, they pulled the trigger, and Mitra placed an 11.25 p.m. call to the station master up the line at the coal town of Asansol. The train was now moments from arriving. He followed up with a telegram:

Arrest B.C. Pande travelling up B.B. mail to-night holding 2nd class ticket No. 0257. Berth in the second class carriage No. 3149

Fair complexioned clean shaven tall stout. May be identified by Kali Das Gupta. Short dark spectacled occupied next 2nd class carriage – charged under section 302/120 I.P.C. Forward under custody to Detective Department, Calcutta.

At 11.30 p.m. Sub-Inspector Molla Nizamuddin Ahmed of the Railway Police took a call from the assistant station master, A.H. Sutton, alerting him that a Calcutta murder suspect was minutes from absconding on the now-idled Bombay Mail. He ran down to the platform with two barefoot constables and met Sutton outside the train where they searched for the right carriage. Sutton and a ticket collector entered Benoy's darkened cabin and woke the three passengers inside, demanding to see their tickets. Benoyendra had been asleep facing the wall in his single-tier berth. He got up and removed his ticket, number 0257, from his baggage for Sutton to inspect under lantern light. This was their man.

Kalidas had lain awake for 115 swaying miles as the Bombay Mail left the incandescent city for the starlit countryside. He said not a word to the other passengers in his compartment, read nothing, ate nothing. His eyes bored a hole through the opposite wall, into the skull of Benoyendra Chandra Pandey. The train had been sitting at the platform for three minutes when the door slid open and Sub-Inspector Nizamuddin poked in his head to ask if a Mr K.D. Gupta were present. He led Kalidas into the next cabin where Benoy now stood near the doorway, the two constables lingering in the dim corridor. Benoy, as ever, kept his cool at the unexpected sight of Kalidas.

'He asked me how I happened to be on the train,' Kalidas recalled. 'I said I was going to Bombay … I said I was going in connection with a civil suit.' Benoy didn't mention the nature of his own business in Bombay, not that it mattered. The raja would never see Bombay again. He was arrested on Kalidas' identification and taken off with his luggage. For the first time in his adult life, Benoyendra was under another man's power. And a more comfortable berth was now available for the long journey to Victoria Terminus. Kalidas left it empty.

The party met Abdus Salam, the Railway Police officer-in-charge, on the platform and they escorted Benoy back to the station, where the officers began an inventory of his belongings. Salam had trouble working the clasps on the big suitcase; Benoy opened it without being asked. The senior officer announced each item as it came out, while Nizamuddin put the list to paper. There, amid the toiletries and the clothes, the silver and gold shirt studs, the mosquito net, the ayurvedic and allopathic medicines, and the hair oil, they found that Benoy was carrying 1,400 rupees cash and two cheque books. There was more.

Among the papers they seized were copies of Kalidas Gupta's confidential memos to both the Calcutta police commissioner and the superintendent of police in Dumka, along with a copy of Amarendra's blood report. There was an eight-page draft of his long-anticipated lawsuit seeking possession of Rani Surjabati's properties, and chits of paper bearing the addresses of people and institutions related to Amarendra's death: the Wasserman Institute, which had provided both the oxygen given to Amar in his last days and their employee, Dr Ghose, who had acted as Sivapada's assistant (and who had refused to produce a death certificate); Santosh Gupta, who had collected and cultured Amarendra's blood sample; an office of the police intelligence branch (which had no role in investigating the murder); the names of several Bombay witnesses; and the home address of someone the Calcutta police hadn't yet heard of – Gauri Sen, a 27-year-old former clerk at Taranath's employer, the Medical Supply Concern.

In the margins of a copy of the *Free India* newspaper found in his bedding, Benoy had jotted in pencil the names of the foes he now saw arrayed against him, including Assistant Commissioner Chakrabarty, Dr Nalini Sen Gupta, Rabindranath Pandey, and the woman who'd devoted her life to him and his siblings, Rani Surjabati.

Benoy spent the first of many nights behind bars. The next morning, he joined Nizamuddin and two constables on a train for Calcutta. Benoy was handcuffed, with a piece of rope tied to the centre steel joint, the other end held by a constable – a dog on a leash, or a goat bound for slaughter. As they pulled into the next station, Benoyendra abruptly complained that he was feeling ill. Nizamuddin said he exclaimed that 'I must get him down for treatment by the civil surgeon at Burdwan. He pressed me. I told him that in the time that it would take to go to the civil surgeon and come back we would reach Howrah.' The sub-inspector asked someone to wire ahead that the prisoner needed medical attention, but when they arrived shortly after 10 a.m., Benoy waved off the doctor waiting to examine him. The stalling had come to nothing. 'As I took the accused along the platform, I saw him talking to a Punjabi, a first or second-class passenger,' Nizamuddin said. 'I asked him not to speak to him, as he was in custody. Then he kept quiet.' An hour later they were inside the walls of Lalbazar. One month into the investigation, S.C. Mitra got his first look at B.C. Pandey.

The raja denied all.

'Regarding the pinprick at Howrah, he said he did not know anything,' Mitra recalled. According to Benoy, Amarendra had 'never complained, nor any other person informed him that Babu received any pin prick'.

The dragnet was in full effect. 'Having once started, we had to go on,' Henry recalled.[10] Sub-Inspector Pabitra Kumar Dutta arrested a bewildered Durga Ratan Dhar from his house on Simla Street and then went hunting for Taranath at the Medical Supply Concern, the home on Tagore Castle Street where he lived with his wife and infant daughter, and his dispensary. (The police were still unaware of his secret laboratory inside the rented garage at Alipore.) Dutta left a note at Taranath's house instructing him to appear at the Amherst Street police station.

Dhar's arrest 'brought a violent reaction from a highly placed member of the medical profession', Henry later recalled, but Deputy Commissioner Bartley, who was holding the fort in Colson's absence, supported him. 'He must have had grave doubts in his mind about the rather meagre evidence on which the arrests had been made,' Henry wrote. 'It was not easy to convince the Commissioner on his return that the arrests were justified.'[11] Indeed, Commissioner Colson's reticence appears to have spared Sivapada from immediate capture. Even though he was at this stage more closely entwined in the emerging police narrative than Dhar or even Taranath, the professor remained free for a full month after the others were taken into custody.

Taranath presented himself at the Amherst Street police *thana* on 18 February. 'He did not answer all the questions that I put to him. He made different answers to the same question,' Sub-Inspector Dutta said. Mitra's quarters were at the Amherst Street police block, and he came down to examine the suspect. 'He said he never went to Bombay with Benoyendra,' Mitra recalled. 'He said he has got no idea of the culture of plague bacilli. He also volunteered the statement that he had never seen Bombay in his life.' When Taranath clammed up, he too was arrested and packed off to Lalbazar.

There he endured with difficulty another round of questioning by Le Brocq, Saktipada, and Dutta, the lawmen boring into his inconsistencies and evasions. 'I have never been to Bombay in my life,' Taranath swore yet again. 'I have never approached any doctor for any letter of introduction to Bombay.' Mitra saw that Benoy's corrupt aide Kalikinkar Misra was being questioned in another room and arrested him on the spot. Police picked up four more of Benoyendra's henchmen during raids on the Gokulpur Palace and other locations in Pakur, and they arrested his mistresses Balika Bala and Chanchala for good measure.

Sivapada came looking for Taranath at the Medical Supply Concern that same day, unaware he had been arrested. It was the first time anyone could remember Sivapada visiting the office.

The investigation was about to take flight, thanks to Kalidas Gupta. Kalidas reached Bombay two days after tipping off the police about Benoy. Among the ranks of touts and scouts waiting for disembarking passengers under the arches at the Victorian Gothic station that morning was the hotel manager and former film actor Ratan Salaria, who booked him into the Royal Punjab. Neither man was yet aware of just how much they had in common. After dropping off his bags, Kalidas attended to the legal case he had come for, and then turned to more vital matters. Back in December, Banabala had found some letters in Amarendra's suitcase that her elder brother had posted from Bombay. Benoy had claimed to be meeting with people in the film industry.

Kalidas hit the pavement, moving from hotel to hotel to discover what Benoy had really been up to. He started at the top with the Taj and the Grand and shoe-leathered his way through more than a dozen establishments – Watson's, Green's, Mellon's, the Apollo, the Majestic. At each hotel the staff willingly showed him the register for July 1933. None had hosted Benoyendra. At the Cosmopolitan Hindoo Hotel, staff recalled that a Mr Pandey had stayed nearby, 'and coming down the [street] there is the Seaview Hotel, and in its register I found the entry of B.C. Pandey ... and of Dr Bhattacharya [sic],' Kalidas said. The desk clerk copied the registry information for him and endorsed it with a signature and the hotel's stamp.

An exhausted Kalidas returned to the Royal Punjab around 11 p.m., but the night wasn't over. Word of his inquiry at the Sea View had reached Ratan Salaria, who supervised both venues. He asked Kalidas about the object of his search and revealed that he himself had been Benoyendra's guide that summer. Kalidas, perhaps beyond the capacity for surprise, politely asked Salaria to write a full account of their activities, but the manager replied that his written English was poor. Would Urdu suffice? Kalidas said it would not. He wrote in longhand as Salaria narrated his days and nights with Benoyendra and Taranath – the visits to the Haffkine Institute and the homes of the different researchers, the trips to P.T. Patel's clinic, the white rats at Crawford Market, and Taranath's work at the lab on Arthur Road. They finished around 1 a.m., and Salaria signed the document. He accompanied Kalidas in a taxi to the central telegraph office, where his guest wired the Calcutta detective department:

Regarding Pakur Conspiracy Case important disclosures Seaview Orient Hotels and Ratan Salaria. Please instruct Commissioner Police Bombay or do needful. Immediate searches, enquiries, statements recorded section 164 criminal code necessary. Activities of Sadhan, Taranath at Haffkines Plague Hospital other places helped by several doctors.
Name and address of sender not to be telegraphed.
Signaller is instructed to observe strictest secrecy.

Le Brocq sent Sub-Inspector Dutta westwards to survey Kalidas' investigative gold mine. Working with a Bombay inspector, he questioned P.T. Patel of the Arthur Road Hospital and his deputy J.M. Mehta. More witnesses were interviewed, including the enterprising rat salesman Jan Mahammad and Jose Mignal Cordeiro at the Bombay Mutual Life Assurance Co. They seized correspondence from the Haffkine Institute, including A.C. Ukil's 1932 wire seeking plague samples for Taranath. Five days later, Dutta left Bombay with enough rope to hang two men.

Taranath and Durga Ratan Dhar were quick to receive bail. So far, the police had submitted little evidence tying either man to Amarendra's last days. Sivapada was still at liberty. On 19 February, Gauri Sen, an aimless former clerk at the Medical Supply Concern, came rapping at Taranath's door. Gauri would often loiter around the drug company's office; the managing director had served as his benefactor since the death of Gauri's father, an early investor in the firm. On several occasions the young man had observed Benoyendra park his car on the street outside and send the driver up to summon Taranath. Sometime in August, Gauri had run into the pair at a movie theatre, where Taranath volunteered that they'd recently been to Bombay. Now, standing just over the threshold inside Taranath's parlour, Sen asked just how deeply his acquaintance was entangled in the Pakur case.

'What really have I done?' Taranath wailed. 'People who did more than me haven't been arrested.'

'He was very excited,' Gauri recalled. 'I wanted to ask him more, but he told me not to … He told me, "Don't ask me any more things," and then I came away.'

19

This Smart Set

Benoyendra was transferred to Alipore Jail, where he was not the only prisoner of note. Jawaharlal Nehru was now a seasoned convict, having already served 1,255 days for his political work.[1] An arrest warrant had been sent to Nehru's home in Allahabad in February 1934 over speeches he had made in Calcutta the previous month. Within three days of his arrest the future prime minister had been transported to Calcutta, tried and convicted for sedition and confined to a 10 by 9ft cell at Alipore Jail. (There is no record of the two men ever meeting.)

New to the arbitrary indignities of life behind bars, Benoy was an uncomplaining detainee. He struck up a sort of friendship with a young guard named Charu Chandra Chakraborty, who decades later would become a top jail official and a best-selling author of prison-inspired fiction. The rookie jailor was drawn to what he saw as Benoyendra's innate, even towering, nobility; still, he grew to regard the raja as a rare specimen of true criminality, possessing 'steady intent, and tireless sincerity' in the pursuit of murder.[2]

Shortly after Benoy was plucked off the Bombay Mail at Asansol, police received an unexpected boon from a target of their investigation. Sivapada had written a letter to Henry Le Brocq seeking to clarify and expand upon the statements he'd made previously. As much as any other piece of evidence or testimony, this correspondence would land the doctor in jail and savage his reputation:

> It occurs to me that I should tell you that between 3 to 4 months ago Dr T.N. Bhattacharjya [*sic*] whom I know as a student of the School of Tropical Medicine came to see me asking for an introductory letter to Parell Laboratory, Bombay, which deals with plague organism. I am not certain whether I gave him the letter he asked for.

Sivapada went on to emphasise his long-standing role as a consulting physician to the Pakur Raj family, and his diligent treatment of Amarendra in December, including the four separate visits he made to Jatin Das Road the day before the boy's death. As for his provision of the death certificate naming septic pneumonia as the cause, he explained that 'Without blood culture no more definite diagnosis could be made'. This was true: the results of Amarendra's blood culture were still unknown at the time of his death. Sivapada also revealed that he had treated Balika Bala at the Calcutta Hotel for several months during the winter of 1933–34 and he disclosed that he had recently seen Benoy over the raja's high blood pressure. (The treatment was in fact for a 'very active' case of syphilis, documents would show.)

Things would soon go badly for Sivapada.

Ratan Salaria, the Bombay hotel manager, had told Le Brocq's men that he saw Benoyendra carrying a letter of introduction to the Haffkine Institute from a Calcutta doctor. They immediately concluded that this letter and the endorsement Taranath had requested from Sivapada were one and the same, linking him directly to the plague plot. But this was a mistake: Sivapada had produced a limp testimonial to his former student; it was never going to open doors and was useless to the conspiracy. The introduction Benoy carried to Bombay was written by Calcutta pulmonologist A.C. Ukil after Taranath brought him a free-spending tuberculosis patient – a fact still unknown to the police.

With his links to Taranath, Taranath's employer, Benoyendra, and Balika Bala; his presence both in Deoghar and at Amarendra's deathbed; multiple witnesses to his speculation that Amar had been murdered; and now this near-admission of having written a letter of introduction to the Haffkine Institute, Sivapada's days as a free man were numbered.

Le Brocq's team would interview more than 200 witnesses and assemble hundreds of pieces of evidence.[3] On 24 February, they spoke with Gauri Sen and learned of Taranath's distraught confession. Two days later, Inspector Luftar Rahman summoned Taranath to his home for a fraught, emotional interview.

The questioning was marked by jags of weeping and long, despairing silences. Taranath finally admitted to visiting Bombay but refused to say why he had done so. He seemed to imply that Sivapada would be imperilled were he to speak freely. 'Sometimes he stated that if he would make any statement he would have to make it against his teacher,' Rahman later said under oath. The noose was tightening. At the Calcutta School of Tropical Medicine, a second round of tests was performed on rats and gerbils to reconfirm the murder weapon as plague. This time the scientists more fully re-enacted Taranath's methods by shaving the animals and rubbing contaminated swabs and plague-infected organs onto the exposed flesh: each died by scarification, just as the rats on Arthur Road had the previous summer.

In court, the public prosecutor N.N. Banerjee argued to have Taranath's bail cancelled, asserting that he had 'approached Dr Sivapada Bhattahcharya [*sic*] of the School of Tropical Medicine and obtained from him a letter of introduction ...' No letter had been shown in court, Taranath's lawyer countered. If there was some letter, why couldn't the Crown introduce it? Taranath was most probably an innocent dupe, his lawyer argued, and Benoyendra, the 'prime mover', had likely stolen the virulent plague he had innocently been culturing for research purposes.[4] Sessions Judge T.H. Ellis, hearing the bail petition, wasn't impressed. Taranath's liberty was revoked on 18 March and he too took up residence behind the walls of Alipore Jail. 'In my opinion, bail should never have been granted,' Ellis said.[5]

Inspector Rahman arrested Sivapada six days later. In a new statement to police, he said he now recalled writing a letter for Taranath, but he insisted – truthfully – that it made no mention of anyone providing facilities to his former student. Police said he made this admission 'after the greatest hesitation ... for obvious reasons'.

Sivapada's lawyer was L.P.E. Pugh, a senior barrister and former president of the European Association who, thirty-seven years earlier, had unsuccessfully defended nationalist leader Lokmanya Tilak against sedition charges following the assassination of Charles Rand, a brutal plague commissioner, in Poona.[6] Pugh ridiculed the government's case while arguing for Sivapada's bail. Not only was Sivapada a pillar of the medical establishment, he was well-off to boot, with significant properties to his name. It was 'childish' to think he could be bought by the likes of Benoyendra Pandey, Pugh said. 'What amount of money could an insolvent raj like the Pakur Raj estate pay to make it worthwhile for the doctor to join the alleged conspiracy?'[7] The case was 'pure speculation'.

Prosecutors confidently replied that Sivapada was mastermind of the whole plot – without him, Amarendra might still be alive. Judge Ellis denied bail, noting his surprise that 'the present petitioner wasn't arrested long ago'.[8] Pugh appealed to the Calcutta High Court, where he highlighted a grinding inconsistency: Sivapada was accused of being a member of a secret conspiracy, while at the same time the government was citing witnesses who said the doctor had straight-up named Benoyendra as the likely culprit. If Sivapada really did call it 'a pure case of murder', as Jyotirmoyee claimed, 'was that the act of a confederate?' Pugh asked. Both could not be true.

The justices were unmoved.[9]

Like Benoy and Taranath, Sivapada too would spend the Calcutta summer sweating out his anxiety in an Alipore cell. ('The entire room would burn like a hot oven,' the nationalist militant-turned-philosopher Sri Aurobindo wrote of his long days as an Alipore detainee.[10]) Only Durga Ratan Dhar remained free. On 9 April, Benoyendra and Taranath were made to stand in a line-up at Alipore Jail, where they were mixed with thirteen other Hindu prisoners and civilians. Ratan Salaria and Dr Mehta of the Arthur Road Hospital pointed out both men; Drs Naidu and Nagarajan selected Benoy. They were good and fingered.

Two days later, police finally filed their long-awaited charge sheet alleging a sprawling plot that closely followed the narrative first suggested by Kalidas Gupta, fortified by interviews in Bombay and Calcutta. The case now moved to the courtroom of Deputy Magistrate Khankar Ali Taib to determine if there was sufficient evidence to send the four accused to trial. Each entered a formal plea of not guilty. 'I have been deliberately involved in this false case,' a defiant Benoy told the magistrate.

After two weeks of hearings, Taib accepted prosecutor N.N. Banerjee's premise with wide-eyed relish, and went on to gild the state's lily in an order committing the four men to trial. With a prudish self-indulgence that Judge Ellis would later emulate, Taib put the spotlight on Benoy's sexual escapades and boozing. Benoyendra hadn't merely starved his brother of funds after their father's death, he 'began to spend away lavishly on himself in wine, women and became an extravagant snob in Calcutta', the magistrate wrote. Taranath was 'a constant companion in his escapades with wine and woman [*sic*] as well has his advisor', while Sivapada and Dhar 'were brought into this smart set and they became familiar with each other'. The plague plot 'could come out from only mature medical brains', Taib concluded.

Benoy's relationships with Balika Bala and Chanchala were at best marginal to the alleged conspiracy, but Taib made time to note how he had forced Surjabati from her home of two decades by 'setting up those prostitutes in the midst of the family residences ...'

The magistrate chundered on. 'It is not unlikely that Taranath was advised by Sivapada,' he asserted without evidence. Dhar, an advisor to a pharmaceutical company called Bengal Immunity, 'had domain over virulent strains of bacteries [*sic*] of different dangerous types ...' After receiving Dhar's injection of tetanus serum, Amarendra didn't just suffer a temporary relapse of symptoms; in Taib's overheated telling, 'his life was again at stake'. Dhar had been paid 400 rupees for his visits to Deoghar (a distance of more than 200 miles each way) 'and he admitted it before the police', Taib wrote triumphantly. And, of course, there was Sivapada's purported letter to the Haffkine Institute.

Taib even used the quality of the defendants' representation as a mark against them, observing that 'they have been spending lavishly' on 'lawyers of eminence'.

He admitted to one weakness – the relative absence of testimony or exhibits implicating Durga Ratan Dhar. 'It cannot but be mentioned that there was no direct evidence to show that Dr Dhar was in any way connected with plague bacilli and [the] subsequent death of Amarendra,' he wrote. 'However, this court cannot usurp the function of the Judge and Jury to ascertain the extent up to which Dr Dhar is liable for his part in the affairs.' Adjudicating probable cause, Taib asserted that it wasn't his job to determine if it existed. He allowed that 'there are some elements to speak in [Dhar's] favour, but this court has no jurisdiction to enter on such deductions on the point of probability'.

All four would go to trial.

Each faced the gallows.

20

Practically Nil

The longest criminal trial in the history of British India began on 23 July 1934, inside the Alipore courtroom of Sessions Judge T.H. Ellis, a lifelong bachelor and a future governor of East Pakistan.[1] The white-columned courthouse had been like an armed camp since the day an assassin had blown out the brains of one of Ellis' colleagues on the bench two years before. Ellis had also been marked for death by the militant underground. Now, bailiffs struggled to manage the unusual crush of spectators eager for a seat at what some were calling the trial of the century. There was 'the clack and mutter of the innumerable voices, muffled laughter, footsteps – the clanging of the iron heels of a Sergeant dashing through the crowd to make the doorway clear, the hiss and rumble of passing trams at a distance and the hurried and feverish steps of the counsels in their blue robes and black jackets', Inspector Luftar Rahman recalled. The budding excitement 'all went to make the scene more morbid than ever'.[2]

The most sensational case in decades was tried before a special jury of six Bengali men, professionals all. Among them was one Brojendra Nath Mukherjee, who taught English at a government school in Ballygunge. Despite Ellis' instructions that jurors were to perform their duty in secrecy, Mukherjee happily spilled the highs and lows of each day's testimony to his wide-eyed adolescent charges, including the future maestro Satayajit Ray. 'Much was being written about this case every day,' Ray later recalled. 'Pamphlets were being printed and distributed at street corners. Each time Brojen Babu returned after a hearing, we badgered him for details. He, too, seemed perfectly willing to share his experiences with us.'[3]

Defence lawyers were outraged at the publicity, or said they were.

The Pakur trial was front-page news around the world, producing hundreds of articles in the US alone, where the Indian germ murder shared space on page 1 with the pavement execution of the notorious bank robber John Dillinger. Eastern horrors made good copy across the Anglosphere. The Pakur case 'Recalls the Borgias', blared one New Zealand headline.[4] But it was the Indian press that most irked the defence. A lawyer for Dhar, N.C. Sen, complained of 'vigorous newspaper propaganda to create sympathy for the deceased and prejudice against the accused'.[5] The media had jumped the gun by referring to the trial as the 'Pakur *Murder* Case', he asserted. 'Whether it was a case of murder or of natural death is to be decided by the court.'[6] Worse, the lawyer said, was a local newspaper's decision to publish a photograph of Amarendra in its pages. Amar's likeness could only serve to unduly influence the public and the jury.

Brojendra Nath Mukherjee and his fellow jurors were treated to a fiery, if lopsided, war for their sympathy and attention.

The Crown was represented by N.N. Banerjee, a popular city councillor and former member of the defence bar whose first courtroom experience had been as a junior lawyer representing the future philosopher Aurobindo Ghose in the Alipore Bomb Case more than twenty-five years before. As public prosecutor, Banerjee had helped convict several members of the famous Chittagong armoury raid; the Pakur murder case would be the biggest – and last – trial of his career.

The prosecutor called eighty-five witnesses, including most of Amarendra's family, everyone Benoy had corrupted or tried to corrupt in Bombay, Taranath's colleagues at the Medical Supply

Concern, the dozen-odd doctors who had treated Amar at different times, and seemingly half the School of Tropical Medicine. Many were the overlapping ties of blood and business. It appeared everyone involved possessed at least one relative who had, at one time or another, received medical care from Taranath, Sivapada, or Dhar. Several witnesses had been classmates, teachers, or students of the accused. The Calcutta of the *bhadralok* was really a small town.

Where Banerjee had stacked dozens of witnesses, the defendants declined to call even a single person to testify. Rather, lawyers for Benoyendra and Taranath threw their all into tearing down the evidence that Amarendra died of plague, and worked to impugn the integrity of the government's witnesses. It was a furious rearguard action by a platoon of skilled advocates – including one who was also a trained physician – against an onslaught of what the legal profession calls 'bad facts', the incontrovertible evidence that can only do harm to one's client. Lawyers for Sivapada and Dhar sought to distance their clients from the odour of culpability that clung to the raja and his sidekick, portraying them as diligent professionals caught up in a wrong-headed police dragnet. All the accused brought formidable representation to the trial: Benoy had a ten-man legal team. Taranath's contingent was nine. Sivapada had six lawyers, and Dhar's table was the smallest with four.

In contrast with modern criminal trials, especially those suffused with scientific evidence, no party – not the police, the prosecution, the defence, or the court – sought to introduce independent experts; each relied exclusively on the experience of doctors and researchers who were already embroiled in the case. These witnesses both boosted and undermined the prosecution's narrative, sometimes with clinical severity.

So it was that Nalini Ranjan Sen Gupta, called to describe Amar's symptoms and the strange story of his pinprick at Howrah Station, was also questioned in depth over Amarendra's tetanus and subsequent infection the prior year – an event to which he hadn't remotely been party. While Sen Gupta was a sterling prosecution witness when it came to Amarendra's plague infection, he helped demolish the case against Durga Ratan Dhar, which centred on his actions in Deoghar.

Prosecutors had harped on the fact that while Dhar was an advisor to the Bengal Immunity company, he had carried Parke-Davis serum to treat Amar in October 1932. Bengal Immunity packaged its anti-tetanus serum in glass ampoules that, once opened, could not be resealed, while the Parke-Davis product was stored in a rubber-topped vial. This, Prosecutor Banerjee confidently told the jury, allowed Dhar to, 'without leaving any trace', adulterate Amarendra's final shot of serum with a poison-filled syringe – the source of Amar's crippling post-tetanus infection.[7]

Sen Gupta, one of Calcutta's most respected physicians, calmly rubbished these notions, explaining that there was nothing suspicious about a patient developing an abscess after an injection. It sometimes happened, he said, despite the best precautions. The fact that Rani Surjabati, against medical advice, had waited more than a month to treat Amar's infection was a further blow to the case against Dhar – one that ought to have been obvious to experienced lawmen like Banerjee and Le Brocq. 'Want of proper treatment delays the cure,' Sen Gupta told the jury.

Despite the drama surrounding Amarendra's illness and treatment at Deoghar, Banerjee struggled to prove the origin of his tetanus. All he could say definitively was that *something* had occurred between the brothers – the jury was told to disregard Amarendra's story of the pince-nez as hearsay. Furthermore, Amar's uncle Rabindranath testified that he hadn't seen any sign of a scratch on Amarendra's nose that evening, further undermining the case that Benoy had purposely infected him. Yes, Taranath had behaved suspiciously in trying to get Amarendra's doctor to replace tetanus serum with morphine, but that didn't establish how he'd got tetanus in the first place.

Plague served as the real battleground.

Benoy's lead counsel was Barada Parsanna Pain, a well-known lawyer and politician, and a former chairman of the Howrah Municipal Corporation. Four months earlier, Magistrate Taib had

alluded to the defendants' pricey advocates; now B.P. Pain (his sur-
name rhymed with *fine*) earned every penny, employing humour
and venom to denigrate everyone associated with the discovery of
plague in Amarendra's blood sample – especially Nalini Sen Gupta's
nephew, Santosh Gupta. Pain went so far as to charge that Santosh
had botched the blood draw and culture and, fearful of disappointing his illustrious uncle, gone on to fake the plague results –wasn't
that so? Santosh denied it. Still, the young researcher admitted to
destroying his original lab notes after sending the extraordinary
blood report to Rabindranath – a baldly suspicious course of action.

Pain attacked every possible angle. Could Santosh have created
fake plague samples from the School of Tropical Medicine's own
inventory? 'At that time there were three sealed tubes containing
plague bacilli in the school,' Professor C.L. Pasricha admitted.
But, he added, they were sealed at the time of Amarendra's illness,
'and are sealed still. They were kept in a different room from that
in which Santosh was conducting his experiments.'

That may be the case, Pain pressed on, but was it truly plague
that they'd found in Amar's blood? Could the killer bacteria not
have been, say, *pseudo-tuberculosis rodentium*, another germ with similar appearance to plague? Alas, B.P.B. Naidu, who had emerged as
the defence's bête noire, replied that infections of *pseudo-tuberculosis
rodentium* were unknown to India; A.C. Ukil reported that it was
found only in guinea pigs; and Santosh explained it was not deadly
to white rats – a half-dozen of which had been fatally infected by
that point with bacteria cultured from Amarendra's blood. There
was no pinning his death on some obscure germ.

Still, even if it was plague that killed Amarendra, the defence
went on to argue, prosecutors still hadn't proved that he was
infected at Howrah. Banabala, who had been walking some
distance behind her younger brother Amar that afternoon, had testified that 'I did not see any man come towards and pushing him'.
Neither had Surjabati, or Ashutosh – or anyone – witnessed the
fatal strike. The story of the pinprick came only from Amarendra's
close family and friends – all sworn enemies of Benoyendra.
Far more likely than the preposterous tale of the mysterious

'blackman', Pain argued, was that Amar's sister Kananbala had actually died of plague, and not the mumps, in September 1933, and that Amarendra had innocently become infected at her home. But Naidu and the others showed it was impossible that a plague-infected flea could have survived the many weeks between Kananbala's death and Amarendra's infection.

While the murder weapon – and the assassin, for that matter – had never been found, prosecutors showed the jury two examples of small syringes that they claimed could have done the job. Defence lawyers replied that it was impossible that an assailant moving at a near-run would have time to discharge enough plague to have an effect. Amarendra had been wearing three layers of clothing – a cotton jersey, a flannel *punjabi*, and a shawl wrapped across his shoulders. How could the supposed needle reach sufficient depth to cause an infection? This question might have gained traction with the jury were it not for the fact that *B. pestis* required minimal penetration into the victim's flesh to take hold – that's what made the tiny rat flea such an effective vector for the disease. The assailant's jab didn't have to go far, or discharge much, Naidu told the jurors. 'An extraordinarily small quantity of infected fluid is sufficient to bring about the death of a man,' Pasricha added.

It was no use. The prosecution had opened a firehose of incrimination. Benoy and Taranath had done nothing to cover their tracks. The raja had barrelled over the line between self-confidence and self-incrimination.

Benoyendra's biggest mistake was failing to anticipate that Amarendra might conjure up the self-confidence to return to Calcutta while his elders were still trying to wish the pinprick away. Had Amar remained in Pakur as Benoyendra expected, he would have died a quiet, pitiful death far from the expertise of physicians like Nalini Sen Gupta and the advanced facilities of the School of Tropical Medicine. Benoy had good reason to believe this was how his brother would exit the stage – murmuring fevered gibberish about murder and regret, cremated at a forlorn backwater, and quickly forgotten. The family's actions suggested – all but promised – that the clan would do nothing until it was too late. Hadn't Surjabati waited a full month to treat Amar's dangerous abscess? Hadn't she cluelessly told Benoyendra their travel plans even after he'd lured Amarendra to Calcutta with a false telegram? Instead, spurred by his cousin Kamala Prosad Pande's letter, Amar had used this last opportunity to take his fate into his hands and boarded a southbound train.

It was also a question of timing. Amarendra made for the city three days after the injection; it was on day four that Santosh Gupta drew blood from his arm and ejected it into a warm flask of broth to culture whatever bacteria might be growing there. Given the history of plague in India, Benoyendra and Taranath had reason to believe that Amarendra would be dead within four days – that was the average life expectancy for a plague victim at the pandemic's murderous height. Even Victor Savage, the victim of an unnamed disease bearing many similarities to septicaemic plague in Arthur Conan Doyle's 'The Adventure of the Dying Detective', was dead within four days. Moreover, Taranath had been working with virulent plague. The assassin's syringe held more *B. pestis* microorganisms than could be delivered by dozens of infected rat fleas.

Amarendra's death was a certainty, but it didn't come to pass until eight days after the pinprick: ample time for some of Calcutta's most respected physicians to hear the tale of the jab at Howrah; for Amarendra to tell disinterested parties that he'd been murdered by his brother; for blood to be drawn and the pathogen painstakingly identified. The only possible explanation for Amar's relatively slow death is that Taranath had stumbled in his repeated subcultures of the stolen plague germs during the scorching summer of 1933. The doctor's pilfered brood must have lost its vigour in the heat, allowing Amarendra's veins to offer up evidence of murder before he finally expired.

Was there more than greed behind Benoy's audacity? Could syphilis have affected his state of mind? It is possible that – like the works of composer Adrian Leverkühn, the protagonist of Thomas Mann's *Doctor Faustus* – Benoyendra's magnum opus was the product of syphilitic mania. As Leverkühn explains in the novel, 'Disease, and most specially opprobrious, suppressed, secret disease, creates a certain critical opposition to the world, to medi-ocre life, disposes a man to be obstinate and ironical toward civil order …'[8] It was an apt description for the Raja of Pakur.

Whether or not the deadly syphilis spirochete affected Benoyendra's judgement, the prosecution and Judge Ellis did their best to ensure that venereal disease and other salacious details of his private life weren't lost on the middle-class jury, from the 'inti-mate' friendship he and Taranath were said to share with Balika Bala, to his relationship with Chanchala, to his daytime visits to Chinatown hotels. Ellis, a future justice on the Calcutta High Court and a future chief justice of the Dhaka High Court, spoke from the bench of Benoy's sexually transmitted infection even though his medical records indicating syphilis were never shown to the jury.

Pain tried to turn the tables by insinuating Amarendra's medi-cal debt was a fiction and that, as a young, single man away at college, he must have owed money to a prostitute. A lawyer for Taranath went further, suggesting that Amar's tetanus symptoms were really those of late-stage syphilis. (At the judge's invitation, he withdrew the statement.)

The defence took similar aim at Gauri Sen, one of the trial's most damaging witnesses. Gauri was the sole eyewitness to Taranath's anguished admission, but he had also confided it to his cousin, Aurobindo Bose. Both were dragged through the Calcutta mud. Pain portrayed Gauri Sen as a lazy sponger, dependent on his late father's former business partner for cash and discipline. 'Is it a fact that you have to go and see your guardian daily so that he can regulate your daily conduct?' the lawyer asked. Gauri had been sued by a silk merchant over an unpaid bill for three saris he'd purchased. Pain alleged these were meant for a prostitute whose services he shared with his cousin. 'Is it a fact that these saris were gifts to a woman named Sona who was in the joint keeping of yourself and Aurobindo?' he asked. Gauri replied that the saris were for his three sisters; he offered to bring them from home if Pain liked. Pain didn't.

As a worldly young man, fluent in English and French, with wealthy parents, Gauri's cousin Aurobindo was harder to push around, though Pain tried. Aurobindo had served as an aide to director Sisir Kumar Bhaduri during a disappointing 1931 production of the play *Sita* on Broadway in New York (for which he had tried to recruit Balika Bala). Aurobindo left the production to complete an engineering degree at Columbia University. Back home in Calcutta he moved in performing arts circles and often saw Benoy and Taranath together at the Natya Mandir theatre, the movies, and at restaurants. Asked about the girl he and Gauri supposedly shared 'on co-operative lines', he angrily replied, 'It is a lie.' When Pain implied he was a pimp and asked about his ties to criminal syndicates, Aurobindo coolly said, 'I do not know the underworld of Calcutta.'

The mud didn't stick.

21

Best of Brothers and Friends

For eight long months, ever since the police first forced him into captivity, Benoyendra had watched mutely as his reputation was turned into a plaything for the police, the prosecution, and the more sensationalist press – a mouse to be batted around by predators and discarded once the trial was over. Newspapers, street corner pamphlets, and weeks of testimony had all identified him as a cold-blooded killer who cared for nothing beyond high living and low women.

By late October, it was at last time for the defence to present its case. This was Benoy's chance to take control of the trial's narrative and show the jury a compelling new interpretation of his maligned life and Amarendra's death. But B.P. Pain and his defence colleagues declined to call a single person to the stand. After hundreds of pages of sworn testimony so damaging to Benoyendra and Taranath as to be almost radioactive, each of the accused now submitted a written statement to the court. If this course of action disappointed the jurors and the spectators, it was the safest way for the raja and his co-defendants to tell their side of the Pakur story; had any of the accused sworn an oath and taken the witness stand, he would have been fair game for Banerjee's cross-examination.

Benoy went first – rather, one of his lawyers went first. Ill health prevented the raja from personally reading his nearly 5,000-word melodrama of nobility and persecution. Jurors would not hear Benoyendra's testament in his own voice; even as he shrank from the chance to narrate his declaration, the statement still captured the man's brazen, entitled essence. A few months before, the Marx Brothers comedy *Duck Soup* had romped through the cinemas of India, sending audiences into stitches with the line, 'Who are you going to believe, me or your own eyes?' In Judge Ellis' courtroom, with his neck on the line, Benoy played the role of Chico Marx.

'I am totally and absolutely innocent, and I did not commit any offence,' his statement began. 'On the other hand, a dangerous conspiracy has been at work against me to implicate me in this false case.' Up was down, black was white. The plotters were legion, each with their own motive to frame the stoic zamindar. Benoyendra named them all.

Benoy charged that, days before his humiliating arrest on the Bombay Mail, Kalidas Gupta had attempted a crude shake-down where the lawyer 'conveyed to me broadest and unmistakable hints that troubles would creep up on me if I could not make matters worth his while'. Surjabati had grave motive to send Benoyendra to prison – he was making moves to seize her properties for himself. Benoy's brother-in-law Ashutosh Chakravarty 'was also in litigation with me' over his sister Kananbala's estate, the raja pointed out. Worse still, 'he and his daughter Anima are the protégés of Surjabati Devi'. Rani Jyotirmoyee had 'taken up and maintained against me a relentlessly hostile attitude, and I was more than once warned that a suitable opportunity was being awaited to wipe me off the face of the Earth'.

In the face of these enemies, Benoyendra argued, no one could dare stand by him. 'Anyone who wanted in any way to help me was threatened with arrest and prosecution for conspiracy – an elastic term indeed under suitable hands,' he said.

As for his alleged feud with Amarendra, Benoy rejected any notion there had been differences between them. 'I did all I could, all that was humanly possible to do, to bring up my brother in a way befitting our position and means, and I spent some of my own money on him, his education, and on his treatment,' Benoyendra swore. 'I had taught him to shoot, and drive, to play tennis and other games, and altogether our relationship had ever been happy and friendly ... There was not a whisper of my ever having tried to do any injury to my brother, so long as he was alive. All sorts of inhuman allegations are cropping up when he is no longer on the face of this earth to refute them.'

While at Deoghar, 'I nursed Amarendra day and night,' he said. As for plague, 'I had nothing whatsoever to do with Dr Taranath's requests for plague culture from the Haffkine Institute. I had no earthly connection whatever with these requests.'

Benoy asserted that Taranath was all but a stranger; he had offered to share his Bombay hotel room with the doctor as a simple act of courtesy, one Bengali helping another. What couldn't be explained was simply denied.

'I had nothing whatsoever to do with the purchase of rats at Bombay,' he said. 'The evidence about it is a tissue of falsehoods.' He had never met Drs Nagarajan and Sathe of the Haffkine Institute, nor did he 'offer them any rewards of any kind whatsoever'. They too were cogs in the conspiracy. All the accounts placing Benoy in the company of a dark-complexioned stranger 'have been deliberately concocted for the purposes of building up a case against me', he said. He had signalled no one outside Howrah Station, and had never seen the glazed, glistening wound on Amar's shoulder that afternoon – much less rubbed it with his bare thumb. Scientists, rat-sellers, teenagers, his surrogate mother: the courtroom had been the setting for nothing less than a months-long parade of liars and schemers.

The public record makes no mention of Benoy's demeanour during the trial; one can imagine him subtly scanning the jury box with those sloe eyes for a sense of whether this bald counter-history might win some converts for the defence.

Benoyendra concluded his statement by returning to the woman who had raised him from the age of 2 and who had aroused his undying resentment by transferring her affection to the newborn, motherless Amarendra some two decades earlier. 'My troubles began with my declared intentions to institute a suit to make certain claim over the whole of the properties which Surjabati Devi has been permitted to call her own,' he said, emphasising his view that the ailing Surjabati had no rights at all.

'Everything possible has been done by my enemies to me.'

★★★

Taranath too declined to read out his own statement, leaving the task to a member of his legal team. So little was known about the anxious doctor that the jury and spectators must have leant in to hear his testament. The audience wasn't left hanging. Taranath provided one of the trial's one true surprises: he all but exonerated Sivapada Bhattacharjee.

The doctor's statement was shorter, and lighter on self-pity, than Benoyendra's. Like Benoy, Taranath laid it on thick for the jury, and maybe for himself. (Unlike Benoy, this would be the last the world would hear from Taranath Bhattacharjee.)

It was the story of a pure-hearted striver of modest means who had devoted his life to the service of humanity – only to stumble due to bad luck and misunderstanding. 'The thought of hurting a human being has never crossed my mind,' he said. 'In fact, since the earliest times about which I remember, I had cherished the ambition to become a doctor so that I could minister to the sufferings of my fellow men.'

Where Taranath's batchmates had devoted themselves to building wealth after graduation, he instead persued profitless research on the conquest of disease. India's hope, he believed, lay in the combination of Western medications and traditional Ayurvedic compounds. He 'set out with the idea of finding out a remedy that will increase the defensive forces of the blood, thereby enabling it to declare victory over invading pathogenic or disease-producing organisms'.

In the doctor's telling, he 'established beyond doubt the surprisingly increased effects of certain Indian drugs when combined with foreign ones'. These successes included the pairing of ayurvedic 'uterine sedative' drugs with haemoglobin, a blood protein, and combining the herbs *kalmegh* and *kulekhra* with haemoglobin in the treatment of bilious diseases.

Throughout his police interrogation and imprisonment, Taranath had kept to himself the ingredients of his putative plague cure but he was now, he told the court, compelled by his legal team to reveal the secret recipe. Taranath's cure harkened back to the 1890s patent plague remedy of the vaccine sceptic Professor T.M. Gujjar and the more recent work of the surgeon Sir Frank Connor, who had been one of his teachers at Calcutta Medical College. 'I had for some time been studying the effect in combination of iodine and the Indian *neem*,' he said, referring to the widely used medicinal leaves of a tree in the mahogany family. 'It struck me that a scientific combination of colloidal iodine with the active principles of neem should furnish an active germicide of no mean order.' The *neem* and iodine formula, he said, 'had striking effects' on the germs *Streptococci*, *Staphylococci*, and *B. coli*.

After hearing the reputed success of iodine against plague, he said, 'I felt that if iodine by itself could affect recovery, the chances of success would be greatly enhanced if the active principles of neem could be combined with it,' he said. Here Taranath came clean about the limits of his purported quest. His innocent search for a plague cure had failed. 'I confess I have not yet succeeded in my attempt, as the additive compound I had made of iodine and neem did not succeed as an effective cure for plague, as the experiments in Bombay actually demonstrated. But I feel assured that success ultimately lies in that direction.'

Then, Taranath took the knees out from under the prosecution's case against Sivapada, revealing that A.C. Ukil had all along been the source of the letter Benoyendra had carried to Bombay – not Sivapada. 'I had obtained a letter of introduction to Doctor Naidu of the Haffkine Institute, asking if he could accommodate me in his house for a few days, as I was new to Bombay and to help me in doing research work with a view to testing the germicidal effect of the medicine on plague I had prepared,' Taranath said. (Ukil had testified that he could not recall writing on Taranath's behalf.)

'I did approach Dr Sivapada Bhattacharjee for a letter of introduction to the officer in charge of the Parel Laboratory,' he allowed. 'Doctor Sivapada gave me only a general certificate as he said he did not know any of the doctors at the Parel Laboratory. The certificate mentioned only the facts that I was a medical practitioner in Calcutta and was going to Bombay.'

The Bombay tour guide Ratan Salaria had testified that Benoy carried a letter from a doctor in Calcutta; Sivapada had admitted writing some kind of letter. The prosecution and the press hadn't shut up about it. Now, with a few lines of text, Taranath had all but got his former professor off the hook. But the revelation did nothing to help Taranath himself. Like Benoy, he had no real answer for his actions in Calcutta, Bombay, and Deoghar – at least none that could discredit the dozens of witnesses arrayed against him.

Sivapada Bhattacharjee, by this time a *former* associate professor at the School of Tropical Medicine, had spent seven despairing months at Alipore Jail, through the heat, the rains, and now the cold. At last he had reason for cautious optimism.

His statement to the court, read by his lawyer, was plain and direct. Sivapada denied outright that he exclaimed on Jatin Das Road that Amar's pneumonia was the handiwork of his elder brother, and that he had told Jyotirmoyee that Amarendra's death was a 'pure case of murder'. He admitted to telling Rabindranath's former teacher that the case was like one from a thriller novel – but insisted his words had been misinterpreted. 'In observing before Captain G.S. Chatterji that it was a case of poisoning the like of which one reads in storybooks, I really meant that the story was hardly credible as a reality,' he said.

Where the Pandeys had painted him as an absentee at Amarendra's sickbed, present only to serve them false hope,

Sivapada insisted he had fought hard for Amar's life against an unknown – and, it turned out, invariably fatal – pathogen. 'I suggested inhalation of oxygen for the patient and [the] calling in of a doctor to attend him throughout the night,' he said. 'I prescribed Feltons's serum, which is a potent remedy against rapidly growing pneumonia. It was with very great difficulty that I succeeded in procuring the serum for the patient.' This was hardly the work of a murderer.

Police and prosecutors had claimed that large deposits to Sivapada's bank account were evidence of payment for his alleged role in the conspiracy; he now persuasively described them as the lawful proceeds of his medical practice and other business dealings – facts a more thorough investigation could have ascertained long before the trial started.

Sivapada concluded his statement by emphasising the fatal flaw in the allegations against him: 'The erroneous belief on the part of the prosecution that the letter produced by B.C. Pandey to Dr Naidu was written by me seems to be the main reasons [*sic*] for my being implicated in this case.'

Durga Ratan Dhar was the only defendant to read his own statement to the court. It was short and to the point, describing how he came to treat Amarendra at Deoghar, his decision to bring tetanus serum from Calcutta in case local dispensaries were poorly supplied, and the successful results of the last serum injection. As for Amarendra's subsequent infection, 'it was the inevitable result of sheer neglect', he said. The public prosecutor had used Benoy's payment of 400 rupees to Dhar as evidence of bribery, but other doctors at the trial had pegged the fee as rather low for a house call to far-off Deoghar. Dhar had actually reduced his normal rate at Benoy's urging; in the end, he told the court, the raja hadn't even paid that much: Benoyendra still owed 150 rupees.

And so, with that overdue bill entered into the trial record, the defence rested.

22

A *Chota* Peg

Barada Pain had one last chance to save his client. He was a wasp-ish, silver-tongued rascal who knew how to sway juries, audiences, voters. He used every tool in the box – flattery, humour, scorn, abjection – during his days-long summation. He hammered at every inconsistency and slip by the Crown's witnesses, no matter how small, and jovially lobbed insults at Public Prosecutor N.N. Banerjee. Representing a defendant who had emerged as an almost cartoonishly villainous figure, Pain made himself the trial's protagonist, and asked the jurors to place their faith in him and his efforts to save an innocent man from execution.

Pain gave it his all. Banerjee had earlier accused the lawyer of trying to 'raise a blizzard' of medical jargon and irrelevant diagnostic procedures to 'obscure the vision of the jurors' during his lengthy cross-examinations. Drawing the jury's attention to Banerjee's complaints over the many days and weeks given over to his harrying of prosecution witnesses, Pain asserted proudly that he wasn't working for the Crown's convenience. If Banerjee wanted to send Benoy to the hangman, it would be without Barada Pain's help in 'gliding and fitting round his neck the noose which has been prepared for him with such a loving and tender care'.[1]

Pain then dropped the unctuous tone to home in on the core weaknesses of Banerjee's case. There were no eyewitnesses to the two key events in the alleged conspiracy – the incident with the pince-nez and the jab at Howrah. The prosecution stood on feet of clay – the second-hand recollections of what Amarendra allegedly told others. The entire case was driven by the supposed murmurings of a dead heir and the animosity of Benoy's enemies, Pain said. Benoyendra's fate rested solely on a scaffold of hearsay, 'statements alleged to have been made by Amar, and great advantage was taken of the fact that Amar was not alive and available for giving evidence and the accuracy of those statements could not be tested,' Pain told the jury. The case was 'purely circumstantial – circumstances that did not happen in reality'.

'On every vital point, where evidence must be decisive and conclusive,' Pain said, the men of the jury were being asked to make 'presumptions and inference to usurp the place of proof'. Where the trial witnesses had been loquacious with Banerjee, Pain said, there had been 'an epidemic of forgetfulness at the time of cross-examination'.

Even the supposed assassin, Pain said, had been invented in such a way as to prejudice the jury and the English judge. By claiming that Benoy's mysterious companion was wearing homespun *khaddar*, the prosecution hoped that Amar's death would be associated with nationalists and terrorists, Pain alleged.

It was a question of decency: despite what the plague experts claimed, a single blood test could not be the basis for convicting a man of murder. Furthermore, Pain added, the presence of plague in Amar's blood didn't even confirm the cause of death; whatever their supposed fears of foul play, the family had not ordered an autopsy before the cremation. Therefore, he said, Amarendra's true cause of death remained unknown. Researchers at the School of Tropical Medicine had examined the diseased organs of their experimental rats and guinea pigs to confirm plague. Was the death of a man – with the fate of four others hanging in the balance – to be held to a lesser standard? Surely the jury would see how preposterous it was.

Pain's only true fear, he said, was that publicity might have clouded the jurors' judgement. 'This case has been intensively reported in the columns of newspapers with sensational headlines and … it has been discussed outside this courtroom,' Pain said. He begged the jury to put aside gossip and newspapers, and to focus only on the evidence. If they did this, Benoy's innocence would become clear.

And he pleaded with the jurors to judge the defendants with the same care they would want if they themselves had been accused in such a nebulous, incredible conspiracy. Had the prosecution really proven its case? The six men were 'sitting here to decide whether [the defendants] should go out of this dock as free men, breathe God's free air again, and go back to their expectant mothers, wives, and children, or whether they should be eternally wiped off the face of the earth'.[2] (Taranath's lawyer, S.C. Chaudhury, did his part as well, taking on the dead Amarendra, Kalidas Gupta, the Haffkine Institute's B.P.B. Naidu, and the prosecution witness Aurobindo Bose in a single caustic sentence. 'An ungrateful patient, a lawyer practising tricks, a dogmatic plague expert and an authority on dancing girls' were 'very poor instruments for the vindication of a nation's justice', he told the jury.[3])

Barada Pain was a survivor. In the coming decade he would regain political control of the Howrah Municipal Corporation, serve as a defence lawyer for independence leader Subhas Chandra Bose just months before Bose's escape to Nazi Germany,[4] and, as a minister in the wartime Bengal assembly, survive a no-confidence vote over charges of extravagant corruption.[5] He had reason to think his address had given the defence some much-needed momentum. And then the momentum was stopped cold. Judge Ellis adjourned the trial for more than four weeks, allowing himself and the rest of the participants an expansive winter holiday. By the time court reconvened in late January 1935, Benoy and Taranath had been 'virtually deprived of the effect of the defence arguments upon the Jury', they claimed.

All that was left was for Ellis to instruct the jurors. His address occupied an unprecedented eight days, stretching from 25 January to 16 February, the longest jury instructions in Indian judicial history. He was thorough, loquacious, biased.

Ellis gave the appearance of fairness during his lengthy summary, but line for line the judge was dependably on Banerjee's side. With his experience trying cases involving nationalist militants, and well aware of the city's deep-seated anti-government mood, Ellis may have had concerns about whether the jury could be relied on to side with the prosecutor. Juries could be unpredictable; a loss in the Pakur case would be a serious blow to the government's authority.

Some of Ellis' statements would have earned him censure in a modern courtroom – or provoked a mistrial. Taking on defence complaints that the jurors were hearing too much about Benoy's drinking, Ellis drew their attention to the whiskies that witnesses saw the raja sharing with the presumed assassin at Kellner's Refreshment Room the night before the attack. 'I do not think that either you or I are likely to be prejudiced against him because evidence is offered that he was seen drinking a *chota* peg on one occasion,' Ellis said. 'But if you do believe that he was seen drinking there,' he added, 'the question that will naturally suggest itself to you is – why should he go all the way from his house in Ballygunge to Howrah Station that evening and whether it was merely to have a drink in the refreshment room.'

Ellis frequently lapsed into commentary, assuming the role of a pitchside pundit at a match he was meant to referee. Addressing the defence suggestion that Santosh had spiked Amarendra's blood sample with *B. pestis* to cover his own incompetence, he shared his opinion that 'Dr Santosh had no reason so far as I can see to introduce plague bacilli into the culture in order to shield himself'. On several occasions he rubbished the defence's arguments, leaving the jury with no doubt as to whom they should trust. He mentioned Balika Bala – who was neither accused nor a witness – twelve times during his address. In recalling the budding friendship between Benoy and Taranath, Ellis described the 'intimacy between the two, founded on a common appreciation of Balika Bala ...'

The judge's thumb was planted firmly on the scales of justice.

After a trial of 140 working days stretched over seven and a half months, Ellis wrapped up his address and the case was ready for the jury. 'The consequences of your verdict do not concern you,' Ellis told the jurors. 'Your task is over as soon as you return your verdict. The sentence is a matter for me alone.'

'Consider your verdict.'

The panel retired at 12.20 p.m. on 16 February and was back with a unanimous decision just four hours later. The jurors found Benoyendra and Taranath guilty of murder and conspiracy. Sivapada Bhattacharjee and Durga Ratan Dhar were acquitted. Sivapada was also found not guilty of producing a false death certificate. The jurors ended their long service with an unusual plea to Judge Ellis: 'Lastly, we all pray that the extreme penalty may not be passed on the first two accused.'

Ellis was in no mood to oblige. 'I am unable to agree with the recommendation to mercy,' he replied. 'The murder was diabolically conceived and cold-bloodedly executed. I see no reason to refrain from passing the extreme sentence of the law.' Benoy and Taranath were each to be 'hanged by the neck until he is dead'. He gave them seven days to appeal. The jury disbanded, each man headed home with one last story to tell.

The verdict was broadcast around the world, and even appeared on the front page of the *New York Times*. The jury had rendered a tidy decision that held the two obvious culprits responsible while leaving unanswered questions about Sivapada Bhattacharjee's conduct. Sivapada had spent enough time around Benoy to have some sense of his innately corrupt character. Benoy would have used their hours together to gain an understanding of what Sivapada could and couldn't be persuaded to do. Sivapada would have been aware that his moral boundaries were being surveyed. There is no evidence he crossed them.

With the blazing exception of Benoyendra, most the actors in the Pakur drama had played their roles with timidity, cowering behind social convention, financial and reputational self-interest, and genuine, sweating fear. Amarendra's closest friend, Ashoke Prokash Mitra, and his cousin, Kamala Prosad Pande, failed to remove him from the Pakur Express the day he was jabbed for fear of causing offence to Amar's chief tormenter. The ailing Surjabati denied under oath that she was aware the brothers were feuding, or that her relations with Benoy were permanently broken. Jyotirmoyee, despite – or because of – her enormous wealth, had been loath to get involved in her nephew's death and twice refused to speak with Le Brocq's investigators before finally agreeing to an interview. As Kalidas Gupta – the only figure in the affair to show real courage – had written shortly after Amarendra's death, 'no step for any inquiry has yet been taken by anyone, as it is apprehended that people of position and money may be found involved'.

In this light, it's not surprising Sivapada denied that he had all but accused Benoy of a terrific murder, or that he filed a death certificate that failed to mention his suspicion of foul play. Like so many others, Sivapada Bhattacharjee was looking out for himself. The high-flying consulting physician disappeared from the public eye after his acquittal; it was rumoured he completed his career as a humble paediatrician.[6] He never published another piece of research. (Durga Ratan Dhar, however, retained most of his reputation and later published a textbook on tropical diseases.)

The Pakur trial left another compromised cohort off the hook: the Indian medical establishment. There is no public evidence of investigatory or disciplinary action against the many doctors and researchers who had used poor judgement, committed material acts of omission, and engaged in apparent corruption. The press took no interest. Magistrate Taib had charged from the bench that 'it appeared some arrangements had been effected' between Benoyendra and P.T. Patel, but Patel kept his job as superintendent of the Arthur Road Hospital and went on to become medical advisor to the Zenith Insurance Co. 'In the present state of human progress such a crime is impossible without the active assistance of the man of science; one of the condemned persons in the Pakur case is a doctor,' the *Times of India* editorialised. 'Happily, the standard of professional honour and the sense of a sacred trust are so high in the medical profession as a whole that such attempts are few and far between.'[7]

Even with the acquittals of Sivapada and Dhar, the conviction of the lead conspirators was a victory for N.N. Banerjee. But the public prosecutor wasn't there to see it – Banerjee died at his home in Bhowanipore after a brief bout of meningitis a week before the jury's announcement, leaving a wife and seven sons. His funeral rites were performed at Keoratola ghat where, fourteen months earlier, Amarendra's body had been cremated in front of his over-joyed, *paan*-chewing brother.

Indeed, the fragility and precarity of life were never far from the trial's antiseptic skirmishes over plague, tetanus, fleas, and syringes. Kalidas Gupta had lost his wife to an unnamed illness just as the Pakur case hearings were getting under way. Saktipada Chakrabarty, Henry's 'most able and dedicated Bengali assistant commissioner', died suddenly in August, before he had a chance to testify.[8] One morning in late September, bailiffs burst through Judge Ellis' doors in the middle of proceedings to drag Sivapada, Dhar, and Dr Naidu into the nearby courtroom of Subordinate Judge D.P. Pal, who had collapsed on the bench. The accused murderers and the prosecution witness strained to save the justice's life, but he never regained consciousness.[9]

One morning before dawn, Betty Le Brocq woke up to find her husband doubled over in pain.[10] She frantically phoned police headquarters for an ambulance, and Henry was rushed into emergency surgery for what turned out to be appendici-tis. 'I must confess,' he later wrote, 'that when I was laid low in the middle of the night without previous warning, I began to wonder if I, too, was to become a victim of the ill-omened Pakur Murder Case.'[11]

23

No Proper Trial

The condemned men were moved to new quarters at Alipore Jail, nearer to the gallows.

Benoyendra kept his nerve. 'Whenever I visited his cell ... he seemed to me a tall white statue made of marble – silent and calm, with an unswerving mentality,' jailer Charu Chandra Chakraborty recalled. 'He always greeted me with a "Namaskar" while wearing a gentle smile on his benign face; it never happened otherwise. He never had any complaint against anything or showed any annoyance or dismay. He had only one answer if asked about his health: "I am fine." But we all knew his health was deteriorating in a new and hostile life for him; he was, in no way, fine.'

Taranath wasn't holding up any better in the adjacent cell. 'He bawled relentlessly, lamented over his fate, and complained about anything and everything,' Chakraborty said.[1]

From behind bars they appealed to the Calcutta High Court. Benoy asserted that, among other outrages, 'the learned trial judge very seriously misdirected the Jury in directing them ... that the onus of proving the truth of their explanations as to incriminating circumstances ... was upon the accused persons'; that 'the omission of the learned Judge to direct the Jury that the alleged statement of Sivapada, implicating your petitioner and suggesting his general bad character, was no evidence against him'; and that Ellis 'failed to caution the Jury against the generally unreliable character of the testimony of experts who are naturally dogmatic in their opinion and biased in favour of the party calling them'.

While their death sentences awaited confirmation, Benoy and Taranath's days were even more regulated than ever. Each was allotted time to work in solitude in the jail garden. Meals were carried to their cells from the dining hall by Brahmin convict cooks. Prison rules governed every aspect of life and even of death. The conspirators could rest easy knowing that, if they were hanged, the rules prevented their corpses from being displayed to the public. Decades-old procedure demanded that 'the bodies of criminals are not to be exposed on gibbets after execution, but are to be burnt or buried, unless claimed by their relations or friends'.[2]

The pair lingered under the gallows for nine months before their appeal was heard, an unusual and unexplained delay for a capital case. The previous June a revolutionary had been hanged at Alipore for the attempted murder of Calcutta Police Commissioner Charles Tegart and the assassination of his Chandernagore counterpart. The uncertainty over the question of if and when the Pakur conspirators might meet the rope played further havoc with Taranath's mental health. Even Benoy cracked under the strain, begging a visiting dignitary to end his torment. 'If you have the authority, please do me this favour,' he told the inspector. 'I've been living with a sword hanging over my head for months now. Please tell them to set it loose on me – that's all I want.'[3] It wasn't until November that a two-man bench took up the case of Benoyendra Chandra Pandey and another v. Emperor. Taranath 'went mad in the interval', according to one account.[4]

When Justices John Rolleston Lort-Williams and Syed Nasim Ali finally released their decision on 10 January 1936, the jurists struck many of the same notes as Benoyendra's appeal. The trial, they concluded, had been anything but fair.

Ellis had 'repeatedly stated the case for the prosecution and the arguments advanced to support it, without clearly pointing out to the jury those parts of it which were not supported by evidence, or depended merely upon glosses of evidence', Lort-Williams wrote.

'Further ... he stated to the jury that they had already heard in the evidence that Benoyendra was suffering from a venereal disease. This was undoubtedly liable to prejudice the accused.' Ellis had 'referred to Balika Bala as the common keep of Benoyendra and Taranath, for which there was no evidence and ... he said that Amarendra's body had been cremated speedily, thanks to Benoyendra's bribe to the Registrar at the burning ghat, of which there was no real evidence.'

Ellis' frequent reference to the defendants having provided no reasonable explanation for their actions also 'amounted to misdirection', Lort-Williams said.

'A good deal of evidence, both oral and documentary, was admitted which was of doubtful relevance,' continued Lort-Williams, a former Conservative Member of Parliament from south-east London. 'When considering the question of admissibility, the Court should lean always in favour of the accused and exclude all evidence tendered by the prosecution which is of doubtful or remote relevance.' Lort-Williams and Nasim Ali chose to discard all the evidence and testimony from Deoghar as insufficient for trial. This was all good news for Benoy and Taranath.

They also set aside the testimony of Gauri Sen, who had heard Taranath's shocking admission, saying there 'may be some doubt' that he was telling the truth.

Nasim Ali, a future chief justice of the Calcutta High Court (and the father of a future chief justice), aligned with Lort-Williams in his concurring opinion. 'In this case the Judge told the Jury that there was no case considering the matter from any point of view other than the point of view presented by the prosecution and that the only course available to them was to bring a verdict of guilty,' he wrote.

'Under these circumstances this Court held that there has been no proper trial.'

This would have been music to the ears of the two crumbling appellants, but for another finding shared by the English and Indian justices: Benoy and Taranath – Judge Ellis' incontinence notwithstanding – were guilty as sin.

However glaring the sessions judge's errors, Lort-Williams said, they were 'no more than comparatively minor blemishes on what was otherwise a careful and very able charge, and a masterly exposition of intricate evidence ...' He commended the work of Le Brocq and Banerjee. None of Ellis' mistakes could obscure 'well-established facts about the existence of which there is not and cannot be any reasonable doubt'.

'The only legitimate inference ... is that the plague culture which was the cause of Amarendra's death was procured from Arthur Road Hospital in pursuance of a conspiracy to murder Amarendra and was supplied to a person at present unknown who injected it into Amar's system,' Nasim Ali wrote. 'Amarendra was murdered in fact by the injection of that sepsis at the Howrah Station on 26th of November 1933 and ... Benoyendra and Taranath were parties to that conspiracy.'

The justices – one the son of a West Midlands solicitor, the other of a Calcutta *maulvi* – were, in effect, finding Benoy and Taranath guilty all over again.

'This court is at least as well, if not better, qualified than the jury to draw the necessary inference,' Lort-Williams wrote. They scotched Benoy and Taranath's plea for a new trial. In light of the excruciating interval between verdict and appeal, and the circumstantial nature of the evidence, they commuted the men's sentences to transportation for life: this typically meant exile to the bleak confines of the Cellular Jail, on the distant Andaman and Nicobar Islands in the southern Bay of Bengal. However, Benoy and Taranath had escaped the noose; and it appears that, ultimately, they were even allowed to serve out their sentences in Bengal.

Lort-Williams and Nasim Ali cited another reason for refusing to confirm the death sentences. They held out hope that the assistance of Benoy or Taranath might eventually 'lead to the discovery and apprehension of the actual perpetrator of this atrocious crime ...' But the assassin was in the wind and, with families vulnerable to reprisal, and their life sentences now affirmed, the convicts had no incentive to help the police nab him.

While it barely came up at trial, the Detective Department had known the killer's identity for more than a year and had failed to run him down. On 16 August 1934, with the trial in full swing, a Mr P. Mukherjee of Old China Bazar Street had posted a confidential letter to Police Commissioner Lionel Colson describing a recent conversation with his friend Jotindra Mohan Dutta. Dutta revealed he had been renting his garage on Mondal Street to Taranath, where the doctor and a dark-complexioned assistant performed experiments on rats and other small animals. For a small fee, Mukherjee wrote, Dutta was willing to identify Taranath's assistant from among the voluminous archive of driver's licence photos maintained by the police. In addition to payment for his services, Dutta's participation would have to be kept secret: he was frightened of the dark-complexioned figure who, Mukherjee said, ran with a gang of hard men.

While Dutta's paid assistance might have helped the investigation to some degree, police had already been on to the killer for more than three months when they received his friend's letter.

The assassin who plunged Taranath's plague cocktail into Amarendra at Howrah Station was one Satish Chandra Das, also known as Patal Das. He was well built, compact, dark complexioned, a former gymnast. Patal Das worked as a mechanic and private driver. He'd been seen chauffeuring Taranath around the city in his Ford; the two were first introduced by Benoyendra, according to police records. Patal Das had been a volunteer with the Indian Life Saving Society during flooding in northern Bengal in the late 1920s, around the same time that Benoyendra served as an assistant secretary for the organisation. It was here, in the context of helping the survivors of disaster, that Benoy first met his hired killer. Patal Das matched the descriptions of the man seen with Benoy outside the Purna Theatre, at Kellner's Refreshment Room, and that of a frequent visitor to Benoyendra's house in Calcutta, where the landlord recalled him as a 'long-haired man' who 'did not appear to be a Mohammedan, nor a Sikh, nor a Punjabi. He was dressed in dhoti and *khaddar*. He might be an upcountry man or a Bengali.'

Das vanished after Amarendra's funeral.

Sub-Inspector Satya Mukherjee was part of the team directed to track him down. Mukherjee was an up-and-coming investigator, 25 years old with a master's degree from Calcutta University, but there was another reason he received the assignment – Mukherjee had known Patal Das when he was a teenager in the Jorabagan neighbourhood of north Calcutta. The future policeman and the future killer had lost touch before reacquainting at a chance meeting in early 1933. Mukherjee scoured Calcutta for signs of his old friend but came up empty. A stake-out of his father's home in the Kadamtola neighbourhood of Howrah produced nothing. Investigators tracked the killer's scent as far away as Rangoon, but Patal Das was never seen again.

'The Pakur murder case has made its last appearance,' the former municipal councillor Henry Hobbs wrote in his diary a few days after the High Court decision.[5] A raconteur of the first order, Hobbs knew the people and byways of Calcutta like the back of his hand. Despite his long experience chronicling the rogues and scoundrels of Bengal, Hobbs was wrong in closing the book on Benoyendra: a deranged sequel was in the works.

24

Vendetta

On 28 August 1947, after more than thirteen years behind bars, Benoyendra walked free out of Alipore Jail thanks to an amnesty celebrating the British departure from India. 'Long years ago we made a tryst with destiny, and now the time comes when we shall redeem our pledge,' the prime minister (and Benoy's erstwhile fellow inmate) Jawaharlal Nehru had said in Delhi fourteen days earlier as the nation awaited freedom at midnight.[1] Released from bondage, Benoyendra, too, was again at liberty to forge his own path. First sentenced to death, and then to life, he was somehow spared exile to the Andaman Islands and now found himself – improbably, fortuitously, indefensibly – free.

Benoy's son Prosunendra, now a young adult, collected his disgraced father at the iron gate. After a few days in Calcutta they journeyed home by train from Howrah to the Gokulpur Palace in Pakur. 'I was anxious to have him amongst us and I did my level best for his release and ultimately he was released,' Prosunendra later recalled.[2]

The killers emerged from incarceration to an India drowning in chaos, and a Bengal weakened by starvation, bloodied by communal violence, and hived by Partition. Benoy and Taranath had spent the entirety of the Second World War in prison; they would have cowered with the rest of the prisoners in December 1943 when Japanese warplanes all but destroyed the Calcutta port in a brazen daylight raid. They survived on dwindling rations through the man-made famine of 1943, which took the lives of as many as 2 million Bengalis and left bodies of the emaciated dead strewn across Calcutta's streets.

Even as Indians had achieved wider self-governance, with elected state leaders and legislatures, the country's institutional politics had hardened along poisonous communal lines. In August 1946 Muslim League supremo Muhammad Ali Jinnah exchanged his tailored, double-breasted suit for sherwani and fez to announce a 'Direct Action Day' demanding the creation of Pakistan. 'We will either have a divided India or a destroyed India,' he promised.[3] In Calcutta, thousands were butchered in the ensuing riots; for the first time, the *bhadralok* took part in the organised slaughter of their neighbours. 'In 1946, the gentry did not shrink from the grisly task, their notions of cultural and moral superiority notwithstanding,' historian Sabyasachi Bhattacharya later wrote.[4]

But the carnage had done its job: the Great Calcutta Killings helped move Gandhi and Nehru to accept the inevitability of partition.[5] The mass murders, rapes, and the despondent flight of hundreds of thousands of refugees were still in progress when Benoy and Taranath blinked at their first unobstructed views in more than a decade.[6] India was broken, exhausted, bleeding. Much of Bengal was now part of newborn Pakistan.

It's not known how Benoyendra spent his first days as a free man, or if he chose to remain in the company of his son. After so long under lock and key, he would have craved quality meals, alcohol, movies, companionship. There was something else he wanted: a firearm. According to Prosunendra, Benoy's first question upon leaving jail was whether his old shotgun was still in the palace.

Father and son reached Pakur on 31 August and Benoy wasted no time in reasserting his authority. He fired his wife's managers and household staff, erased a large portion of the debts owed to the estate by his Santhal and Muslim tenants (winning their allegiance after long absence), assembled his former gang of toadies, and cracked open the treasury for long nights of booze, opium, and sex. 'Instead of leading a sweet home life amidst his children and other members of his family,' Prosunendra said, he 'took to his old habits of drinking and other vices in the company of his old associates'.[7]

He also took possession of the double-barrelled 12-gauge. Pritilata had registered the weapon in her own name a few years after Benoy's conviction; he confiscated the gun licence and 200 rounds of ammunition as well. He was obsessed with the need for arms, she later said. It was unnerving. One afternoon Pritilata stole into Benoyendra's quarters while he slept, hoping to remove a box of shotgun shells, but he awoke and snatched it from her with the snarling desperation of an addict. A few days after his return from prison, Benoy asked a local lawyer for help in obtaining a gun licence – money was no object. When the lawyer explained that it would be impossible for a murder convict to legally own a firearm, Benoy tried to persuade a distant cousin, Rama Prasad Pandey, to loan him a rifle. His idea was that Rama would license it to one of Benoyendra's retainers, who would live with him at Gokulpur Palace. The cousin strung Benoy along for weeks before extricating himself.[8]

Prosunendra's hopes for 'a sweet home life' notwithstanding, Benoy made it clear he needed his wife for one thing only: money. He harried her for funds; she doled out some 3,000 rupees over a few weeks. From their first meeting after his release, Benoy addressed Pritilata as *apni*, as one would a stranger, rather than the familiar *tumi*. As for their son, Benoy declared he had no affection or use for him – except as a source of cash. Prosunendra had a bank account in Calcutta, and Benoy wanted its contents. He threatened to slay their son and bury his corpse on the palace grounds if he didn't get the money within seven days, Pritilata later told police. Prosunendra left to collect the funds; Pritilata sent a servant to follow him with a message not to return.[9]

It's hard to imagine the swirl of compassion, resentment, and fear Benoy's wife and son must have experienced after Benoy's return. He hired a carpenter to build a pair of timber barricades fitted with eye slits and barrel holes, each thick enough to absorb gunfire, but light enough for one man to move about. With this, the shotgun, and a collection of 6ft-long, sharpened poles of *sal* wood, Benoyendra was preparing for war. The police could never have succeeded in taking him off the train at Asansol if he'd been armed, Benoy told Pritilata. After the humiliation of arrest and trial, and the long, degrading years as a prisoner, never again would Benoyendra submit to uniformed oppression. On a visit to the nearby village of Ilami, he pledged to forever protect his tenants against trouble with the law.

On the day of Prosunendra's scheduled return, Benoy drove out to meet him – and his cash – at the station. When the boy didn't show, Benoyendra stormed home and ordered Pritilata out. She fled to one of her father's properties and never saw her husband again.[10] Five weeks after leaving prison, Benoy was living alone in the palace with one Santhal bearer and a local prostitute. He had stocked food in the upstairs chambers along with more than 50 gallons of water in a stone tank.

Benoy's wife and son regrouped. Prosunendra approached the deputy police superintendent at Dumka, a childhood friend of his father's, for advice about Benoy's obsessive grip on the family shotgun. There was no question, the friend said: they would have to file a complaint. Authorities promptly cancelled the gun licence, and a local sub-inspector travelled the 3 miles out of Pakur town to retrieve the weapon. Benoy refused to open up and the officer left empty-handed. Now an official search warrant was drawn up, and a magistrate, a police inspector, and two constables marched up Benoy's drive on 21 October to demand access to home and the weapon both.

Gokulpur Palace was built to withstand an army. One of Benoy's ancestors, the Rani Kshemasundari, had nearly lost her head during the Santhal *Hool* of 1855–56, when the region's hard-put indigenous tenant farmers rose against the British East India Company and the cruel local gentry. In the aftermath of that brief reign of terror, the Pakur Raj clan built a new, impressive redoubt, one that would hold fast against any future rebellion.

The palace was designed on the lines of a medieval castle, complete with battlements and turrets. The walls of dense brick were held and finished with a mortar of lime, quarry dust, jaggery, and millions of egg whites. The palace sat on an open plain, with lines of sight in every direction. The front portion consisted of ante-rooms on either side of a parlour hall, followed by ground-floor chambers and a kitchen, leading to an enclosed, narrow, U-shaped stairway to the first floor; and another leading from there to the second. As the builders intended, this was the sole route up; future insurgents could be held at bay from the top of the stairs by a small party of spear and swordsmen – or a lone rifleman. The two upper floors were riddled with blind passageways and other defensive traps.[11] 'Any single occupant of the house gifted with courage and possessing plenty of ammunition could easily give battle at the head of every stair and cause a number of injuries to the attacking party,' a local official recalled.[12]

Speaking from behind the slightly ajar door, Benoy warned the magistrate's party to keep its distance. After half an hour of bitter negotiation, the police inspector lunged for the raja to force his way in, but Benoy bolted the door. The constables then took turns with an axe, hacking their way in until Benoy opened fire, splintering the door. He retreated under fire into the corridor, behind the cover of one of his wooden barricades, and up the stairs while the intruders scattered. The scene went quiet. After catching their breath, the police party gingerly entered the ground-floor court-yard with an eye to reaching the stairs inside, but Benoy had the space covered from a vantage on the first floor balcony and sent them off with explosions of birdshot. The police withdrew and the first night fell on a bizarre siege that would embarrass the new Indian government, create a political storm in Pakur, and make a marquee hero of Benoyendra Chandra Pandey.

Sentries surrounded the palace. The doors leading out were sealed with iron, and the well was ruined with kerosene. Police reinforcements arrived under the command of Superintendent B.B. Mishra, who sent some of Benoy's cronies into the courtyard with a local delegation to try coaxing him out. As the fruitless parley ended, Benoy said 'he considered himself as good as dead and hence did not care for what we thought to do', a local official reported.[13] The police believed that, in addition to Benoy, they also heard a feminine voice from the balcony. This complicated matters. It was bad enough their quarry was a zamindar; nobody wanted a woman's blood on their hands. There also appeared to be a second gunman – his Santhal servant – somewhere inside the palace.

As Mishra's party searched in the dusk for possible escape routes Benoy might exploit, the fugitive slipped down the stairs and shot the nearest police sentry. The next-nearest fled, giving Benoy time to grab his barricade from near the doorway and haul it up to the first floor. Mishra and braver constables came running to find Benoyendra, dressed entirely in black with matching headwrap, trying to wrest away the wounded sentry's rifle as he lay splayed and semi-conscious in a pool of blood. They traded shots as Benoy again retreated up the stairs.[14]

'It is obvious that B.C. Pandey is bent upon creating serious trouble,' B.C. Ghosh, deputy commissioner for the Santhal Parganas, told his superiors. 'He is a desperate character.' Two days into the stand-off Ghosh described his nettlesome position. The immediate police strategy was to sit tight and 'starve him to surrender', Ghosh said. But police morale would surely suffer over a long operation given that Benoyendra had already shot two constables, with plenty of ammunition to spare. 'He is quite adept in the use of a gun,' Ghosh noted, adding that Benoyendra was believed to have at least 144 shells remaining. 'It is, therefore, necessary that this matter should be liquidated as early as possible. If necessary, B.C. Pandey may have to be shot dead if he tries to do further mischief or to fight his way out.'

Ghosh and Mishra wanted more firepower. 'The Superintendent of police thinks that if we mobilise at least one section of the Military with tommy guns and requisition the help of a tear gas squad and also automatic weapons the operation might be more effective,' he wrote. The subdivisional officer in Pakur added a note of caution: 'One difficulty in utilising the military is that there is one female with Sadhan,' he said. 'If the military take the operation over, the chances are that the female would also be killed. This may expose us to great criticism.'

The request for army assistance was debated in Dumka, Bhagalpur, and Patna, the state capital. With each round of discussion, the menace of Benoyendra Chandra Pandey appeared to grow, either thanks to natural exaggeration or the police's need to ensure the military took up their slack; top officers feared a bloodbath if their ill-equipped men were ordered to seize Benoy by force. 'His intention is to come out of the house as soon as the police vigilance is withdrawn and then murder all those who had given evidence against him in the Pakur Murder Case,' wrote B.N. Mullick, deputy inspector general for the Eastern Range. Were it not for the siege, 'His next step would have been to go out and murder his enemies one by one ...' A detachment of forty constables was now guarding Gokulpur Palace. 'It is impossible for me to spare this force any longer and even on the dark nights he may escape by means of a rope,' Mullick added.[15]

Six days into the stand-off, a procession of 400 Santhal and Muslim tenant farmers – some armed with bows and arrows – marched on the palace demanding freedom for their zamindar. The ancestors of these exploited, debt-ridden tillers had risen against the region's landlords, moneylenders, and petty royals in 1811, 1820, 1830, 1855, and 1872. Their children would take up arms against these same oppressors in 1968.[16] But today they rallied to their embattled ruler.[17] The managers hired by Benoy's wife had reportedly been ruthless with the tenants,[18] while the raja had forgiven a portion of their debts after returning from prison. 'He was, during that time, their king,' recalls Emmanuel Marandi, a retired crop scientist who watched the stand-off as a young boy. 'People are questioning in their mind, "Why are they going to kill this man?" Because he was good to them.'[19, 20]

The authorities banned public assembly for five days to forestall another jamboree in Benoyendra's honour. Public sympathy for the raja only grew. Local leaders peppered officials with pleas and warnings that Benoy must be taken alive. Hrishikesh Mukherjea, a local politician of the ruling Congress party, wired the Bihar governor to request 'a last chance for honourable surrender'. Benoy had been 'obliged to resist for self-defence alone and for having received cold behaviour from near ones on arrival after fourteen years absence', Mukherjea explained. 'If Benoyendra fails to avail of such gracious opportunity', to surrender, 'the local indignant masses, ninety percent of which are *adibasis*[21] and Muslims, including thousands of his tenants, will have nothing to say'. Here Mukherjea raised a sensitive topic – indigenous organisations were advocating for a new, tribal-majority state called Jharkhand to be carved out of Bihar. The state Congress party had recently held a meeting in Dumka urging its members to 'counteract the evil' of the separatist movement.[22, 23]

The government was meant to be the embodiment of Gandhi's ideals, Mukherjea chided the governor in the clipped cadence of his telegram, and 'not [the] new sheath of ... [the] blood-stained old sword of bureaucratic regime with Churchillian vanity'.[24]

On 29 October, Benoy agreed to a parley with the local magistrate but it was only to demand more opium.[25] The following day he shot and wounded three more constables. On 5 November, troops from the Rajputana Rifles arrived in Pakur carrying machine guns and other heavy weapons. Benoy almost shot the unit's commanding officer, a Captain Kilgour, as he crept up the steps for a first look at the situation. The blast tore the lapels off the captain's uniform and he rolled down to safety, losing his sidearm along the way – an undignified start. The next morning, the Raj Rifles poured machine gun fire into the palace, hoping to remove the upstairs doors and shutters one slug a time. It didn't work. Kilgour requested mortars and rifle-fired grenades. Each escalation begat another.

Meanwhile, police snipers were taking shots at Benoy whenever he showed himself on one of the balconies. On at least two evenings, they were led to believe the raja had been hit, only for him to appear again at sunrise ambling about unharmed. 'These miraculous escapes made Sadhan more cautious but affected the morale of his attackers, some of whom even credited him with supernatural powers,' Mishra recalled. 'Oracles circulated rumours about his invincibility.'[26]

'I need not say that this prolonged siege and inability of the police and the military to effect his arrest is damaging the

Administration,' a district official complained to the state's chief secretary. 'It is absurd that a desperate criminal like him with three cases of attempted murder already instituted and with his past history should be able to successfully evade arrest.'[27]

With the bold luck of a Bengali Douglas Fairbanks, 'Benoy was like a colossus astride the police force', Mishra told his superiors.[28]

On 7 November, another procession, led by a group of mullahs, approached the palace. Mishra convinced them to disperse. At 5 a.m. on 11 November, Benoy shot and wounded a sentry as he walked to his post carrying a lantern. Doctors pulled twenty pellets from his arm. Dozens of teargas shells were fired onto the balconies and verandas but the raja wouldn't be smoked out. The next day he took aim at another constable, but police fire sent him scurrying back to safety. More local entreaties were sent to Patna begging for Benoy's life.

'Above all there must not be any BRAHMAYA HATA in your regime in a merciless way,' the politician Hrishikesh Mukherjea wrote to a minister in the Bihar government, referring to the apex sin of slaying a brahmin. Mukherjea explained that his plea was not made 'as an admirer or well-wisher of Sadhan ... though the public now commends his valour, stamina and stand for his self-respect at this time'.[29] A telegram from another local declared that the entire district stood with Benoyendra.

Twenty-five days into the siege, two army tanks reached the town. Residents were awed by the clanking diesel war machines.[30] No one had ever seen the like. Villagers had already become accustomed to the popping of gunfire from Gokulpur; now they flinched under the explosions of artillery. Tank crews fired 216 shells at the upper levels of the palace that first day – with little to show for it. The palace's nineteenth-century builders had done their job well. 'It is a very solid structure,' Mishra reported. Munitions 'that easily penetrate armour plates ... were [only] capable of breaking one brick at a time'. Benoy's storehouse caught fire and burned for six hours, but the walls remained intact. At least ten mortar rounds were fired at the palace. The bombs arced across the sky and landed with loud explosive thuds – but none struck home. Officials complained the weapon was defective. Residents celebrated. Something had to give.

On 17 November the tanks started again, shelling the palace simultaneously from two sides to break open a walled corridor that had provided Benoyendra foolproof cover. Amid the cannon fire, Mishra spied Benoy crawling on the second-floor rooftop, where he took a firing position through a broken portion of the balustrade and was sent back by a Bren light machine gun. The raja retreated on hands and knees towards the stairway leading to a third-floor room that sat atop the roof. This was the moment the siege party had been waiting for. With the tanks blasting away, the Brens firing nonstop, and amid a volley of teargas shells, a helmeted squad of Rajputana Rifles stormed the building. They took the first floor without incident and gingerly mounted the U-shaped staircase leading to the second. The door at the top was closed but unbolted. Through a crack the soldiers could see Benoyendra lying on the roof, his side resting against the balustrade, shotgun trained on the stairs. A sword, a dagger, and a bag of ammunition lay beside him. He fired as the door creaked open and the blast ricocheted off the stair head, destroying a harmonium in one of the side rooms.

Seconds later Benoyendra was dead, cut down with a view of all he once commanded. The town fell silent. But how did he die?

In an after-action report, Mishra wrote that Benoy was fatally shot by the raiding party. In a memoir of the siege published eleven years later, he said it was a grenade that finished the raja. Among Benoyendra's loyal partisans, there was no question: Benoy wasn't killed at all – he kept his dignity by taking his own life. 'Finally, when he ran out of his ammunition, his supplies for food, water, he killed himself,' Emmanuel Marandi said, speaking for many. 'They never got him.'[31]

A search of the smoking palace found no confederates, no damsel. Benoy's companions had slipped away the first night of the stand-off and the cops had been hoodwinked over four long weeks. Benoyendra's last deception – fooling the police into thinking there was another gunman in the palace – has echoes in the popular 1924 adventure novel *Beau Geste* and its 1926 Hollywood adaptation. In the film's climax, the last two survivors of a desert siege use clever misdirection to convince a party of attackers that their fortress is teeming with gunmen. Benoyendra, with his insatiable hunger for the movies, was in his early 20s when *Beau Geste* first reached India, where it was received with a fervour matching the debut of *Star Wars* or Steven Spielberg's *Jaws*, breaking attendance records.[32]

Benoy had 'rapidly shown himself in a variety of dresses to convince the police that he was not alone but had a woman, and someone else armed, with him', Mishra recalled. 'He had done the acting so well that each room had to be searched with the utmost care for the second man who was supposed to be his associate. To the end, we were sure that a woman was inside.'[33]

It was a bravura performance.

By refusing to yield in the face of certain defeat, Benoy had guaranteed himself a most cinematic exit. Unlike Amarendra, he died the hero of his own epic and chose the moment of his own death.

25

Rajbansha

Prosunendra Chandra Pandey gaped at the blasted walls of the Gokulpur Palace, turned from the dried pool of his father's blood, and resolved to rehabilitate the family name. In January 1948, the new Raja of Pakur wrote to state officials seeking compensation for the injuries Benoyendra's stronghold had suffered by the army and police. The first and second floors were 'entirely damaged and all the belongings are converted to into heaps of ruins', he said. It would take 'enormous expenditure' to fully restore the property, but 15,000 rupees would 'make it habitable'.[1]

A new wind was blowing through India, and it threatened to carry away a great deal of feudal income. 'In these days of hardships and in view of the proposed abolition of the Zamindari system in the near future it is a problem to me as to how to meet this heavy expenditure,' Prosunendra wrote.[2]

The Pakur Raj's glories dated back to the days of Akbar the Great. Prithvipal Tewari had joined the formidable Raja Man Singh in his conquest over the Raja of Jessore in 1612, was hosted in Delhi, and returned home with gifts from the emperor himself. Pakur had suffered through famine, invasion, rebellion, and cruel nawabs. It had always bounced back.

In the mid-1700s, the Rani Chandanmayee, new to her late husband's throne, had rallied the war-weary people of Pakur to trap and exterminate a raiding party of Maratha lancers after years of rape and murder by the western horsemen. 'Sending all the females and old men with the children to the impassable hill-fastness, she assembled all the able-bodied youths and supplying them with arms she herself got upon a palanquin and proceeded to give battle to the Marathas,' a family account recalled. 'Not a single "Bargee" escaped with his life.'[3]

In 1806, Prosunendra's ancestor, Raja Prithvichandra, a scholar of Sanskrit, Persian, and Bengali, had authored the *Gaurī-mangala*, an important, nearly lost epic composed to honour the goddess Durga. Encoded within the *Gaurī-mangala* is an allegorical retelling of Britain's conquest of India – and the equally allegorical story of how the different peoples and kingdoms of Hindustan might unite one day to remove their oppressors. 'A Zamindar, whose position and property depended on the favour of the British rulers, could not afford to be more explicit,' historian Bimanbehari Majumdar wrote of the call to arms Prithvichandra had stitched between the lines of his text. Still, 'Raja Prithvichandra was the first writer to prepare the mind of the people for asserting national independence'.[4] In 1859, Raja Gopilal Pande first established the Pakur Raj High School, as well as a girls' school not far from the Gokulpur Palace. And Protapendra Chandra Pandey, father of Benoy and Amarendra, had served in elected office while also risking his position and freedom by secretly funding a member of Bengal's revolutionary underground.[5]

Just as the palace was brought back to working order, Prosunendra worked to restore his family's honour. Like his grandfather before him, Prosunendra was elected to public office and represented Pakur in Patna as a member of the post-Independence state assembly. There, he advocated for the special needs of the Santhal Parganas region, joining a movement that decades later would bring about the new state of Jharkhand. His mother Pritilata, Benoy's widow, lived into the 1960s; those who knew her recall Pritilata as a spirited old woman who broke with convention by drinking tea – a pleasure that custom still denied women who outlived their husbands.

Benoy's fellow defendants returned to obscurity. Taranath Bhattacharjee was freed from Midnapur Jail in August 1947 and returned to a quiet life with his wife and daughter on Tagore Castle Street in Calcutta. In 1938 a judge had denied Taranath's request to regain possession of his professional certificates; he was barred for life from the practice of medicine.[6]

Sivapada Bhattacharjee never escaped the erroneous charge, repeated in the courts and the press, that he had written Taranath's introduction to the Haffkine Institute. Eighty-five years after the Pakur charge sheet was filed, an elderly, retired gynaecologist living next door to Sivapada's former home still recalled him as the man who helped Taranath acquire plague germs – and she hadn't even been born then.

Durga Ratan Dhar was the only defendant to escape the Pakur murder case with his reputation. In 1948, a year after Benoyendra's spectacular suicide-by-police, Dhar was teaching at the National College of Medicine and had published a 400-page treatment guide for general practitioners, with a foreword written by the director of the Calcutta School of Tropical Medicine – an unmistakable sign of establishment support.[7] While Dhar had been welcomed back to the fold by his fellow professionals, he was still tainted by scandal in the popular imagination. At least one person close to the case misremembered him as a villain. 'Such is the perversity of human nature,' Betty Le Brocq wrote nearly fifty years later, that Dhar's practice 'was greatly enhanced by clients thinking that if Dr D could get away with murder he must be a very clever man!'[8]

Rani Surjabati died in 1956; of the four children she raised inside Gokulpur Palace, only Banabala outlived her. She remained haunted by murder. In her old age, Banabala, recalled as 'very fair, very beautiful, and a very aristocratic looking lady', became fixated on the notion that someone was out to get her. As the terrors of her youth infected Banabala's final years, she was 'constantly suspicious and scared that someone was going to poison her', an acquaintance remembers.[9]

★★★

Three decades after he left the set in a blaze of glory, Benoyendra Chandra Pandey finally made it to the big screen. Benoy's name was nowhere on the credits, but the story – slathered in artistic licence – was unmistakably his.

A 1976 Bengali feature inspired by the plague murder, *Rajbansha*, or '*Dynasty*', tells the story of an aggrieved noble who murders his father and brother to take his rightful place on the throne of a wealthy zamindarate. The long, eventful years since Amarendra's murder had given director Piyush Bose the breathing room needed to recreate the cold-blooded germ murderer as an emotionally complex anti-hero. More social drama than murder mystery, *Rajbansha* portrays in luminous black and white the casual abuse of women and lower-caste communities by unscrupulous landlords.

The film tells the story of Pratap Babu, illegitimate son of the violent raja of Moinamoti, who lives in poverty with his mother, a former lady-in-waiting who was exiled over her pregnancy. Following the death of his saintly mother, Pratap returns to Moinamoti and blackmails the raja into allowing him to live in the palace. The raja intends to leave the estate to his second, legitimate, son, Rajnarayan, but Pratap Babu has other ideas. He conspires with the palace physician – who bears his own mortal grudge – to slay the zamindar before he can complete his will.

Pratap Babu's murder weapon is tetanus, which he smears onto the blade of his father's straight razor. Pratap then antagonises the prickly raja during his morning shave, provoking him to leap violently from the barber's chair and suffer a cut with the contaminated blade. Just as Amarendra was saved by medical treatment at Deoghar, the raja too appears to be recovering before he finally succumbs to the tetanus and is killed. Pratap Babu follows this success by having his pure-hearted brother murdered with an injection of snake venom.

The film opens in August 1947, with the murder convict Pratap learning that he is about to be released from prison thanks to the same amnesty that freed Benoy and Taranath. But the fictional protagonist begs to remain behind bars and laments that his death sentence wasn't carried out.

'I don't want mercy,' the murderer says.

In the end, neither did Benoyendra.

Afterword

I covered my first homicide one roasting New York summer when a 12-year-old boy called June-Bug was shot dead on the midday street in a dispute over 25 cents. June-Bug was followed by dozens, scores, and even hundreds of other victims. The city was never short of violence and its tabloid newspapers ran each killing down in a nearly psychotic spirit of competition. People murdered for big money and small. They killed over self-respect, out of despair, and they shot and stabbed and bludgeoned for the hatred of women. Eventually the blood got old. I left New York and broadened my horizons.

While moving my base from South Asia to Africa and back again, I became interested in public health and the history of medicine, especially cholera – especially in India. One day, while searching for clues to an unpublished biography of Waldemar Haffkine, I came across a curious 1930s news item reporting that plague germs used to murder a young man on a Calcutta railway platform had come from some place called the Haffkine Institute. What? Who? *Plague?* Some murder cases are too good to pass up. I felt the ink-stained urge to run down yet another homicide.

Setting aside my work on *Vibrio cholerae*, I dug into this strange germ murder, working my way through libraries and archives on three continents. After years spent interviewing presidents and

Nobel laureates, investigating politicians and corporations, and travelling the length of the Nile and Ganges rivers, I was still a police reporter at heart. The assassination of Amarendra Chandra Pandey presented a marvellous chance to combine the appetites of my earliest days as a journalist with a fascination for the history of pandemics and peoples.

Here you had the very oldest of crimes, fratricide, executed with utterly modern tools, inspired by mass media in the form of Sherlock Holmes, fiction's greatest detective. Benoyendra Chandra Pandey's love of the movies, his contempt for tradition, his dreams of remaking himself as a film impresario – not to mention his defiant, blood-splattered exit – all suggested a sociopathic twentieth-century archetype. He'd even shared a prison address with Jawaharlal Nehru, and his lawyer would later defend the nationalist icon Subhas Chandra Bose. Benoy's correspondence revealed a remorseless manipulator. In other words: a perfect villain.

The Pakur murder case was part of a new chapter in the story of homicide, one tailor-made for a world tumbling midway between mustard gas and the atomic bomb. Amarendra's death provided the eye-popping core narrative for a story encompassing topics as diverse as pandemic disease, popular film, and the social and political cauldron of a tabloid-ready Calcutta on the verge of war and independence. It's the story of a fascinating, overlooked time and place – one that won't be seen again.

Dan Morrison

Acknowledgements

More than anyone I am grateful to my irreplaceable companions: Lauren, Oona, and Sol.

I want to remember the late historian Srimoy Roy Chaudhury of Shiv Nadar University. Moy and I mined the Pakur case in parallel for more than a year before realising our common object. He was gracious, generous, funny – a man of great integrity.

Vaaswat Sarkar was a dedicated legman when I was unable to return to Kolkata. He performed critical work under difficult conditions.

In Pakur, warm thanks to Meera Singh, P.K. Singh, Emmanuel Marandi, and Maqsud Alam. In Patna, I am lucky for the friendship and guidance of Nalin Verma. In Kolkata, thanks to Aishwarya Mondal, Ruby Palchoudhuri, Ananda Bhattacharjee, Amitabha Ray, Souhardyo Chatterjee, Vibha Mitra, Monica Shie, Adrian Pratt, Jaydeep Das of the Calcutta Police Museum, and Murlidhar Sharma, IPS. Delhi: Grateful salaams to Chiki Sarkar and the judicious Anjai Puri at Juggernaut Books, to Prakash Ray, Pritha Sen, William and Anjali Bissell, and to Sarah Chamberlain. In Banaras, I am blessed with the friendship of Navneet Raman, Petra Manefeld, and Ajay Panday; and in Jaipur, of Rohit Gupta. Thanks to Mohammad Saiful Islam in Dhaka for his translation of Charu Chandra Chakraborty's *Louha Kapat*.

On the Isle of Jersey, I am in debt to Philip and Sally Le Brocq, Jo and Philip Forster, and Roland Quintaine. In the UK, great thanks to the stand-up Max Edwards at Aevitas Creative Management, Nicholas and Alison Connor, Alex Von Tunzelmann, Richard Colson, Catharine Tucker and, at The History Press, Mark Beynon, Laura Perehinec, Rebecca Newton and Graham Robson. I don't recall just how I wound up as Kirti Narayan Chaudhuri's guest in the south of France, but I learned much from this singular historian.

Closer to home I am ever-grateful for Jack Morrison, Ena Marrero, Ashley Chen, Cora Morrison, Bette Cabot, Ed Morrison, and Irv Leibowitz; Sharon Lovelace, Paul Lovelace, and Garrett Graddy; and Schon Bryan, Maria Golia, Mohamad Bazzi, Eileen Markey, Miriam Hagans, David Morrison, Renee Torres Simo, Derzula Aguila, Robin Shulman, Chris Tyree, Heidi DeRuiter, Marwa Ali Sabah, Liz Van Hoose, and Rebecca Friedman.

Special thanks to Solomon Morrison; to Leonard Levitt, Les Payne and Jim Dwyer; and to Joe Morrison and Rae Cabot.

Notes

1. Every Inch an Aristocrat

1. B. Dey, 'Summer in Calcutta', in K. Bardhan (ed.), *Oxford Anthology of Bengali Literature*, Vol. I, Oxford University Press, 2010, pp. 70–72.
2. S. Dorin, 'Jazz and Race in Colonial India', *Jazz Research Journal*, 2010, pp. 123–40.
3. S. Kurien, *Finding Carlton* [Motion Picture], retrieved from YouTube, 29 April 2011, www.youtube.com/watch?v=zU6shKTo38M.
4. 'Calcutta Letter: Plain Words Terrorism', *Times of India*, 7 December 1933, p. 3.
5. 'Women Waitresses Wanted', *The Sun* (Baltimore), 25 February 1934, p. 8.
6. *Calcutta Gazette*, 1935.
7. 'Calcutta Letter: Black Record of Midnapore', *Times of India*, 3 September 1933, p. 7.
8. 'Pandit Nehru and the Mahasabha', *Times of India*, 29 April 1933, p. 9.
9. C.C. Chakraborty, *Louha Kapat* (M.S. Islam, trans.), Mitra and Ghosh, 1967.

2. These Jealous Impulses

1. S. Freud, 'Lecture XXXIII: Femininity', in S. Freud, *New Introductory Lectures in Psycho-Analysis* (J. Strachey, trans.), Norton, 1965, p. 123.
2. K. Datta, *Gauri-Mangala: With a Short History of the Pakur Raj*, Asiatic Society, 1971.
3. Ibid.
4. Ibid.
5. Pakur and the Santhal Parganas were part of the Bengal Presidency until 1912, when they were included in the newly created province of Bihar and Orissa. Bihar and Orissa were split into separate provinces in 1936, and Pakur remained a part of Bihar until the birth of Jharkhand state in November 2000.

6. K. Datta, 1971.
7. L.M. Roy, *Degradation of Bengal Zamindar*, Indian Patriot Press, 1893.

3. The Nervous *Bhaiya*

1. A reputedly abstemious religious community of merchants. See indpaedia.com/ind/index.php/Bhakat.
2. A bazaar in Pakur.
3. Kautilya, *Arthashastra* (L. Rangarajan, ed.), Penguin, 1987.
4. H. Das Gupta, *The Indian Stage*, Vol. IV, M.K. Das Gupta, 1944.
5. D. Sengupta, 'A City Feeding on Itself ', in T. Sarkar, & S. Bandyopadhyay (eds), *Calcutta: The Stormy Decades*, Social Science Press, 2015.
6. K. Ballhatchet, *Race, Sex, and Class under the Raj*, St Martin's Press, 1980.
7. Ibid.
8. M.A. Mackirdy and W.N. Willis, *The White Slave Market*, Stanley Paul, 1912.
9. P. Levine, 'Venereal Disease, Prostitution, and the Politics of Empire: The Case of British India', *Journal of the History of Sexuality*, 1994, pp. 579–602.
10. R.B. Roy, 'Sexually Transmitted Diseases and the Raj', *Sexually Transmitted Infections*, 1998, pp. 20–26.
11. K.N. Chaudhuri (D. Morrison, Interviewer).
12. R. Gopal, *Trials of Jawaharlal Nehru*, Book Centre, 1962.
13. J. Nehru, *Autobiography*, Jawaharlal Nehru Memorial Fund, 1982.
14. P.C. Ray, *Life and Experiences of a Bengali Chemist*, Vol. II, Chuckervertty, Chatterjee & Co., 1935.
15. Ibid.

4. As Meat Is Dangerous for the Child

1. J.R.B.J., 'Letter to the Editor', *Times of India*, 10 July 1946, p. 6.
2. Mananda Devi, *Autobiography of an Educated Fallen Woman*, R. Chakravartty, Mymensingh, 1939.
3. S. Ray, *On Cinema*, Columbia University Press, 2013.

5. The Viper's Tooth

1. F. Daly, Report on Native Papers in Bengal for the Week Ending 9 February, 1907, Bengali Translator's Office, Bengal, Inspector-General, 1907.

2. A.C. Doyle, *His Last Bow: Some Reminiscences of Sherlock Holmes*, John Murray, 1917.
3. 'The Strand', *London Daily News*, 28 November 1913, p. 3.
4. 'Conan Doyle Brings Back Sherlock Holmes', *New York Times Review of Books*, 28 October 1917, p. 1.
5. Medico-Legal Congress at New York, *Journal of the American Medical Association*, 1895, pp. 463–64.
6. W. Birchmore, 'Science in Crime', *Courier-Journal*, 1 September 1895, p. 3.
7. H. Bernstein, 'The Doctor Who Killed His Patients with Germs', *New York Times*, 19 February 1911, p. 45.
8. W.S. Carus, *Bioterrorism and Biocrimes*, Center for Nonproliferation Research, 1998.
9. Ibid.
10. Ibid.
11. 'German Bluebeard Beheaded', *Hamilton Daily Times*, 23 March 1914, p. 9.
12. E. Geissler and J.E. Moon, *Biological and Toxin Weapons: Research, Development, and Use from the Middle Ages to 1945*, Oxford University Press, 1999
13. H.O. Yardley, *The American Black Chamber*, Bobbs-Merrill, 1931.
14. D. Kahn, The Reader of Gentlemen's Mail, Yale University Press, 2004.
15. A. Lorenz, 'Germ Slaying Cycle Feared by Professor', *San Francisco Examiner*, 19 April 1925, p. 7.
16. 'German Tragedies', *Bombay Gazette*, 14 February 1914, p. 9.
17. 'Murder by Germs Case: Trial at Chicago', *Times of India*, 12 June 1925, p. 7.
18. Colonel George Montagu, retrieved from 'Shellers from the Past and Present', www.conchology.be/?t=9001&id=25237.
19. 'Bombay Amusements', *Times of India*, 24 January 1931, p. 5.
20. B. Roden, 'Who Did It?', *The Case Files of Sherlock Holmes*, Calabash, 1998, pp. 145–48.
21. B. Dean, *The Return of Sherlock Holmes* [Motion Picture], retrieved 19 December 2022, from the Library of Congress, FBC 2853–5854 (16mm reference print), AFI/Jonathan Sonneborn Collection, 1929, rb.gy/ui0rl.

6. Savour of Self-Interest

1. A.K. Samanta, *Terrorism in Bengal,* Vol. 5, Government of West Bengal, 1995.

7. A Specially Virulent Strain

1. E. Lutzker and C. Jochnowitz, 'The Touchstone', Unpublished manuscript, n.d.
2. Plague at this time was known either as *B. pestis* (for *Bacillus pestis*) or *P. pestis* (for *Pasteurella pestis*), the name Alexandre Yersin assigned the bacteria in honour of Louis Pasteur, one of the leading founders of medical microbiology. The plague bacterium was renamed *Yersinia pestis* in 1944.

8. Taut

1. Report of the Drugs Enquiry Committee, Government of India, 1931.
2. D. McCullough, *The Great Bridge*, Simon and Schuster, 1972.
3. Colonel George Montagu, 'Shellers from the Past and Present', n.d.
4. Aretaeus; Francis Adams (ed. and trans.), *The Extant Works of Aretaeus*, The Cappadocian, Boston Milford House Inc., 1972 (republication of the 1856 edition).
5. N. Ohler, *Blitzed: Drugs in Nazi Germany*, Allen Lane, 2016.
6. E. Wilson, 'Neurosurgical Treatment for Tetanus', *Journal of the History of the History of the Neurosciences*, 1997, pp. 82–85.
7. W.F. Gibb, 'Sequel to a Case of Acute Tetanus Treated by Intracerebral Injections of Antitoxin', *BMJ*, No. 9, 1899.

9. I Will See You, Doctor

1. G. Cheema, 'The Grandeur of Haffkine Institute Under Dr Sahib Singh Sokhey', *The Panjab Past and Present*, 2013, pp. 100–09.
2. *Greater Bombay Gazetteer*, Government of Maharashtra, 1986.

10. *Cito, Longe, Tarde*

1. J.M. Barry, 'The Site of Origin of the 1918 Influenza Pandemic', *Journal of Translational Medicine*, 2004.
2. J.K. Taubenberger and D.M. Morens, '1918 Influenza: The Mother of All Pandemics', *Revista Biomédica*, 2006, pp. 69–79.
3. J. Kelly, *The Great Mortality*, HarperCollins, 2005.
4. L.F. Hirst, *The Conquest of Plague*, Oxford University Press, 1953.
5. M. Echenberg, 'Pestis Redux: The Initial Years of the Third Bubonic Plague Pandemic, 1894–1901', *Journal of World History*, 2002, pp. 429–49.
6. R. Nathan, *Plague in India: 1896, 1897*, Government of India, 1898.

7. Ibid.
8. *Minutes of Evidence of the Indian Plague Commission*, Vol. 1, Government of India, 1900.
9. E. Lutzker and C. Jochnowitz, 'The Touchstone', Unpublished manuscript, n.d.
10. I. Catanach, 'Plague and the Tensions of Empire', in D. Arnold (ed.), *Imperial Medicine and Indigenous Societies*, Manchester University Press, 1991.
11. E. Lutzker and C. Jochnowitz, n.d.
12. 'The District of Mandvie', *Bombay Gazette*, 30 September 1896, p. 3.
13. E. Lutzker and C. Jochnowitz, n.d.
14. W. Churchill to Lady Randoph, 14 October 1896, in R.S. Churchill (ed.), *Winston S. Churchill: Companion Volume I (Part 2), 1896–1900*, Houghton Mifflin, 1967, pp. 686–89.
15. M. Echenberg, 2002.
16. 'Plague in Calcutta', *Indian Medical Gazette*, 1947, p. 137.
17. L.F. Hirst, 1953.
18. I. Catanach, 'Poona Politicians and the Plague', in J. Masselos (ed.), *Struggling and Ruling*, Sterling, 1987.
19. P.-L. Simond, 1898.
20. C. Lynteris, 'Zoonoses et recherche en laboratoire', 21 October 2022, retrieved from www.translitterae.psl.eu.
21. 'The Plague in Bombay', *Manchester Guardian*, 5 October 1896, p. 5.
22. Ibid.
23. 'The District of Mandvie', *Bombay Gazette*, 30 September 1896.
24. D. Arnold, *Colonizing the Body*, University of California Press, 1993.
25. 'The Question of the Segregation', *Bombay Gazette*, 28 December 1896, p. 4.
26. 'Excitement of the Mill-Hands', *Bombay Gazette*, 30 October 1896, p. 5.
27. C.N. Bose, Report on Native Papers for the Week Ending 27th March 1897, Bengali Translator's Office, 1897.
28. 'Attack on the Infectious Disease Hospital by Mill-Hands', *Bombay Gazette*, 30 October 1896, p. 5.
29. I. Klein, 'Plague, Policy and Popular Unrest in British India', *Modern Asian Studies*, 1988, pp. 723–55.
30. M. Echenberg, 2002.
31. W. Deverell, *Whitewashed Adobe: The Rise of Los Angeles and the Remaking of Its Mexican Past*, University of California Press, 2004.
32. F. Feldinger, *A Slight Epidemic*, Silver Lake Publishing, 2008.
33. E. Lutzker and C. Jochnowitz, n.d.
34. 'The Prophylactic Lymph Prepared by Prof. Haffkine', *Bombay Gazette*, 21 January 1897, p. 5.
35. E. Lutzker and C. Jochnowitz, n.d.

36. 'Professor Gajjar's Cross-Examination', *Bombay Gazette*, 21 February 1899, p. 6.
37. *Minutes of Evidence Presented to the Indian Plague Commission*, Vol. 3, Her Majesty's Stationery Office, 1900.
38. W. Churchill, in R.S. Churchill (ed.), *Winston S. Churchill: Companion Volume I (Part 2), 1896–1900*, Houghton Mifflin, 1967, pp. 686–89.
39. Indian Plague Commission, 1898–99.
40. D. Arnold, *Colonizing the Body*, 1993.
41. J.N. Cook, *Plague in Calcutta*, Calcutta Municipal Press, 1898.
42. 'Indian Vital Statistics for 1933', *Nature*, No. 159, 1936.

12. The Poisoned Spear

1. J. Kelly, 2005.
2. R. Gupta, 'Horrors of the East', *Hindu BusinessLine*, 23 January 2018, retrieved from www.thehindubusinessline.com/ blink/explore/ horrors-of-the-east/article7137420.ece.
3. M. Maskiell and A. Mayor, 'Killer Khilats, Part 1: Legends of Poisoned "Robes of Honor"', *Folklore*, 2001, pp. 23–45.
4. F. d'Errico, L. Backwell, P. Villa, I. Degano, J.J. Lucejko, M.K. Bamford, ... P.B. Beaumont, 'Early Evidence of San Material Culture Represented by Organic Artifacts from Border Cave, South Africa', *PNAS*, 2012, pp. 13214–19.
5. 'Tawlar Case', *Times of India*, 25 March 1932, p. 14.
6. 'Brothers Appeal Against Death', *Times of India*, 19 March 1932, p. 18.
7. 'Zamlar Poisoning Case Appeal', *Times of India*, 25 April 1932, p. 11.
8. 'Wife and Children Burnt on Charcoal Heap', *Bombay Chronicle*, 23 June 1933, p. 1.

14. *Boro Ghori*

1. J. Devi, *The River Churning* (E. Chatterjee, trans.), Kali for Women, 1995.
2. F. Hauswirth, *Purdah: The Status of Indian Women*, Kegan Paul, Trench, Trubner & Co., 1932.
3. S. Lamb, *White Saris and Sweet Mangoes*, University of California, 2000.
4. J. Hutton, *Census of India, 1931*, Manager of Publications, 1933.
5. Isabel Colson, wife of the future Calcutta police commissioner L.H. Colson, wrote of sailing for India in 1919 in the company of a 21-year-old fellow passenger who had not seen her husband since she was first wed at age 14. ('Memoirs of Isabel Colson', unpublished.)

6. C. Banerji, 'The Propitiatory Meal', *Gastronomica*, 2003, pp. 82–89.
7. N.C. Chaudhuri, *Thy Hand, Great Anarch!*, Addison, 1987.
8. J. Devi, 1995.
9. K. Datta, 1971.
10. *India: A Reference Annual*, Ministry of Information and Broadcasting, 1954.

15. Like Something Out of a Foreign Novel

1. J. Boyd, 'Leonard Rogers, 1868–1962', *Biographical Memoirs*, Royal Society, 1963, pp. 260–85.
2. J.M. Johnston, 'Lobar Pneumonia and Its Serological Treatment', *Edinburgh Medical Journal*, 1935, pp. 265–79.

16. Hello!

1. President's Secretariat, 'Ball at Belvedere – 12th January, 1934', 1933–34, retrieved from www.abhilekh-patal.in/jspui/handle/123456789/2763963?
2. 'Memoirs of Isabel Colson'.
3. Ibid.
4. B. Le Brocq, unpublished memoirs, 1983.
5. A.C. Doyle, *The Sign of Four*, Penguin Classics, 2014.

18. Forward Under Custody

1. 'Why Hindu Said Muslim Prayers', *Times of India*, 13 January 1934, p. 6.
2. 'Arrested After Eight Years', *Times of India*, 23 January 1934, p. 3.
3. 'Alleged Fraud', *Indian Express*, 31 January 1934, p. 1.
4. 'Jawahar's Message to Young Bengal', *Bombay Chronicle*, 18 January 1934, p. 1.
5. *Bengal Legislative Council Proceedings*, Bengal Government Press, 1935.
6. 'Police Department', *Supplement to the Calcutta Gazette*, 22 August 1935, p. 1183.
7. E.H. Le Brocq, *The Pakur Murder Case*, n.d.
8. Ibid.
9. Ibid.
10. Ibid.
11. Ibid.

19. This Smart Set

1. R. Gopal, 1962.
2. C.C. Chakraborty, 1967.
3. M.L. Rahman, 'Pakur Murder Case', *Calcutta Police Journal*, 1940, pp. 112–28.
4. 'Murder Conspiracy Charge', *The Statesman*, 13 March 1934, p. 4.
5. 'Bail Cancelled', *The Statesman*, 15 March 1934.
6. S. Setlur and K. Deshpande (eds), *A Full and Authentic Report of the Trial of the Hon'ble Mr Bal Gangadhar Tilak*, Education Society's Press, 1907.
7. 'Bail Petition for Accused Doctor', *The Statesman*, 4 April 1934.
8. 'Bail Petition of Doctor Dismissed', *The Statesman*, 5 April 1934.
9. 'Doctor to Remain in Custody', *The Statesman*, 13 April 1934.
10. S. Aurobindo, 'Tales of Prison Life', *Bengali Writings Translated into English*, Sri Aurobindo Ashram Trust, 1991.

20. Practically Nil

1. Sir Thomas Ellis, *Times of London*, 21 December 1981, p. 10.
2. M.L. Rahman, 1940.
3. S. Ray, *Childhood Days*, Penguin, 2016.
4. 'Recalls the Borgias', *Evening Herald* (Wellington), 5 June 1934, p. 9.
5. Pakur Murder Case: cross-examination of Sreemati Banabala Devi.
6. Ibid.
7. 'Public Prosecutor's Address to the Jury Continues', *Amrita Bazar Patrika*, October 1934.
8. T. Mann, *Doctor Faustus* (J.E. Wood, trans.), Vintage International, 1997.

22. A *Chota* Peg

1. 'Defence Address Begins', *Amrita Bazar Patrika*, November 1934, p. 7.
2. Ibid.
3. 'Dr Chowdhury's Defense Argument Continues', *Amrita Bazar Patrika*, December 1934.
4. 'Subhas Bose Trial Opens', *Bombay Chronicle*, 11 September 1940, p. 1.
5. Official Report, Bengal Legislative Assembly, 1944.
6. S.R. Chaudhury (D. Morrison, Interviewer), 2019.
7. 'Crime and Science', *Times of India*, 26 February 1935, p. 8.
8. E.H. Le Brocq, *The Pakur Murder Case*.
9. 'Judge Collapses in Court', *Times of India*, 26 September 1934, p. 9.
10. B. Le Brocq, 1983.
11. E.H. Le Brocq, *The Pakur Murder Case*.

23. No Proper Trial

1. C.C. Chakraborty, 1967.
2. *Calcutta Gazette*, Bengal Printing Office, 1935.
3. Ibid.
4. P. Lacey, 'Murder by Pin-prick', *The Straits Times*, 11 May 1950, p. 10.
5. H. Hobbs, journal entry, Calcutta, 14 January 1936.

24. Vendetta

1. J. Nehru, *Autobiography*, 1982.
2. P.C. Pandey, 'To the Deputy Commissioner, Santhal Parganas', 19 January 1948.
3. M. Bourke-White, *Halfway to Freedom*, Simon and Schuster, 1949.
4. S. Bhattacharya, *The Defining Moments in Bengal: 1920–1947*, Oxford University Press, 2014.
5. Ibid.
6. 'Situation Grows Worse in West Punjab', *Bombay Chronicle*, 30 August 1947, p. 1.
7. P.C. Pandey, 1948.
8. R. Mondal, Confidential Memo No. 326/C, 1 December 1947.
9. Ibid.
10. Ibid.
11. B.B. Mishra, 'Postscript to the Pakur Case', *Indian Police Journal*, 1958, pp. 177–81.
12. B.B. Mishra, 'Untitled memorandum', 25 December 1947.
13. Subdivisional Office, P, D.O. No. 269/C, Pakur, 23 October 1947.
14. Mishra, 'Postscript ot the Pakur Case', 1958.
15. B. Mullick, Confidential Home No. E.R.C. 20-5-47, 3 November 1947.
16. M.K. Gautam, 'Santal Uprising and the Use of Weapons', *Ethnographic Museum, University of Oslo, Yearbook 1970*, 1970, pp. 61–90.
17. 'Sensation at Pakur', *The Indian Nation*, 2 November 1947.
18. H. Mukherjea, Letter to Governor Binodananda Jha, Pakur, 14 November 1947.
19. E. Marandi, Retired Agronomist (D. Morrison, Interviewer), 1 March 2019.
20. B.B. Mishra, 'Untitled memorandum', 1947.
21. Adivasis, or indigenous people, including the Santhals.
22. 'Separatist Movement in Santhal Parganas', *The Searchlight*, 6 November 1947.
23. 'Separate Jharkhand Is an Anachronism To-Day', *The Searchlight*, 11 November 1947.

24. H. Mukherjee, Telegram to Governor Jairamdas Daulatram, Pakur, 6 November 1947.
25. Mishra, 'Postscript to the Pakur Case', 1958.
26. Ibid.
27. C. Raman, 1947.
28. Mishra, 'Untitled memorandum', 1947.
29. H. Mukherjea, 1947.
30. E. Marandi, 2019.
31. Ibid.
32. '"Beau Geste" to be Repeated', *Times of India*, 30 July 1927, p. 16.
33. Mishra, 'Postscript ot the Pakur Case', 1958.

25. *Rajbansha*

1. P.C. Pandey, 1948.
2. Ibid.
3. N.K. Singh, 'The Depredations of the Marathas in the Pakaur Raj', *Quarterly Review of Historic Studies*, 1974, pp. 46–48.
4. B. Majumdar, 'Introduction', *Gauri-Mangala: With a Short History of the Pakur Raj*, Asiatic Society, 1971.
5. A.K. Samanta, 1995.
6. 'Doctor Not to Practise', *Times of India*, 14 March 1938, p. 4.
7. D. Dhar, *Medical Treatment in General Practice with Recent Advances*, Monica Dhar, 1948.
8. B. Le Brocq, 1983.
9. Acquaintance of Banabala (D. Morrison, Interviewer).

Bibliography

'2 held in toxic scheme', *Dayton Daily News*, 20 February 1998, p.1.

'Adventures of Binoyendra Chandra Pandey of Pakur Murder Case Fame' (1947). File 2351 of 47. Government of Bihar.

'A European Zamindar', *Times of India*, 11 September 1913, p.8.

A Review of the Administration of the Bombay Presidency. Bombay: Bombay Presidency, 1926.

Adeoti, O.E., & Imuoh, U.A. (2016). 'The Contribution of Dr Oguntola Obunbaku Sapara Williams to Colonial Medical Service in Lagos'. *IOSR Journal of Humanities and Social Sciences*, pp.50–54.

Advertisement (1922). *Motion Picture News*, pp.3188–3189.

Advertisement: 'Enlighten Thy Daughter', *Bombay Chronicle*, 16 September 1922, p.3.

'Alleged Fraud', *Indian Express*, 31 January 1934, p.1.

'Alleged Murder of Step-Brother', *The Statesman*, 4 March 1934.

'Alleged Rioting and Murder', *Times of India*, 11 May 1933, p.4.

Anderson, R. (1922). *Drug Smuggling and Taking in India*. Calcutta: Thacker & Spink.

Arnold, D. (1993). *Colonizing the Body*. Berkeley: University of California Press.

'Arrested After Eight Years', *Times of India*, 23 January 1934, p.3.

Associated Press, 'Zamindar of Thar Murdered', *Bombay Chronicle*, 10 June 1930, p.1.

Associated Press, 'India Deports Nila Cram Cook; Put on Ship, Feigning Blindness', *New York Herald-Tribune*, 11 February 1934, p.1.

'Attack on the Infectious Disease Hospital by Mill-Hands', *Bombay Gazette*, 30 October 1896, p.5.

Aurobindo, S. (1991). 'Tales of Prison Life'. In S. Aurobindo, *Bentali Writings Translated into English*. Pondicherry: Sri Aurobindo Ashram Trust.

Bacot, A., & Martin, C. (1914), LXVII. 'Observations on the Mechanism of the Transmission of Plague by Fleas'. *J Hyg*, pp.423–39.

'Bail Cancelled', *The Statesman*, 15 March 1934.

'Bail Petition for Accused Doctor', *The Statesman*, 4 April 1934.
'Bail Petition of Doctor Dismissed', *Straits Times*, 21 April 1934, p.12.
'Bail Petition of Doctor Dismissed', *The Statesman*, 5 April 1934.
Ballhatchet, K. (1980). *Race, Sex, and Class Under the Raj*. New York: St Martin's Press.
Bandyopadhyay, B. (2008). 'Canvasser Krishnalal'. In A. Chaudhuri (ed.), *Memory's Gold: Writings on Calcutta*. New Delhi: Viking, pp.421–35.
Banerji, C. (2003). 'The Propitiatory Meal'. *Gastronomica*, pp.82–89.
Barber, N. (1973). *Lords of the Golden Horn*. London: Macmillan.
Barker, A., 'Too Much Cleopatra Turns U.S. Girl From Gandhi to Whoopee', *New York Daily News*, 3 December 1933, pp.38–39.
Barry, J.M. (2004). 'The Site of Origin of the 1918 Influenza Pandemic'. *Journal of Translational Medicine*.
'"Beau Geste" to Be Repeated', *Times of India*, 30 July 1930, p.16.
Bengal Legislative Council (1925). *Official Report, Bengal Legislative Council, 18th Session*. Calcutta: Bengal Book Depot.
Bengal Legislative Council Proceedings. Calcutta: Bengal Goverment Press, 1935.
Bernstein, H., 'The Doctor Who Killed His Patients With Germs', *New York Times*, 19 February 1911, p.45.
Bhattacharya, S. (2014). *The Defining Moments in Bengal: 1920–1947*. New Delhi: Oxford University Press.
Birchmore, W., 'Science in Crime'. *Courier-Journal*, 1 September 1895, p.3.
'Bombay Amusements', *Times of India*, 24 January 1931, p.5.
Bombay Plague Committee (1898). *Report of the Bombay Plague Committee*. Bombay: Times of India Steam Press.
Bose, C. (1901). 'Original Research in India'. *The Indian Review*, p.247.
Bose, C. (1913). 'Cocaine Poisoning'. *BMJ*, pp.16–17.
Bose, C.N. (1897). *Report on Native Papers for the Week Ending 27th March 1897*. Calcutta: Bengali Translator's Office.
Bose, K.C. (1902). 'Cocaine Intoxication and its Demoralizing Effects'. *BMJ*, pp.1020–22.
Bourke-White, M. (1949). *Halfway to Freedom*. New York: Simon and Schuster.
Boyd, J. (1963). 'Leonard Rogers 1868–1962'. *Biographical Memoirs*, London: Royal Society, pp.260–85.
'Brahmin Murderer on Trial', *Chicago Daily Tribune*, 4 November 1897, p.4.
'Brothers Appeal Against Death', *Times of India*, 19 March 1932, p.18.
Calcutta Gazette, 1935.
'Calcutta Letter: Black Record of Midnapore', *Times of India*, 3 September 1933, p.7.
'Calcutta Letter: Plain Words Terrorism', *Times of India*, 7 December 1933, p.3.

'Calcutta University Looted', *Indian Express*, 3 January 1933, p.1.

Carr, G. (2019). *Victims of Nazi Persecution in the Channel Islands*. London: Bloomsbury Academic.

Carus, W.S. (1998). *Bioterrorism and Biocrimes*. Washington, DC: Centre for Nonproliferation Research.

Catanach, I. (1987). 'Poona Politicians and the Plague'. In J. Masselos (ed.), *Struggling and Ruling*. New Delhi: Sterling.

Catanach, I. (1991). 'Plague and the Tensions of Empire'. In D. Arnold (ed.), *Imperial Medicine and Indigenous Societies*. Manchester: Manchester University Press.

Central Committee, Jubbulpore Exhibition (1866). *Once in a Way: A Jubbulpore Miscelleny*. Calcutta: George Wyman.

Chakraborty, C.C. (1967). *Louha Kapat* (M.S. Islam, Trans.). Calcutta: Mitra and Ghosh.

Chan, E.D., & Dorn, W.S. (2018). 'It Is Infallibly Deadly'. *Baker Street Journal*, pp.32–36.

Chatterjee, M. (1999). *Do and Die*. New Delhi: Penguin India.

Chaudhuri, N.C. (1987). *Thy Hand, Great Anarch!* Reading: Addison.

Chaudhury, S.R. (2018). 'Toxic Matters: Medical Jurisprudence and the Making of the Indian Poisons Act (1904)'. *Crime, History, and Societies*, pp.83–107.

Cheema, G. (2013). 'The Grandeur of Haffkine Institute Under Dr Sahib Singh Sokhey'. *The Panjab Past and Present*, pp.100–09.

Chopra, R., & Chopra, G.S. (1931). 'Cocaine Habit in India'. *Indian Journal of Medical Research*, pp.1013–46.

Churchill, W. (1967). WSC to Lady Randoph, 14 October, 1896. In R.S. Churchill (ed.), *Winston S. Churchill: Companion Volume I; Part 2 1896–1900*, pp.686–89. Boston: Houghton Mifflin.

'Clever Phosphorous Trick in Murder Case', *The Standard*, 29 September 1913, p.9.

Colson, I. (n.d.). 'Memoirs of Isabel Colson'.

'Conan Doyle Brings Back Sherlock Holmes', *New York Times Review of Books*, 28 October 1917, p.1.

Connor, F. (1929). *Surgery in the Tropics*. London: J. & A. Churchill.

Connor, F.P. (1914). 'Iodine in the Treatment of Plague'. *Indian Medical Gazette*, p.208.

Cook, J.N. (1898). *Plague in Calcutta*. Calcutta: Calcutta Municipal Press.

Crawford, E.A. (1996). 'Paul-Louis Simond and his Work on Plague'. *Pespectives in Biology and Medicine*, pp.446–58.

'Crime and Science', *Times of India*, 26 February 1935, p.8.

Curry, J. (1932). *The Indian Police*. London: Faber.

d'Errico, F., Backwell, L., Villa, P., Degano, I., Lucejko, J.J., Bamford, M.K., ... Beaumont, P.B. (2012). 'Early Evidence of San Material Culture Represented Byorganic Artifacts from Border Cave, South Africa'. *PNAS*, pp.13214–19.

Dahlinger, S. (1998). 'Of Mites and Men'. In C. Roden, & B. Roden (eds), *The Case Files of Sherlock Holmes: The Dying Detective*. Ashcroft: Calabash Press, pp.41–52.

Daly, F. (1907). *Report on Native Papers in Bengal for the Week Ending 9 February 1907*. Calcutta. Bengali Translator's Office.

Das Gupta, H. (1944). *The Indian Stage* Vol. IV. Calcutta: M.K. Das Gupta.

Datta, K. (1971). *Gauri-Mangala: With a Short History of the Pakur Raj*. Calcutta: Asiatic Society.

Dean, B. (Director). (1929). *The Return of Sherlock Holmes* [Motion Picture]. Retrieved 19 December 2022, from catalog.afi.com/Film/5033-THE-RETURNOFSHERLOCKHOLMES?sid=d683c349-5363-4d46-b726-aad9a1f4a931&sr=12.456681&cp=1&pos=0.

'Death of Accused in Murder Case', *Times of India*, 18 October 1932, p.7.

'Defence Address Begins', *Amrita Bazar Patrika*, November 1934, p.7.

Deverell, W. (2004). *Whitewashed Adobe: The Rise of Los Angeles and the Remaking of its Mexican Past*. Berkeley: University of California Press.

Devi, J. (1995). *The River Churning* (E. Chatterjee, trans.). New Delhi: Kali for Women.

Dey, B. (2010). 'Summer in Calcutta'. In K. Bardhan (ed.), *Oxford Anthology of Bengali Literature* Vol. I. New Delhi: Oxford University Press, pp.70–72.

Dhar, D. (1948). *Medical Treatment in General Practice with Recent Advances*. Calcutta: Monica Dhar.

'Divine Hand Behind the Quake Havoc', *Indian Express*, 1 February 1934, p.1.

'Doctor Not to Practise', *Times of India*, 14 March 1938, p.4.

'Doctor to Remain in Custody', *The Statesman*, 13 April 1934.

Dombrowski, F.A. (1988). 'Internment of Members of the Royal Family in Ethiopia, Turkey, and India'. *Rassegna di Studi Etiopici*, pp.45–57.

Dorin, S. (2010). 'Jazz and Race in Colonial India'. *Jazz Research Journal*, pp.123–140.

Doyle, A.C., 'Guinea Pig or Man?' *Daily Express*, 1 November 1910, p.4.

'Dr Chowdhury's Defence Argument Continues', *Amrita Bazar Patrika*, December 1934.

'Dr P.B. Naidu Further Cross-Examined', *Amrita Bazar Patrika*, September 1934.

Echenberg, M. (2002). 'Pestis Redux: The Initial Years of the Third Bubonic Plague Pandemic, 1894–1901'. *Journal of World History*, pp.429–49.

Ehrenkranz, N.J. (1987). 'A. Conan Doyle, Sherlock Holmes, and Murder by Tropical Infection'. *Reviews of Infectious Diseases*, pp.222–25.

Ellis, Thomas Hobart. Papers of (Sir) Thomas Hobart Ellis (1894–1981), Indian Civil Service, Bengal 1919–47, Sessions Judge; Comprising Transcripts of Proceedings in the Pakur Murder Heard by Ellis in the Sessions Court, 24-Parganas (1934–35) and the Appeal before the High Court, Bengal (1936), and Newscuttings Relating to the Case. BL: Mss Eur F375: 1932–1936.

Evidence: Indian Cinematograph Committee (1928). Calcutta: Government of India.

'Excitement of the Mill-Hands', *Bombay Gazette*, 30 October 1896, p.5.

Feldinger, F. (2008). *A Slight Epidemic*. Los Angeles: Silver Lake Publishing.

Fenn, E.A. (2000). 'Biological Warfare in Eighteenth-Century North America: Beyond Jeffery Amherst'. *The Journal of American History*, pp.1552–80.

'Film of the Popular Novel', *Times of India*, 19 July 1927, p.10.

Finney, P. (n.d.). *The Chandernagore Raid*. Unpublished Memoir.

'First Jersey Hanging Since 1907', *Coventry Evening Telegraph*, 9 October 1959, p.3.

'Frankly Speaking', *Bombay Chronicle*, 10 November 1933, p.6.

'Free Fight With Police', *Times of India*, 14 November 1931, p.5.

Freud, S. (1965). 'Lecture XXXIII: Femininity'. In S. Freud, *New Introductory Lectures in Psycho-Analysis* (J. Strachey, trans.). New York: Norton, p.123.

Frischknecht, F. (2003). 'The History of Biological Warfare'. *EMBO Reports*, pp.47–52.

Frith, J. (2012). 'Syphilis: Its Early History and Treatment Until Penicillin, and the Debate on its Origins'. *Journal of Military and Veterans' Health*, pp.49–58.

Gascoigne, B. (1971). *The Great Mughals*. New York: Harper and Row.

Gautam, M.K. (1970). 'Santal Uprising and the Use of Weapons'. *Ethnographic Museum, University of Oslo, Yearbook 1970*, pp.61–90.

Geissler, E., & Moon, J.E. (1999). *Biological and Toxin Weapons: Research, Development, and Use from the Middle Ages to 1945*. Oxford: Oxford University Press.

George, T. (1964). *Krishna Menon: A Biography*. London: Jonathan Cape.

'German Bluebeard Beheaded', *Hamilton Daily Times*, 23 March 1914, p.9.

'German Tragedies', *Bombay Gazette*, 14 February 1914, p.9.

Gibb, W.F. (1899). 'Sequel to a Case of Acute Tetanus Treated by Intracerebral Injections of Antitoxin'. *BMJ*, p.9.

Gomez, M.A. (2019). *African Dominion*. Princeton: Princeton University Press.

Gooptu, S. (2011). *Bengali Cinema*. London: Routledge.

Gopal, R. (1962). *Trials of Jawaharlal Nehru*. Bombay: Book Centre.

Greater Bombay Gazetteer (1986). Bombay: Government of Maharashtra.

Guha, R. (2019). *Gandhi: The Years That Changed the World, 1914–1948*. London: Penguin.

Gupta, R. (23 January 2018). 'Horrors of the East'. *The Hindu BusinessLine*. Retrieved from www.thehindubusinessline.com/blink/explore/horrors-of-the-east/article7137420.ece.

Harris, S.H. (1994). *Factories of Death*. London: Routledge.

Hauswirth, F. (1932). *Purdah: The Status of Indian Women*. London: Kegan Paul, Trench, Trubner & Co.

Hirst, L.F. (1953). *The Conquest of Plague*. London: Oxford University Press.

Hobbs, H., journal entry. Calcutta, 14 January 1936.

Hobbs, H. (1937). *Indian Dust Devils*. Calcutta: H. Hobbs.

Huang, Z., *Imperial China's Bloody Succession Struggles Show Why Failed Princes Like Kim Jong-nam are Doomed*. Retrieved from Quartz: qz.com/913516/imperial-chinas-bloody-succession-struggles-show-why-failed-princes-like-kim-jong-nam-are-doomed, 19 February 2017.

'Hunger Strike in Alipore Jail', *The Statesman*, 24 February 1934, p.10.

Hutton, J. (1933). *Census of India, 1931*. Delhi: Manager of Publications.

'Hypnotism Used in Crime', *Chicago Chronicle*, 7 September 1895.

'In Another Column', *Bombay Gazette*, 25 September 1896, p.4.

'In Nigeria' (1956). *BMJ*, p.881.

India: A Reference Annual (1954). 'Delhi: Ministry of Information and Broadcasting.

Indian Vital Statistics for 1933' (1936). *Nature*, p.159.

Interdepartmental Political-Military Group (1969). *US Policy on Chemical and Biological Warfare and Agents*. National Security Council. Retrieved from nsarchive2.gwu.edu/NSAEBB/NSAEBB58/RNCBW6a.pdf.

'Iodine Terchloride and Plague', *Times of India*, 5 June 1901, p.4.

'Jawahar's Message to Young Bengal', *Bombay Chronicle*, 18 January 1934, p.1.

Johnston, J.M. (1935). 'Lobar Pneumonia and its Serological Treatment'. *Edinburgh Medical Journal*, pp.265–79.

'Judge Collapses in Court', *Times of India*, 26 September 1934, p.9.

Kahn, D. (2004). *The Reader of Gentlemen's Mail*. New Haven: Yale University Press.

Kamath, M.S. (1914). *The Census of India: An Analysis and Criticism*. Madras: Theosophical Publishing House.

Kautilya. (1987). *Arthashastra*. (L. Rangarajan, ed.) New Delhi: Penguin.

Kelly, J. (2005). *The Great Mortality*. New York: HarperCollins.

Klein, I. (1988). 'Plague, Policy and Popular Unrest in British India'. *Modern Asian Studies*, pp.723–55.

Kurien, S. (Director), *Finding Carlton* (Motion Picture). Retrieved from YouTube: www.youtube.com/watch?v=zU6shKTo38M, 29 April 2019.

Lacey, P., 'Murder by Pin-prick', *The Straits Times*, 11 May 1950, p.10.

Lahiri, N. (2015). *Ashoka in Ancient India*. Cambridge: Harvard University Press.

Lamb, S. (2000). *White Saris and Sweet Mangoes*. Berkeley: University of California.

Le Brocq, B. (1983). Unpublished Memoirs.

Le Brocq, E.H. (n.d.). *Bengal Police at War*.

Le Brocq, E H. (n.d.). *The Pakur Murder Case*.

L'Etang, H. (1959). 'Some Observations on the Black Formosa Corruption'. *The Sherlock Holmes Journal*, pp.58–60.

Levine, P. (1994). 'Venereal Disease, Prostitution, and the Politics of Empire: The Case of British India'. *Journal of the History of Sexuality*, pp.579–602.

Lorenz, A., 'Germ Slaying Cycle Feared by Professor', *San Francisco Examiner*, 19 April 1925, p.7.

Lutzker, E., & Jochnowitz, C. (n.d.). 'The Touchstone'. Unpublished Manuscript.

Lynteris, C. (2022). 'In Search of Lost Fleas: Reconsidering Paul-Louis Simond's Contribution to the Study of the Propagation of Plague'. *Medical History*, pp.1–22.

Lynteris, C. (21 October 2022). 'Zoonoses et recherche en labouratoire'. Paris. Retrieved from www.translitterae.psl.eu/seminaire-danthropologie-europeenne-des-relations-entre-humains-et-animaux-2022-23.

Mackirdy, M.A., & Willis, W.N. (1912). *The White Slave Market*. London: Stanley Paul.

Majumdar, B. (1971). 'Introduction'. In Raja Prithvichandra of Pakur, *GAURI-MANGALA*. Calcutta: Asiatic Socity.

Mandal, R., Memo No. 311C. Pakur, 19 November 1947.

Mann, T. (1997). *Doctor Faustus* (J.E. Wood, trans.). New York: Vintage International.

Mantle, B., 'India's Drama, "Sita", Is Overlong', *Daily News* (New York), 16 January 1931.

Maskiell, M., & Mayor, A. (2001). 'Killer Khilats, Part 1: Legends of Poisoned "Robes of Honour"'. *Folklore*, pp.23–45.

McCullough, D. (1972). *The Great Bridge*. New York: Simon and Schuster.

McLean, K. (2015). *A Revolutionary History of Interwar India*. London: Hurst.

Medico-Legal Congress at New York (1895). *Journal of the American Medical Association*, pp.463–64.

Milne, W. (1917). *Collier's Municipal Manual*. Calcutta: Thacker, Spink & Co.

Minney, R. (1922). *Night Life of Calcutta*. Calcutta: Muston.

Minutes of Evidence of the Indian Plague Commission, Vol. 1. Calcutta: Government of India, 1900.

Minutes of Evidence Presented to the Indian Plague Commission, Vol. 3.
London: Her Majesty's Stationery Office, 1900.
Mishra, B.B., untitled memorandum, 25 December 1947.
Mishra, B.B. (1958). Postscript ot the Pakur Case. *Indian Police Journal*,
pp.177–81.
Mondal, R., Confidential Memo No. 326/C, 1 December 1947.
'Montagu, George (Colonel)' (n.d.). Retrieved from Shellers from the
Past and Present: www.conchology.be/?t=9001&id=25237.
Morgan, R.W. (1979). *The Sopono Cult and Smallpox Vaccination in Lagos.*
Boston: African Studies Centre, Boston University.
Mukherjea, H., Letter to Governor Binodananda Jha. Pakur,
14 November 1947.
Mukherjee, H., Telegram to Governor Jairamdas Daulatram. Pakur,
6 November 1947.
Mukhoty, I. (2018). *Daughters of the Sun.* Delhi: Aleph.
Mullick, B., Confidential Home No. E.R.C. 20-5-47, 3 November 1947.
'Murder by Germs Case: Trial at Chicago', *Times of India*, 12 June 1925,
p.7.
'Murder Conspiracy Charge', *The Statesman*, 13 March 1934, p.4.
'Murder of a Zamindar', *Times of India*, 10 June 1930, p.10.
'Murder of a Zemindar', *Times of India*, 6 October 1909, p.7.
'Murder of Big Zamindar', *Times of India*, 25 December 1929, p.14.
'Murder of Mr Lawrence Barber', *Bombay Chronicle*, 17 April 1915, p.10.
Najmi, Q., 'Memories of Forgotten Heroes to Come Alive in Pune's
Chapekar Wada', *Indo Asian News Service*, 21 August 2022.
Nathan, R. (1898). *Plague In India 1896, 1897.* Simla: Government of India.
Nehru, J. (1982). *Autobiography.* New Delhi: Jawaharlal Nehru Memorial
Fund.
'Nila Cram Cook, Once Gandhi Aid, Held as Vagrant', *New York Daily
News*, 11 January 1934, p.50.
Official Report, Bengal Legislative Assembly. Alipore: Bengal Government
Press, 1944.
Ohler, N. (2016). *Blitzed: Drugs in Nazi Germany.* London: Allen Lane.
'Pakur Zamindar's Bid For Vendetta', *The Searchlight*, 7 November 1947.
Pandey, P.C., 'To the Deputy Commissioner, Santhal Parganas',
19 January 1948.
'Pandit Nehru and the Mahasabha', *Times of India*, 29 November 1933,
p.9.
Patel, P.T. (1929). *Infectious Diseases and Other Fevers in India.* Calcutta:
Butterworth.
'Plague in Bombay', *The Singapore Free Press and Mercantile Advertiser*,
20 October 1896, p.5.
'Plague in Calcutta', *Indian Medical Gazette*, 1947, p.137
'Police Department', *Supplement to the Calcutta Gazette*, 22 August 1935,
p.1183.

'Poona Bomb Outrage On Mahatma', *Bombay Chronicle*, 26 June 1934, p.1.

President's Secretariat (1933–34). Ball at Belvedere – 12 January 1934. Calcutta. Retrieved from www.abhilekh-patal.in/jspui/handle/123456789/2763963.

'Professor Gajjar's Cross-Examination', *Bombay Gazette*, 21 February 1899, p.6.

'Public Prosecutor's Address to the Jury Continues', *Amrita Bazar Patrika*, October 1934.

Rahman, M.L. (1940). 'Pakur Murder Case'. *Calcutta Police Journal*, pp.112–28.

Raman, C., D.O. No. 557/C, 8 November 1947.

Rao, C.H. (ed.) (1915). *Indian Biographical Dictionary*. Madras: Pillar & Co.

Ray, P.C. (1935). *Life and Experiences of a Bengali Chemist* Vol. II. Calcutta: Chuckervertty. Chatterjee & Co.

Ray, S. (2013). *On Cinema*. New York: Columbia University Press.

Ray, S. (2016). *Childhood Days*. New Delhi: Penguin.

'Recalls the Borgias', *Evening Herald* (Wellington), 5 June 1934, p.9.

'Refugee Train Attacked', *Bombay Chronicle*, 28 October 1937, p.1.

'Remarkable Story of a Conspiracy', *Englishman's Overland Mail*, 11 September 1913, p.7.

Report of the Drugs Enquiry Committee. Madras: Government of India, 1931.

Report of the Indian Cinematograph Committee, 1927–1928 (Government of India Central Publication Branch, Calcutta, 1928); Evidence of the Indian Cinematograph Committee, Volumes 1–5; 1927–1928 (Government of India Central Publication Branch, Calcutta, 1928).

Roden, B. (1998). 'Who Did It?' In *the Case Files of Sherlock Holmes*. Ashcroft: Calabash, pp.145–48.

Rodin, A.E., & Key, J.D. (1984). *Medical Casebook of Doctor Arthur Conan Doyle*. Malabar: Robert E. Kreiger.

Roy, L.M. (1893). *Degredation of Begal Zamindar*. Calcutta: Indian Patriot Press.

Roy, R.B. (1998). 'Sexually Transmitted Diseases and the Raj'. *Sexually Transmitted Infections*, pp.20–26.

Roy, T. (2012). *Life and Times of Dr Syamaprasad Mookerjee*. New Delhi: Ocean Books.

'Russian Poisoners Are Found Guilty', *New York Times*, 17 February 1911, p.4.

Samanta, A.K. (1995). *Terrorism in Bengal* Vol. 5. Calcutta: Government of West Bengal.

Sapara, O. (1977). 'Dr Sapara's Report to the Colonial Government on Smallpox Epidemic in Yoruba Country; Lagos 1 September 1909'. In A. Adeloye, *Nigerian Pioneers of Modern Medicine*. Idaban: Idaban University Press, pp.53–71.

'Separate Jharkhand is an Anachronism To-Day', *The Searchlight*,
    11 November 1947.
'Scenery a Laugh, Hindu Premiere for 400 is Off', *Daily News*,
    29 October 1930.
'Scenery Shortage Delays Hindu Play', *The New York Times*,
    29 October 1930.
'Searches Continue In Patna', *The Searchlight*, 11 October 1947, p.1.
Seigel, B.R. (2018). *Hungry Nation*. Cambridge: Cambridge University
    Press.
Sengupta, D. (2015). 'A City Feeding on Itself'. In T. Sarkar, & S.
    Bandyopadhyay (eds), *Calcutta: The Stormy Decades*. New Delhi: Social
    Science Press.
'Sensation at Pakur', *The Indian Nation*, 2 November 1947.
'Separatist Movement in Santhal Parganas', *The Searchlight*,
    6 November 1947.
Setlur, S., & Deshpande, K. (eds) (1907). *A Full and Authentic Report of
    the Trial of the Hon'ble Mr Bal Gangadhar Tilak*. Bombay: Education
    Society's Press.
Shoesmith, B. (1988–89). 'The Problem of Film: A Reassessment of the
    Significance of the Indian Cinematograph Committee, 1927–28'.
    Continuum, pp.74–89.
Simond, M., Godley, M.L., & Mouriquand, P.D. (1998). 'Paul-Louis
    Simond and His Discovery of Plague Transmission by Rat Fleas'.
    Journal of the Royal Society of Medicine, pp.101–04.
Singh, N.K. (1974). 'The Depredations of the Marathas in the Pakaur
    Raj'. *The Quarterly Review of Historic Studies*, pp.46–48.
Sinha, D. (2012). 'The Last Hundred Years'. In *The High Court at Calcutta*.
    Kolkata: Indian Law Institute.
'Sir Thomas Ellis', *Times of London*, 21 December 1981, p.10.
'Sisir Kumar Bhaduri and Hindu Troupe in Belated Delight', *Daily News*,
    13 January 1931, p.39.
'Situation Grows Worse in West Punjab', *Bombay Chronicle*,
    30 August 1947, p.1.
'Sons' Story in Shobi Talao Murder Case', *Bombay Chronicle*,
    21 October 1932, p.8.
Source Material for a History of the Freedom Movement in India, Vol. 2.
    Bombay: Government of Bombay, 1958.
Spargo, J.W. (1936). 'Clarence in the Malmsey-Butt'. *Modern Language
    Notes*, pp.166–73.
Sri Dharmarajika Vihara Hall (1926). *The Maha-Bodi*, pp.64–65.
Stevens, D. (2022). *Camera Man*. New York: Atria.
Subdivisional Office, P., D.O. No. 269/C. Pakur, 23 October 1947.
'Subhas Bose Trial Opens', *Bombay Chronicle*, 11 September 1940, p.1.
Supriyac, *Venereal Disease and the Prostitution Policy of the British Raj*.
    Retrieved from krentely.in, 3 August 2020.

Swellengrebel, N.H. (1950). 'Plague in Java, 1910–1912'. *The Journal of Hygiene*, pp.135–45.

Taubenberger, J.K., & Morens, D.M. (2006). '1918 Influenza: The Mother of'. *Revista Biomédica*, pp.69–79.

'Tawlar Case', *Times of India*, 25 March 1932, p.14.

Tegart, C., Memo #7782-83. Calcutta, 2 September 1930.

'The District of Mandvie', *Bombay Gazette*, 30 September 1896, p.3.

'The Fatal Accident at St. Saviour's', *Morning News*, 9 November 1915, p.1.

The House of Commons, *Cocaine Traffic, Calcutta. Oral Answers to Questions – India. – in the House of Commons on 14th December 1925*. Retrieved from They Work for You: www.theyworkforyou.com/debates/?id=1925-12-14a.939.6&s=cocaine+speaker%3A22436#g939.7

'The Plague in Bombay', *Manchester Guardian*, 5 October 1896, p.5.

'The Probhat of Hyderabad', *Amrita Bazar Patrika*, 8 April 1898, p.4.

'The Prophylactic Lymph Prepared by Prof. Haffkine', *Bombay Gazette*, 21 January 1897, p.5.

'The Question of the Segregation', *Bombay Gazette*, 28 December 1896, p.4.

'The Resident in Mysore' (1932). *Report for the Second-half of December 1932*. Mysore.

'The Shooting Case at Highfield', *Jersey Weekly Post*, 13 November 1915, p.1.

'The Strand', *London Daily News*, 28 November 1913, p.3.

'The Supposed Outbreak of Plague', *Bombay Gazette*, 25 September 1896, p.5.

Todd, S. (2004). 'Young Women, Work and Family in Inter-War Rural England'. *Agricultural History Review*, pp.83–98.

Turkhad, N., 'Production of an Indian "Talkie"', *Bombay Chronicle*, 25 July 1932, p.6.

Untitled editorial, *Bombay Gazette*, 21 January 1897, p.4.

Walsh, C. (1929). *Indian Village Crimes*. London: Ernest Benn.

Walsh, C. (1930). *Crime in India*. London: Ernest Benn.

'West Punjab Still Disturbed', *Bombay Chronicle Weekly*, 31 August 1947, p.9.

Wheelis, M. (1999). 'Biological Warfare before 1914'. In E. Geissler, & J.E. Moon (eds), *Biological and Toxin Weapons*. Stockholm: Stockholm International Peace Research Institute, pp.8–34.

'Why Hindu Said Muslim Prayers', *Times of India*, 13 January 1934, p.6.

'Wife and Children Burnt on Charcoal Heap', *Bombay Chronicle*, 23 June 1933, p.1.

Wilson, E. (1997). 'Neurosurgical Treatment for Tetanus'. *Journal of the History of the History of the Neurosciences*, pp.82–85.

'Women Waitresses Wanted', *The Sun* (Baltimore), 25 February 1934, p.8.

Wujastyk, D. (1985). *The Roots of Ayurveda*. New Delhi: Penguin.

Yardley, H.O. (1931). *The American Black Chamber*. Indianapolis: Bobbs-Merrill.

'Zamlar Poisoning Case Appeal', *Times of India*, 25 April 1932, p.11.

Libraries and Archives

United Kingdom
The British Library
The National Archives

India
Bihar State Archives
Calcutta School of Tropical Medicine
Jagjivan Ram Institute for Parliamentary Studies, Patna
Kolkata Police Museum
National Library of India, Kolkata
Natya Shodh Sansthan, Kolkat
The Sinha Library, Patna
West Bengal State Archives

United States
New York Public Library
Library of Congress
National Library of Medicine

Jersey
The Jersey Archive

Ireland
National Library of Ireland

Digital
Abhilekh Patal: National Archives of India
National Library of Singapor
Papers Past: National Library of New Zealand
The British Newspaper Archive
The Internet Archive
Trove: National Library of Australia

Index